D1791229

THE ASSASSINATION PLEASE ALMANAC

Tom Miller

HENRY REGNERY COMPANY · CHICAGO

Published by Henry Regnery Company
180 North Michigan Avenue, Chicago, Illinois 60601
Manufactured in the United States of America
Library of Congress Catalog Card Number: 76-55654
International Standard Book Number: 0-8092-7903-7

Published simultaneously in Canada by
Beaverbooks
953 Dillingham Road
Pickering, Ontario L1W 1Z7
Canada

Library of Congress Cataloging in Publication Data

Miller, Tom.
    The assassination please almanac.

Includes index.
    1. Kennedy, John Fitzgerald, Pres. U.S., 1917-1963—
Assassination.   2. Assassination—United States.
I. Title.
E842.9.M53   1977   364.1'524'0973   76-55654
ISBN 0-8092-7903-7

Permissions

The author wishes to acknowledge permission to reprint the following material:

Quotations cited from *Fact Magazine* © 1966 Fact Magazine, Inc. All rights reserved.

Quotations from *If You Have a Lemon, Make Lemonade*, by Warren Hinckle, © 1974, G. P. Putnam's Sons.

Quotations from "The Rolling Stone Interview With Seymour Hersh, Part II" by Joe Esterhaus; "The JFK Assassination: Why Congress Should Reopen the Investigation" by Robert Blair Kaiser; "New South Burn" by John Belushi and Dan Aykroyd; and "American Grandstand" by Dave Marsh © 1975 and 1977 by *Rolling Stone* magazine. All rights reserved. Reprinted by permission.

"Elegy for John F. Kennedy" was written for the "November 22 Coalition" rally in Boston, Massachusetts, 1975. "The Age" was first read at the New Year's Day 1976 reading of poets at St. Marks Church, New York City and initially appeared in *Crawdaddy* magazine. Both poems © 1975 by Ed Sanders. Used by permission of the poet.

"Newspoem" © 1976 by Tuli Kupferberg originally appeared in the *Soho Weekly News*, February 26, 1976. Used by permission of the poet.

"Cover-Up Lowdown" cartoons used by permission of Paul Mavrides and Jay Kinney. "Cover-Up Lowdown" will be published as a comic book by the Rip-Off Press in San Francisco in 1977.

Quotations excerpted from *The Eye in the Pyramid: Illuminatus, Part I* by Robert J. Shea and Robert Anton Wilson copyright © 1975 by Robert J. Shea and Robert Anton Wilson. Reprinted by permission of Delacorte Press.

Other permissions and credits appear throughout the book. Every effort has been made to credit and secure permission for copyrighted material. Publishers of any material for which permission was not secured or credit not given are asked to write the author for proper acknowledgment in any future editions.

A section of Chapter 1 originally appeared in a slightly different form in *Crawdaddy* magazine, August 1975, under the title "The Assassination Please Almanac."

CONTENTS

PREFACE

President Lyndon Johnson receives the final report from the Warren Commission, September 24, 1964. Left to right: JOHN J. McCLOY (quoted from *Inquest*), Commission Chief Counsel J. LEE RANKIN (from a commission meeting 1-27-64), RICHARD RUSSELL (from *Whitewash IV*), GERALD FORD (from *Portrait of the Assassin*), EARL WARREN (from a commission meeting 2-10-64 to Marguerite Oswald), LYNDON JOHNSON (on receiving the report), ALLEN DULLES (from a commission meeting 1-22-64), JOHN SHERMAN COOPER (from *Inquest*), and HALE BOGGS (from *Inquest*).

Who killed JFK? If anyone tells you that he or she knows, don't believe it. False solutions are worse than no solutions in this subject of all-consuming interest. Penn Jones, one of the earliest and most durable researchers in the field, gratuitously warns novices not to get their toes muddied on the banks of the good river conspiracy, for there is no soap powerful enough to wash the dirt off.

Who killed JFK? The question serves as a conversational icebreaker, and, conversely, has caused good friends never to speak to each other again. It is America's deepest running mystery. There is no one who doesn't have something to say on the subject.

On a magazine assignment in the fall of 1973, I traveled through the South with assassination lecturer Bob Katz, whose two-hour presentation on the Kennedy murder was booked into colleges of all sizes, sophistication, and locale. His talk at the University of Tennessee to a packed auditorium had been the best received lecture on the tour, and afterwards we celebrated at a nearby restaurant. Returning to our hotel just after midnight, we found a new desk clerk on duty. The elderly gentleman had no idea what Katz's business was, nor did he know about the presentation earlier that evening. We checked for messages with him, and exchanged small talk about the newly appointed vice-president, Gerald Ford, when the desk clerk abruptly changed the subject. "You know," he said slowly, "this country hasn't been the same since they killed Kennedy."

"They?" replied Katz. "Who do you think did it?"

Without hesitation the desk clerk answered. "It was the Texas mafia."

"Don't you think Oswald did it?" Katz responded.

"Nawww," came the confident reply. "It was Lyndon Johnson and the Texas mafia."

With all due respect to the night desk clerk at the Sheraton Campus Inn, I do not think it was Lyndon Johnson and the Texas mafia. But I couldn't suggest who it was, either. Enough years have elapsed that we can tell which interests benefited from the assassination, who was capable of engineering it, and what elements in and out of government desired national policies quickly changed.

The purpose of this book is not to propose yet another theory, uncover another gunperson in the bushes, or expose a clandestine cabal between parties A, B, and D (party C died mysteriously six months ago). What this book sets out to do is make available enough information and concrete leads that each reader can intelligently pursue the subject, and in so doing, learn how public opinion of the assassination of John Kennedy has taken shape in the press, on stage, in books, on records, in people's imaginations, in libraries, and on sketchpads.

It is not enough to focus on that one assassination as a singular event in American history, for it is not. People in and out of office have been the target of murder for political purposes since the country began, and many of those incidents are represented toward the end of the book.

How we go about solving a crime—particularly a political crime—can be almost as important as the solution itself. Be wary of motives and preconceptions. There should be enough data in this book for you to start with. If it gets you thinking about how and why American history is riddled with assassination, you've taken the most difficult step. Just don't let it get you down.

Tom Miller
Tucson, Arizona
January 1977

ACKNOWLEDGMENTS

Numerous people have offered suggestions, research assistance, direction, advice, and support. Of those kind enough to help out, the following have been of particular value: the Assassination Information Bureau, Walter and Peggy Bowart, the Citizens Commission of Inquiry, *Crawdaddy* magazine editors Peter Knobler and Greg Mitchell, David Dunaway, Mary Fritz, Larry Harris, Gerald Harwood and Alison Whitehead of Cave Canyon Associates, John and Lynn Long, Frank Milan, Charles Miller, Modern Times Book Store, Beverly Ogden, Charles Oldham, Theron Raines, and Steve Weeks. Without their help and support, this book would have taken much longer and been considerably more difficult to prepare.

A special note of gratitude goes to Mary Ferrell, librarian of the truth.

CONTRIBUTORS

Chip Berlet, who researched the chapter on assassination attempts against officeholders, is a free-lance writer and photographer living in Washington, D. C. He was a co-founder of the College Press Service Collective in Denver, Colorado, and has been published widely in the alternative media. *Jeff Cohen,* who served as a consultant on the Kennedy assassination chapters, is the West Coast representative of the Assassination Information Bureau. He lectures extensively on the Kennedy murder conspiracy and is considered an expert on the assassination of Martin Luther King, Jr. He lives in Los Angeles. Illustrator *Paul Mavrides* is co-author, with Jay Kinney, of "Cover-Up Lowdown," a comic book to be published in 1977 by the Rip-Off Press in San Francisco. Mavrides, whose art work has appeared in the alternative press, lives in Berkeley, California. Research for the chapter on assassinations against non-officeholders was prepared by *Scoop Sweeney,* a former news director at KPFT-FM in Houston, Texas. In addition to a nine-to-five job, Sweeney is a free-lance broadcast journalist. He lives in Oakland, California, where he is a shop steward for local # 29 of the Office and Professional Employees Union, AFL-CIO. *David Williams,* who helped research and gave advice on the Kennedy assassination section, is a founding member of the Assassination Information Bureau in Cambridge, Massachusetts. His presentation on the Kennedy death has been given at more than a hundred campuses. Williams has also prepared videotape programs on clandestine power in America.

INTRODUCTION: JUDGMENT AT WASHINGTON

BY DONALD FREED

. . . It happens to be to our interest, as well as the interest of the Commission and of the country, to obtain as wide a distribution of the document as we can . . . .

—Letter from the then assistant managing editor of the *New York Times*, Clifton Daniel, to J. Lee Rankin, Chief Counsel to the Warren Commission, May 21, 1964 (four months prior to publication of the Warren Report)

"Truth crushed to earth, will rise again," prophesied Martin Luther King, Jr., quoting William Cullen Bryant in his poem The Battlefield.

On November 22, 1963, something happened. What went before, what led up to "the day the music stopped" and the decade of murder in the streets that followed? The prologue years of the 1950s and the Korean War had determined the blood sacrifice of two ordinary people, Julius and Ethel Rosenberg. The 1960s, the era of the megalomania of the American empire, required the assassinations of heads of state. In Guatemala, the Congo, Cuba, Chile, and finally America, the homicidal clandestine apparatus of the new American "Invisible Government" came home.

The American political process has been inching toward mania for twenty-five years. But a movement is afoot that could reverse the pathology. The need to know—what the Greeks called *Anánke*—is the driving impulse of this new Freedom of Information movement and its media. In the big propaganda wars of this century of death, the prize is historical truth.

The tremendous social realities of our time are ghosts, specters of murdered gods and our own humanity returned to haunt and destroy us.

—R. D. Laing

Is "Truth" some categorical imperative that will vanquish "Untruth" on the grand battlefield of moral history? Is it a Hegelian orchestration of raw phenomena and propaganda? Or is it really "truth" with a small "t"—a matter of mass history that builds up in the flesh and blood of millions of people over time? The work of the free-lancers and independent investigators, who have followed the blood-red footprints from Dallas through Watergate and beyond, is dedicated to the belief that ordinary people will finally make a coherent summary of their experience whatever the official mythology may be.

This interrupted process of national maturation began again, in the 1960s. Behind the murder of black leaders in that decade lay centuries of obscured racial violence; in America three times again as many black people were murdered as were Jews under the Nazis. The Gestapo actually studied the American techniques of genocide against the Indians in their training schools. And the Salem witches, the Wobblies, Sacco and Vanzetti, the

Scottsboro boys were all innocent political victims. American democracy has a long red underside.

The free-lancer believes that the people who faced with courage and resourcefulness the terrors of the Great Depression and of World War II can face the terror and pity of Dallas and Memphis and all the other killing grounds. From the execution of Malcolm X at the Audubon Ballroom in Harlem to the assassination of Fred Hampton as he lay drugged in his Chicago apartment to the dreaded "Adjustment Center" at San Quentin, where George Jackson was set up for the kill, Americans will be able to face the fact that, as Franz Fanon had predicted, the third phase of violence always returns to plague its inventor.

History is the trick the living play on the dead.

—George Bernard Shaw

The process of demythologizing official propaganda begins, sometimes, with a lone wanderer such as Mark Lane, who like a town crier in Pompeii, wanders through the Western World with the good news that the murderers of the president live and move among us in the jungles of our cities.

For their pains the first voices of dissent were battered; their characters were assassinated by the big media that would, a decade later, begin to stir as the accumulated conspiracies and cover-ups began to make America the name of a nervous disease. It was as George Orwell had said, there was truth and there was untruth, and if you clung to the truth, even against the whole world, you were not mad. Only individuals can cling, and only to a truth with a very small "t." This individual truth is then pitted in unequal struggle against the "Truth" of the State's propaganda engines. Now, thirteen years later, the world knows that the critics, the demystifiers of the official reports, the free-lancers, all those who clung to the truth, that they were not mad.

[It was important] to show the world that America is not a banana republic, where government can be changed by conspiracy.

—John J. McCloy,
Warren Commission member

Now the truth, so long covered up, is rising up through the flesh and blood, the nervous systems of people. And there is a purgation, a catharsis of terror and pity about to break over this nation that has been bound hand and foot with lies.

Then will we see how we were all defined and driven mad by secrecy and psychological warfare. We will understand that the doctored photograph of Lee Harvey Oswald with his rifle in one hand and his Marxist newspapers in the other was a materialization of the obligatory monster born out of the Cold War: the mad, subversive nonentity who, we were to believe, would crawl up out of the Dallas sewers to change history with the metaphysics of his magical communist hunting rifle.

I'm just a patsy. I didn't kill anyone.

—Lee Harvey Oswald

Something happened. America lost a weekend in November 1963. Instead of the ritual autumn leaf raking and sports viewing, the nation huddled in front of the hypnotic television tube. Millions watched the big heads of the commentators reading conflicting reports, heard the defiant pro-red defector maintain his innocence, wept as the incessant beat of the military funeral pounded the bloody images into our memory.

We all watched our first live murder on Sunday morning. Horns sounded and a patriotic Dallas nightclub owner strolled through police lines to execute the accused assassin. The image of Lee Oswald's agony is forever framed in the collective American unconscious. And the *New York Daily News* editorialized: "The only good murderer is a dead murderer, and the only good Communist is a dead Communist."

The identity of the real Lee Harvey Oswald (FBI informer, pawn of U.S. intelligence) was irrelevant on November 24, 1963, when that "police buff" Jack Ruby (triple agent: FBI, organized crime, anti-Castro gunrunner) was ushered into the Dallas Police and Courts building. Run and rerun on television as part of this spectacle of that autumn weekend was the ritual murder of the mad communist who had somehow escaped from the confinement of our Cold War consciousness. On that day Jack Ruby's handgun pointed straight out from the television screen at the head of every watching citizen. We put up our hands and shut our mouths.

The real Lee Harvey Oswald was a twenty-four-year-old throwaway of the military-intelligence machine, but the mythic Oswald had a long American genealogy. He was first and foremost an atomic mutant, the generic descendent of the myth of Julius and Ethel Rosenberg.

The future determines the past.

—Morton Sobell

The case—what the government always called "the atom spy ring"—was a generation's political baptism. Whether it was as Jean-Paul Sartre called it, "the start of World War III," or not, it certainly was the start for many of us in the 1950s of what was to become known in the 1960s as "the movement."

In those days the headlines rather than the tube handed down the fateful news of doomsday. It was the government men that dominated the stage with their federal agents, lawyers, judges, elected red hunters, and armies of functionaries. It was the United States versus the USSR and the "spies" were only attendant lords in the surreal drama. We in the public received our mythology from the front pages. Thousands of people who were later —through dint of hard study of transcripts and evidence—to become either expert in or obsessed with the case, followed from day-to-day the cartoonlike melodrama of the editorial imagination. At first we tender liberals thought the Rosenbergs and Sobell guilty; just as years later some of us—a small number now—would try to fit Oswald into the same Cold War mold of treason.

We are the first victims of American fascism.
—Ethel Rosenberg's
last death house letter

Following a generation behind bars for "conspiracy to commit espionage," Morton Sobell talked about the future controlling the past. That is, the past becomes received myth until artists and critics begin a revision or de-

mythologization. Existentially, the public past of America is gone and dead as the Rosenbergs or the Kennedys and Dr. King. If it were not gone, then we could change it. None of us can change the political cruelty of the past, but we can, if we are sufficiently lucid, *determine* it, given the weight of information now available about our collective Cold War madness. The new antimyths of the freelancers and the Freedom of Information movement do not invoke terror and pity in the old way. Rather, they try for anguish and a rooted solidarity.

The predicate for the tribunal now build-

Copyright 1976 Jules Feiffer

ing in the American consciousness is based on collective suffering and shame. We now realize that we are not, as we were told, guilty of the great crimes of violence perpetrated in our era. But we do feel shame for silence in the face of official evil and its cover-up. Shame, the only revolutionary emotion according to Marx, posits the reality of freedom, thus choice. Shame is the libido of the national judgment of the Cold War now forming, the releasing mechanism for hope in modern man and woman.

We do have a dirty rumor [Oswald's FBI link] . . . and it must be wiped out.
> —J. Lee Rankin, Warren Commission Chief Counsel

The conveyers of twentieth-century myth are film, tape, trials, technology, confessions —in short, the State and its visible paraphernalia. The infrastructure of the myth is the agony and confrontation between Science and Magic. The Rosenbergs and Morton Sobell were players in this myth.

The Cold War maimed and spoiled the American dream. Our "best and brightest" intellectuals committed collective treason, twitching to the signals and magic of science and power like so many Dostoyevskian pale criminals. Next there were the "creatures of the State," as Whittaker Chambers called himself and others, the professional prosecution witnesses condemned to talk and point forever.

We need a tribunal now so that we can be made to remember. A vast mnemonic device, a time capsule of lies to be exorcized: "The Bomb," "The Spy Ring," "The Korean Police Action," "The Lone Assassin," "The Vietnam Nation Building." We need to remember the past so that we want to change it. After feeling shame that the past cannot be changed, then will we know that we are free.

In the twentieth century we have begun to frighten ourselves to death with grotesque and mindless abstract blocs—"The Government," "The Masses," "The Power Structure," "The Outsider." These are our myths, and—like the ancients—we really believe them. The difference is that their myths were theirs and served them, whereas ours are invented from above and have made us sick. Racial and political myths can best be subverted by those who should know the most about storytelling—the playwrights. The artists take the baton from the free-lance investigator, on to the next order of abstraction and disenthrallment.

There is, now, a deep yearning for sanity and a great nausea at the spectacle of Bicentennial consolatory mythology. While the media heaps kudos on itself for saving the nation and exposing all the president's men, the scandal of their cover-up of the violence and conspiracy of the State itself continues.

The individualism of American assassins is what Europeans, and some Americans too, find hard to grasp. In other parts of the world, political assassination is usually the result of an elaborate plot. The object is to bring about a shift in power. No such plan appears to guide the American assassin.

—Time Magazine

The dereliction of the national media has been unprecedented. The *New York Times* hailed the Warren Report as the "final truth" after "the most painstaking, exhaustive investigation." The dissenting investigators who pored over the twenty-six volumes of evidence were labeled "scavengers." For two years no major news outlet would air one word of doubt! The report was above debate in the corporate media.

The loudest silence came from the liberal press, which had just begun to speak out against the red purges and racial discrimination of the 1950s. Not since the Rosenberg frame-up had liberals been so slow in reacting to official deception. Relieved that the commission had not found a leftist conspiracy behind the "pro-Castro defector," liberal journals were happy to forget about the whole affair.

While the media slept, working people carried home the tabloid press in grocery bags and found articles on the JFK murder wedged in between pieces on UFOs, cancer cures, and Liz and Dick's latest breakup. The government/media repression was bound to result in delusions: "JFK STILL ALIVE IN DALLAS HOSPITAL!"

Now from official Washington, the city of lies, comes the progress report that the "long nightmare is over." The terror bombers of Southeast Asia have been charged with a few white-collar crimes. The assassins of Guatemala, Cuba, Indonesia, Vietnam, Chile, and Angola have been convicted of misdemeanors as if the board of directors of Murder, Inc., had been caught cheating on their income tax.

It's a case of the chickens coming home to roost . . . Hate, allowed to spread unchecked, finally has struck down this country's chief of state.

—Malcolm X

After the first demystifiers like Sylvia Meagher and Mark Lane, other books and articles followed to question the report's "final truth" and to put the case before the American people. The wave of criticism swept the *New York Times, Life,* and CBS toward independent reviews of the evidence. But each investigation was aborted when the trial led toward conspiracy. After holding solidly for twelve years its minority opinion that Oswald acted alone, the corporate media is now pushing the scandalous fiction that Fidel Castro manipulated the murder in Dallas. It is a clear signal that the cover-up and the Cold War are down to their last revetment. The creatures from the Bay of Pigs that first spread the myth of the Castro conspiracy, like Frank Sturgis of Watergate, have reappeared.

In its cowardice, the media now intends to blame the FBI and CIA for not investigating the Cuban links to the crime when all along the major organs of opinion have known that the answers were here at home. In this country, the media does not cover up for communists.

During the long nightmare of the Cold War, we were assured from on high that we were being stabbed in the back. The men who told us that knew whereof they spoke. It was the cold warriors of the Invisible Government wielding the long knives (HUAC, Execution Action, Operation Chaos, CO-INTEL-PRO, etc.).

No, if health returns to America the remission will come from below. The time for a quick accounting is at hand. The action shifts from Dallas and Memphis to the Capitol at Washington, D. C.

There is a shit-storm coming.
—Norman Mailer

There, where it all began, an antispectacle is unfolding. For the first time since World War II the American public may undergo a positive and unifying mass experience. Television alone can build on the grammar of the Kefauver, Army-McCarthy, and Ervin inquiries and saturate the public with the terrible information of those megacides from Dallas to Watergate. This new electronic tribunal must also reach into every home, run and rerun, day after day, until the truth about the generation of official violence bleeds into the popular psyche and until the ghosts of the great victims are finally buried in the national memory. It is, of course, true that only a defeated nation must submit itself to a war crimes tribunal. But America *has* been defeated: The opening salvo of the war rang out in Dealey Plaza all those years ago! Charged with crimes against humanity, the red-handed conspirators will soon be in the historical dock.

With defeat, we must begin over again at ground level. The new history books of revision and demystification are in the stalls. The years from *Rush to Judgment* to *The Pentagon Papers* to *Inside the Company—CIA Diary* to the "Schweiker Report" are only moments in historical time.

We Americans have bided our time; *we* did not rush to judgment, *we* had faith and hope in the system; while we waited we saw our beloved country—which Frost called "the gift outright"—debauched and transformed into a gigantic and damned city of the plain. We saw Washington come to be like Dostoyevsky's St. Petersburg—the city that cannot be trusted.

Someone is coming who will take the ball out of the hands of the terrible players.
—Nellie Sachs, Nobel Prize-winning poet of the Holocaust

The need-to-know has reached a kind of critical mass for the American people. The "Red Menace" cover-story—for the machinations of the old secret government that held up for twenty-five years—has been blasted apart. Billions of preinflation dollars, hundreds of thousands of casualties, strangled priorities have ground to a halt the imperial propaganda machine that had infantalized our people and driven official America mad.

Time has run out now on the "terrible players" of the American Garrison State, on the traitors and the war lovers, on the assassins of the American people. Further patience on our part and on the part of Congress would be an insupportable historical scandal.

The time has come at last for sanity, for judgment, and for justice.

Donald Freed is coauthor of *Executive Action*, the first major novel (and Hollywood film) based on evidence from the John Kennedy murder investigation. His Broadway play about the Rosenberg-Sobell "spy ring" case, *Inquest*, was performed in 1970, and his book on the black liberation movement, *Agony in New Haven*, was published in 1973. His novel, *The Killing of R. F. K.*, came out in 1975. Freed lives and teaches college in Los Angeles.

PART 1
THE JOHN KENNEDY ASSASSINATION

1 STALKING THE WILD CONSPIRACY

It all started with the *National Guardian*, a politically progressive weekly newspaper. A five-page legal brief defending the ghost of Lee Oswald against charges from the Dallas police, the federal government, and the national press appeared in its December 19, 1963, issue. The author, a former New York state legislator named Mark Lane, sensed that the conclusions about Oswald came far too rapidly, were much too convenient, and clumsily contradicted themselves.

The *Guardian* piece was picked up by newspapers in Rome, Paris, Tokyo, Mexico City, and elsewhere. By virtue of his early article—quickly followed by a couple of others in the progressive press—Lane became the focal point for the public's desire for information on the subject, information neither the government nor the conventional press would willingly provide.[1] Having a good sense of dedication, organization, and self-promotion, attorney Lane set up shop on Fifth Avenue in lower Manhattan. His group was called the "Citizens Commission of Inquiry." C. C. I. chapters—sometimes no more than correspondents writing in for literature—quickly sprang up on dozens of U. S. campuses and in Europe.

Attending an early Lane lecture was a true

adventure. Nothing quite like it had happened before in American history; a new and fertile field of politics and history was unraveling. The sheer novelty of a man traveling through the country engaging the government in evidentiary combat made Lane's mission all the more intriguing. With little more than skepticism, press reports, and government pronouncements, Lane demonstrated how the known facts in the assassination of John Kennedy had been twisted, turned, obfuscated, and distorted to present the official line: that Lee Oswald, with no encouragement from any other party, killed John Kennedy. This was before the Warren Report was issued in September 1964, and although it appeared to the public that Lane was the one officer in a soldierless army, he was, in fact, the only one who made himself highly visible.

Others had the same doubts about the conventional wisdom propagated by the government. In Philadelphia attorney Vincent Salandria wrote and spoke on the subject. In Midlothian, Texas, Penn Jones, Jr., editor of the weekly four-page *Midlothian Mirror* hammered out editorials of skepticism. In Dallas a tiny group of people—secretaries, financiers, and others—started cataloging every scrap of evidence from the press and private conversations around town. Publications such as *The New Republic, Liberation,* and *Minority of One* were among the few where one could read dissenting words on Os-

1. The same week, a Gallup Poll revealed that fifty-two percent of the United States adult population thought some group or element was responsible along with the man who shot Kennedy. Oswald was not mentioned by name.

wald's presumed guilt. Shirley Martin, Margaret Field, and Sylvia Meagher in Oklahoma, California, and New York, respectively, pursued less publicized investigations of their own. Unencumbered by the overwhelming hostile press feedback Lane was receiving, these early amateur detectives undertook what government and media personnel did not dare: to explore and collate evidence that two or more people were involved in a plot to kill John Kennedy.

The publication of the Warren Report was supposed to finally silence the vocal but small band of critics. Here at last, seven wise men handed down the scroll based on months of painstaking investigation. The critics—often branded "leftists," "greedy," and "exploiters" (sometimes all three)—would see the error of their ways and slowly resign themselves to historical footnotes.

"As for the 1960 election, Mrs. Dixon thinks it will be determined by labor and won by a Democrat. But he will be assassinated or die in office . . ."
—JACK ANDERSON and FRED BLUMENTHAL
writing about forecaster Jeanne Dixon in *Parade,* May 13, 1956

The leading media in the country, CBS-TV, *The New York Times, The Washington Post,* and the Associated Press, treated the report with awe, placing it between Numbers and Deuteronomy. Still, skepticism around the country had not abated. A Louis Harris poll taken in the weeks following the report's publication showed that forty-five percent of the adult population still felt there were unanswered questions. Fully three of every ten surveyed felt that Lee Oswald had accomplices. The statistics indicated that one stated

" . . . we can't afford to make a mistake in America. So if this young Kennedy makes a mistake, he's got to be impeached immediately. We can't wait for a second."
—HENRY LUCE
to a private dinner party, circa 1961; quoted in *Heartland,* by Mort Sahl

purpose of the report—to quell the wild rumors of conspiracy—was not met. The release of the report and the twenty-six volumes of evidence and testimony allowed the masses of people to read for themselves what the freelance sleuths had been talking about.

In Europe there was no question from the start that the assassination of John Kennedy and the subsequent murder of the accused were carried out by a conspiracy. The press there reversed the process followed by the conventional news media in the United States. Contradictions, suppositions, rumors, reasoned theories, and logical hypotheses dominated coverage of the assassination investigation; pronouncements from the U.S. government received sidebar status.

A June 1964 visit to Britain by Mark Lane led to the formation of the British "Who Killed Kennedy?" committee under the aegis of philosopher Bertrand Russell. Lord Russell quite properly saw himself as an international citizen with the obligation to speak out on issues regardless of national boundary. His early criticism of U.S. involvement in Vietnam helped establish European feelings on the subject. In 1963 he met with Helen Sobell, wife of imprisoned "atom spy ring conspirator" Morton Sobell, as she traveled through Europe enlisting support for her husband. And so it was not out of character

for Russell to question the official assassination investigation. Unfortunately, most of the effort in this direction under Lord Russell's "Who Killed Kennedy?" committee was hot air.

"We cannot, as a free nation, compete with our adversaries in tactics of terror, assassination, false promises, counterfeit mobs and crises."

—JOHN KENNEDY
Edmundson Pavillion, Seattle, Washington, November 16, 1961

Russell himself had little to do with the committee. It was, from the start, the work of his assistant Ralph Schoenman, who manipulated evidence and personalities to his advantage. The "committee" was never a committee. It never once met. At most it was a letterhead of prestigious names, such as playwright John Arden and Oxford modern history professor Hugh Trevor-Roper. Schoenman would issue releases in the committee's name, statements which committee members would find harder and harder to support, branding them "sophistries." In the opinion of some, it was a complete sham. At least one member, Professor Trevor-Roper, broke off relations entirely. During this same time period, Russell's name appeared over an article entitled "Sixteen Questions on the Assassination" in the American publication "Minority of One." The article contained many errors of fact. Unfortunately, constructive criticism from American sympathizers was not forthcoming. Russell's position on the issue did, however, merit an attack from *New York Times* editor Harrison Salisbury in his glowing introduction to the highly profitable *Times* paperback version of the Warren Report. The other substantial attack on Russell was from journalist I. F. Stone,[2] who, curiously, gave his immediate and unequivocal endorsement to the Commission and its findings.[3]

Elsewhere in Europe attention was focused on writer Joachim Joesten. Born in Cologne in 1907, later escaping Hitler's Germany where the Gestapo branded him an undesirable leftist, Joesten gained U. S. citizenship in 1948, although his primary residence became Munich. By November 1963 Joesten had already written twenty-six books. The assassination set Joesten upon his most ambitious project yet. He traveled to Dallas, Washington, and elsewhere tracking down leads in the conspiracy. Hastily assembling research into books, Joesten became Europe's most prolific

Warren Report critic. Unfortunately, much of his information came secondhand or via unchallenged news clippings from America. Joesten was at a distinct disadvantage in that he could not pick up a phone and double-check information, and he used material from sources shown to be unreliable. The continuum many researchers follow of developing theories based on carefully gathered facts was more like a merry-go-round for Joesten. While his findings were many, and his early work proved valuable in awakening many to flaws in government investigations, his later volumes were top-heavy with specu-

---

"We are under pressure from our military to use force against Cuba. . . . If the situation continues much longer, the president is not sure that the military will not overthrow him and seize power."

—ROBERT KENNEDY
to Soviet Ambassador Anatoly Dobrynin, Autumn 1962 (during the 'Missile Crisis'); quoted in *Khrushchev Remembers*

---

2. Lord Russell had obtained a press copy of the Warren Report a few days before the official release so he would be prepared to discuss and attack it. Stone, usually a meticulous fact checker, assumed that Russell's information on the newly released report came via telephone from Mark Lane and chastised the Briton for speaking out of turn.

3. "I believe the commission has done a first rate job, on a level that does our country proud," Stone wrote in the "Weekly" for October 5, 1964. "I regard the case against Lee Harvey Oswald as the lone killer of the president as conclusive."

lation. Despite this, Joesten was for years the primary source of information for the European community which followed the subject. In 1968 he started a biweekly news bulletin called the "Truth Letter," which kept the small list of subscribers up to date on assassination facts and theories. The newsletter ceased publication in October 1972 when Joesten's health made continued efforts im-

From Europe: anarchist art blends fact and fantasy, avoiding speculation altogether. Left—from England, right—from Italy.

Socialist Worker—London

From the Montreal 13th International Salon of Cartoons

possible. A courageous man despite the subjective errors in his works, Joesten died in August 1975, a little-known but nonetheless quite important critic.

"I talked with some of the leading people there [in Dallas]. They wondered whether the president should go to Dallas, and so do I."
—ADLAI STEVENSON
following his nasty reception in Dallas October 25, 1963; quoted in *A Thousand Days,* by Arthur Schlesinger, Jr.

Back in the United States little legitimacy was granted the growing band of critics. The legal profession, which, like the rest of us, observed the travesty of justice in Dallas and the subsequent investigation, remained silent. For a case generally acknowledged to be the major murder investigation of the century,

one in which numerous significant legal questions arose, the American Bar Association's lack of activity is curious.[4] The closest that prestigious organization came to commenting on the investigation was a January 1965 article in the *A.B.A. Journal* by Warren Commission staff attorney Alfredda Scobey. The author raised the question of whether Oswald was properly "represented" and afforded his rights in commission hearings; she concluded he was.

The American Medical Association was no better. The only action the A.M.A.'s House of Delegates took was to pass a resolution extending sympathy to the widow Kennedy and her two children. Periodically, the *A.M. News* would print articles on medical evidence considered by the Warren Commission.

---

4. A past president of the A.B.A. was appointed to a somewhat confused role as Lee Oswald's attorney during the Warren Commission hearings. He "participated" in two commission sessions.

REPORTER: *Mr. President, Fidel Castro claims to have captured some Americans whom he says are CIA agents, and he says he is going to execute them. Is there anything at all you can tell us about this?*
JOHN KENNEDY: *No, no.*
Press conference exchange, October 31, 1963

One report, in the issue of January 4, 1964, showed that the autopsy results were at odds with the official conclusion, but this discrepancy was not followed up. Now and then letters would appear in the *A.M. News* about the medical evidence, but as an organization, the American Medical Association did nothing to resolve the problems created by the medical evidence.

Criticism did come from other medical sources. The American Academy of Forensic Sciences, whose members are trained in conducting autopsies, spoke out about the examination of John Kennedy's body in Dallas and Bethesda as early as 1966. It was, perhaps, the most important autopsy in the country's history, and it had been badly botched. They wanted to rectify the situation as best they could. Factors such as the angle of bullet entry and exit, and the amount of bullet fragments left in the body were left unresolved. Eight presidents of the Academy have called for reopening the investigation for scientific tests.

The personalities of both Lee Oswald and Jack Ruby were for years the subject of abstract psychological study. One of the more ponderous conclusions was prepared by University of Cincinnati psychiatrist James Hamilton, who presented his findings at a meeting sponsored by both the A.M.A. and the American Psychiatric Association. Oswald, according to Hamilton, lived in a fantasy world, and spent most of his time trying to master the feelings related to his father's death (two months prior to Lee's birth). Kennedy was a "father-figure" to Oswald, Hamilton noted, and in November 1963 the assassin "nestled in the womb-like setting of the warehouse, surrounded by cartons of books (he had been an avid reader) and he re-enacted the situation that he had omnipotently fantasized had taken place two months before his birth, striking from above and behind to control his own fears of such attacks upon himself."

The assassination and its effect upon Americans provided academicians with subject matter for abstract research in almost every field. Esoteric studies, such as "Resolu-

REPORTER: *Mr. President, in view of the changed situation in South Vietnam [coup d'etat and assassination of Diem], do you still expect to bring back 1,000 troops before the end of the year, or has that figure been raised or lowered?*
JOHN KENNEDY: *No, we are still going to bring back several hundred before the end of the year. . . .*
Press conference exchange, November 14, 1963

Attitudes on the Warren Commission's conclusions change over the years. At left, Herblock, September 1964; on the right, Herblock, May 1976.

"It's a Light and I Don't Like It"

Copyright 1964 by Herblock in the Washington Post

"EXACTLY! IF WE HAD SHARED OUR SECRETS WITH PEOPLE LIKE THAT, IT MIGHT HAVE ENDANGERED NATIONAL SECURITY"

Copyright 1976 by Herblock in the Washington Post

tion of the Liberal Dilemma in the Assassination of President John Kennedy,''[5]

5. Using classic survey techniques, this study, published in the December 1965 *Journal of Personality*, concluded that liberals found it hard to accept that Oswald was both liberal and guilty, while those with a more conservative foreign policy outlook found it easier to believe. The survey was underwritten by the National Science Foundation.

dotted professional journals through the mid-sixties, taking up library space but adding virtually nothing to the body of knowledge accumulated on the assassination. One reason is that most of them began with the premise that Lee Oswald was guilty as charged.

The years 1966 and 1967 were pivotal in the movement to reopen the investigation into

John Kennedy's murder. Critical books such as *Inquest, Six Seconds in Dallas, Rush to Judgment, Whitewash, Accessories After the Fact,* and *Forgive My Grief* gave support to the widespread underground of buffs throughout the country.[6] Finally, one did not have to attend a Mark Lane lecture to have assassination information intelligently spelled out. The dissenters had invaded the bookstores.

To a lesser extent, dissenting opinion also came to the newsstand. Both *Life*[7] and the *Saturday Evening Post*[8] suggested a new investigation was in order, but their follow through—especially that of *Life*—was lacking. The most aggressive periodical at the time was *Ramparts,* a muckraking lefty magazine with universal appeal. Guided by an editorial policy which blended flash, controversy, and vanguard politics, *Ramparts* editor Warren Hinckle imported a team of experts in the field to prepare a special report on the subject.

Many leftists at the time thought conspiracy investigation was a silly and time-wasting business. What difference did it make who killed Kennedy in 1963 when his successor was shipping off thousands of soldiers to Vietnam every month? One *Ramparts* editor,

6. The word buff, always a slight embarrassment to followers of the assassination, refers to those who follow the case exclusively through public dialogue, books, newspapers, and magazines.

7. November 25, 1966.

8. January 14, 1967.

Robert Sheer, characterized involvement in the controversy as "moral masturbation." More than anything else, the sleuths were simply tolerated by political activists, who found the raging controversy over one tiny bullet somewhat amusing.

" . . . J. A. Milteer [National States Rights Party official] on November 9, 1963 at Miami, Florida, made a statement that plans were in the making to kill President John F. Kennedy at some future date. . . . "
FBI report, Warren Commission Document No. 1347

By the time the *Ramparts* issue on the assassination appeared, the work of the special research team became subordinate to what became known as the "strange deaths list." While the strange deaths list never furthered the assassination investigation one bit, its universal appeal attracted tens of thousands more to the subject than any well-reasoned theory ever could.

The strange deaths list was the province of Penn Jones, Jr., the small-town newspaper editor from Midlothian, Texas. Jones, an aggressive, likable, and highly opinionated populist, had noticed a disturbing pattern among people whose lives touched on the Kennedy assassination: They seemed to be meeting quick, unnatural deaths. Jones began to editorialize about this in the four-page weekly *Mirror,* and soon presented all his in-

GUILE BY JURY

SCRIPT: TOM MILLER • ART: CHAS. OLDHAM
WITH APOLOGIES TO GILBERT & SULLIVAN

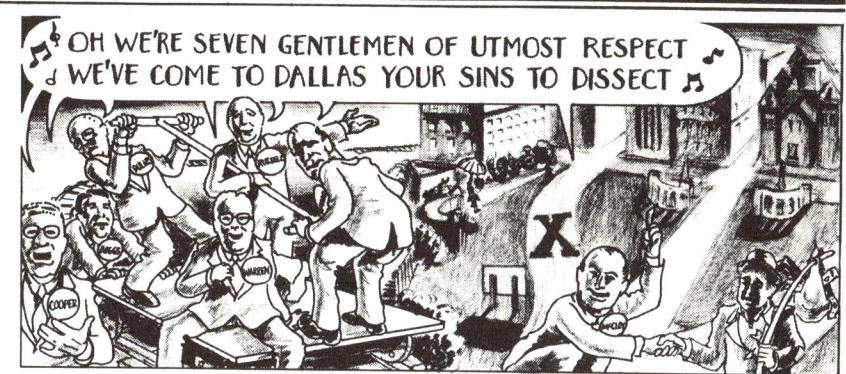

formation in his ongoing *Forgive My Grief* series, volumes I-IV. To *Ramparts* this was just the right angle. A mystery growing out of mystery. Something everyone could relate to. Nationally, the media seized on it, and Jones's strange deaths list became legendary.[9] As *Saga* magazine headlined a Penn Jones article in 1968: *"One by one they die under the most mysterious circumstances—'suicides,' auto 'accidents,' and 'apparent' heart attacks. Can it all be extraordinary coincidence, or is it all part of a sinister plot to liquidate the*

"Well, on November the 17th [1963] . . . I was on duty at the FBI office in New Orleans from twelve midnight until eight in the morning, and that was, as I remember it, a Sunday morning. I received a teletype from FBI headquarters, Washington. It was a normal movement teletype indicating that the president was going to be in Dallas on the 22nd, and that the FBI in Washington had information that an attempt would be made on President Kennedy's life in Dallas."

—WILLIAM WALTER
former FBI employee on *CBS Reports Inquiry,* November 26, 1975

---

9. Details of *Ramparts* involvement in the JFK controversy are in Warren Hinckle's *If You Have a Lemon, Make Lemonade,* chapter 6: "Give Us This Day Our Daily Paranoia." "I wanted [to get] people talking about the Warren Report with the cynicism they did about the weather report," Hinckle wrote.

people who hold the key to the murder that still nags at the world's conscience?" Even today, in any barroom across the country when the talk drifts to the Kennedy assassination, someone will inevitably mention the strange deaths as part of the mystery. It has become proletarian folklore.

Because the strange deaths list served its purpose so well, few people took a closer look at it. The unspoken hypothesis is that numerous people associated with the assassination and its aftermath have been silenced by a dread unknown force determined to keep The Truth forever sealed. Taking a few names from the list at random, we find Earlene Roberts, Dorothy Kilgallen, Delilah Walle, Edward Benevides, and David Ferrie. Here is how they became part of the strange deaths list:

Earlene Roberts was the housekeeper on Beckley Street in Dallas where Lee Oswald had a room 11-22-63. She testified to the Warren Commission that in the brief time Oswald was home that afternoon at one o'clock, a Dallas police car drove up to the house, honked lightly twice, and pulled away. She "had opportunity to talk with Oswald after the assassination," Jones has written. Mrs. Roberts's sister knew Jack Ruby. At age 60, on January 9, 1966, Mrs. Roberts died of "an apparent heart attack."

Dorothy Kilgallen, syndicated columnist and game show panelist, had an interest in the assassination and attended Jack

Ruby's March 1964 murder trial. Some reports say she had an exclusive interview with Ruby during the trial, making her the only person to talk with him in total privacy at the time. Others say this is myth, and her interview consisted of a brief exchange of pleasantries. At the beginning of November 1965, Kilgallen

---

"I don't think that there is any doubt that Fidel Castro, as a symbol of revolution in this hemisphere, has failed badly. . . ."
—JOHN KENNEDY
to the Florida Chamber of Commerce, November 18, 1963

told a friend she was going to break the assassination mystery wide open. At age 52, on November 8, 1965, she died at her home. An autopsy report on November 16 said she died of barbiturates and drink. Asked Jones two weeks later: "Is she another victim of possibly knowing the secret that still moves in the troubled mind of Jack Ruby?" (Ruby's death by cancer fourteen months later is also on the list.) To fuel the mystery, two days after Kilgallen's death, a confidant of hers, Mrs. Earl T. Smith, died of undetermined causes, which earned her a spot on the list.

Delilah, a stripper at the Carousel Club in November and December 1963, was later reported to be working on a book about the assassination. In August 1966, still a stripper, she married Leonard Walle of New Orleans, and they moved to Omaha, Nebraska. In the fourth week of their marriage, Delilah's husband killed her, for which he received a twenty year prison sentence. "We do not know why Delilah was killed," Jones wrote in volume II of his series. "Was she considered too important to remain alive?"

Edward Benevides had a brother named Domingo, who witnessed the killing of Dallas policeman J. D. Tippit. Domingo's description of the assailant did not fit Lee Oswald, who was charged with the murder. Jones reports that Domingo received threats on his life, and in February 1964, brother Edward died in a beer-hall brawl. "Both Domingo and his father-in-law, Mr. W. J. Jackson, felt the murder was a case of mistaken identity," Jones reported.

David Ferrie, a very strange investigator, pilot, low-level mob functionary, CIA contract agent, and cultist, was the primary suspect in New Orleans District Attorney Jim Garrison's investigation of the assassination in 1967. A few days after this became public, Ferrie died of a "brain hemorrhage," while at the same time leaving a couple of suicide notes.

Others on the strange deaths list include Dallas sheriff Hiram Ingram, age 53. In volume III, Jones writes that "while at home, he fell and broke his hip. He was taken to a hospital where he died of cancer three days later. Ingram was a special friend of former deputy sheriff Roger Craig," whose testimony to the Warren Commission showed clear evidence of conspiracy in the assassination. The strange deaths list has many more equally dubious entries.

The biggest element in the strange deaths folklore is an essentially meaningless statistic which the *London Sunday Times* developed. An actuary said that the odds of fifteen material witnesses to the assassination dying within 39 months of the event were 100,000 trillion to one. It's a provocative figure, and assassination lecturers use it constantly to make a point. The article it comes from, however, shows the scare tactic to be more tactical than scary.

After relating the "suicide" of David Ferrie,

"The CIA will have to be dealt with."
—JOHN KENNEDY
to staff members mid-November 1963; quoted in *To Move a Nation,* by Roger Hilsman

---

which does indeed appear connected to his culpability, the *Sunday Times* of February 26, 1967, explained that they had an actuary compute the life expectancy of fifteen of the dead, concluding that on the morning of November 22, 1963, there was one chance in about 10 to the 29th power that they would all be dead by late February 1967. "More crudely," the article stated, "the odds against all 15 dying were 100,000 trillion to one. This statistic is not grounds for any sinister conclusion. The odds against a randomly selected sample of fifteen Americans all dying

---

"Kennedy could be an even greater president than Lincoln . . . Kennedy is a man you can talk with. I have gotten this impression from all my conversations with Khrushchev. . . . Personally, I consider him [Kennedy] responsible for everything, but I will say this: He has come to understand many things over the past few months, and then too, in the last analysis I am convinced that anyone else would be worse."

—FIDEL CASTRO
to French journalist Jean Daniel, November 20, 1963

in a similar period of time would be much the same. . . . '' They concluded that the "statistics are not proof of anything. . . . They simply introduce an element of cool science into a very irrational situation."

That was the *Times* early edition. Between that article and the final edition that same day

---

"I am sure that all but a handful of our citizens will cordially welcome the President of the United States to Dallas."
—JESSE CURRY
Dallas Police Chief, November 1963

---

the article was "lawyered," with the new version omitting the sensational strange death odds. A more accurate statistical sampling was established, and they concluded that "there is no reason for surprise at the mere numbers" of violent deaths among witnesses. The unnatural deaths, said the actuary, warranted "a tremor of suspicion."

The fifteen people in the actuary's list are Lee Oswald, Jack Ruby, Edward Benevides, Dorothy Kilgallen, J. D. Tippit, David Ferrie, Delilah Walle, Bill Hunter (see 4-4-64 in Chapter 3), H. T. Killam (see 3-17-64 in Chapter 3), Jim Koethe (see 9-21-64 in Chapter 3), Lee Bowers (railroad employee positioned behind the School Book Depository, who saw two men in a likely assassination position behind a nearby picket fence, died in a one car accident at Midlothian, Tex., (!) on 8-9-66), Nancy Mooney (evidently they meant Betty Mooney MacDonald, whose connection to the assassination was that she was at a February 1963 party the Lee Oswalds attended, and who was the alibi for a man accused — and subsequently cleared—of shooting a used car salesman who saw Officer Tippit's assailant leaving the murder site; MacDonald was jailed in early 1964 after a fight with her roommate, and was found hanged by her toreador pants in the Dallas jail an hour after imprisonment), Frank Martin (head of the Juvenile Department of Dallas Police, testified before the Warren Commission, died 6-16-66 of cancer), Harold Russell (saw someone fleeing the Tippit killing, his description did not fit that of Oswald; at a party in Oklahoma 7-23-65 he started acting uncontrollably, police came to quiet him down, hit him on the head with a pistol, and he died a few hours later), and James Worrell (saw a rifle in Depository window at the time of the shooting, saw a man fleeing the building minutes later, died in a motorcycle accident 11-9-66).

After carefully appraising the strange deaths linked to the Kennedy assassination, the mystery is not so much why all these peo-

---

"Henry, the Secret Service told me that they had taken care of everything—there's nothing to worry about."
—JOHN KENNEDY
responding to Congressman Henry Gonzalez's fears about Dallas, on the plane to Texas, November 21, 1963

---

ple were killed, but rather, why they were included on the list in the first place. Asked at a conspiracy researchers conference in 1975 how high the list had gotten, Penn Jones replied: "Hell, I don't know what it's at now. I think I've made my point."[10] Indeed he had.[11]

The Garrison investigation, which began in late 1966 and lasted through the Clay Shaw trial in March 1969, became the arbitrary dividing line between first- and second-generation researchers. First-generation critics, those who started investigations within a year or so of the assassination, were too small in number to allow room for destructive personality conflicts. Except for propagandist Mark Lane, who relied on the work of others, most of the critics were content to stay home with mountains of books, documents and clippings, methodically piecing together

10. When forensic pathologist Cyril Wecht was allowed in 1972 to view medical evidence in the Kennedy case at the National Archives in Washington, he was heading back from lunch with researcher David Lifton when a U.S. military car came within a hair of hitting him. "I often wonder what Penn Jones might have written if Wecht has been run over by an Army car in front of the National Archives," Lifton mused later.

11. In a silly attempt to outdo the Kennedy assassination, the supermarket tabloid *Midnight* headlined its 7-12-76 article about Watergate "30 KEY WITNESSES MET VIOLENT DEATHS." The newspaper said that "Watergate had surpassed" the dead witness list of the Kennedy assassination. This is the same publication that told us two years earlier that Oswald was possessed by the devil when he shot JFK, and that exorcism may have prevented the assassination where the Secret Service could not.

hypotheses of the assassination and showing fallacies in the Warren Commission's work. Their living rooms resembled oversized filing cabinets.

Defenders of the Warren Commission simply referred to the report as the final arbiter of truth and benevolently dismissed all critics as loonies. Books defending the commission and attacking the critics rarely showed evidence of research beyond what we were told in the weeks following the assassination. One of the few commission defenders who was open to a semblance of public dialogue was Wesley Liebler, a commission staff attorney who taught law at UCLA. In addition to his specialty, antitrust law, Liebler held a seminar on the Warren Commission for interested law students, in which each student was assigned an area of investigation to see if conclusions other than those found by

the commission would arise. First-generation researcher David Lifton was invited to play devil's advocate in the class, which was itself run like a miniature Warren Commission. Lifton's experience with the class gave him insight into how the commission itself operated. The fault lay not so much with a commission staff cover-up, Lifton concluded, but rather with the way lawyers operate. The students, to no one's surprise, ended up supporting the commission findings.

"I am convinced from that class that lawyers are simply trained to think that way. They took things at face value," Lifton said later. "It has to do with the way lawyers see the world. They perceive reality through this overlay of evidence. My inferences regarding conspiracy were perceived by them as being unreasonable. Period. If you give them the Mannlicher-Carcano rifle, they *assume* it's the murder weapon. If you suggest that the rifle or bullet was a plant, that seems irrational to them. To assume that someone lied to the commission or to show fudgery by the authorities is not something students trained in law school feel comfortable with. They simply don't think that way." Liebler, while evidently the most skeptical of the staff attorneys, has never publicly renounced the commission's findings.[12]

"Oh my God! They've shot my husband!"
—JACQUELINE KENNEDY

By the time New Orleans District Attorney Jim Garrison's investigation into the Kennedy assassination became public in February 1967, the Harris survey showed that fifty-nine percent of adult Americans thought there were still unanswered questions about the assassination, and forty-four percent felt there was a broader plot than we had been

told. Garrison's main suspect, David Ferrie, had the background and contacts which made him a likely candidate for conspirator of the year. His rather untimely death, virtually coinciding with public knowledge of his impending arrest, left Garrison without a focal point for his investigation.

The D.A.'s activities in the ensuing months had a double effect. First, the conventional press, looking for solid leads in the case, was continually offended by Garrison's ever-changing pronouncements of when or if the case would be solved, and who was involved. Disappointed, the pack reporters who flocked to New Orleans for The Story could only wire back that Garrison was a slick, grand, egotistical, and hardnosed investigator, but that there was nothing there.

The truth is that there was too much there. Garrison was fed lead after lead, some of which checked out, many of which didn't. On occasion, false evidence was planted to divert him. By the time he arrested local businessman Clay Shaw on conspiracy, Garrison's information was too diffuse to gain a conviction. Evidence of conspiracy he had solid; evidence against Clay Shaw as a conspirator was too flimsy to sway a single juror.[13]

When Garrison began his probe, Warren Commission critics set out for New Orleans. Here was a man with an entire police and investigative force at his disposal who was will-

---

12. At a party in Liebler's home in late 1967, researcher Lifton was introduced to another commission staff attorney, David Slawson, who it turned out, like Liebler, taught antitrust law in the area. "Oh, you also teach antitrust law!" Lifton remarked on meeting Slawson. "That's right," chimed in Liebler. "After we fucked it up on the Warren Commission, we all got a chance to come out to California and teach antitrust law."

13. When Clay Shaw died in August 1974, the following notice appeared in *Variety:* "CLAY SHAW. America didn't kill him, but we didn't keep him alive. —Rod McKuen and the staff of Stanyon Records."

ing to subpoena people! Put them on the stand! Unlock dark secrets of the Warren Commission! To a large extent, the Garrison probe did just that. Despite all the misinformation flowing in and out of the district attorney's office, a substantial body of knowledge about the assassination was added to

David Milne

"My God! They're going to kill us all!"
—JOHN CONNALLY
realizing that both he and the president have been hit, November 22, 1963

information already accumulated, and this brought on the second effect. The Garrison probe was the major turning point in public opinion on the subject. It heightened awareness like no other single factor since Ruby shot Oswald. Surveys at the time showed that the number of people feeling there was a broader plot jumped by a third in the space of three months. Garrison came on like a people's hero rather than someone ordained from on high. Despite accusations of strong-arm investigative tactics, which could have been true, Garrison's activity successfully dealt a serious blow to the carefully maintained line from Washington that the conclusions of the Warren Commission were impregnable.[14] (A resolution introduced in September 1966 by

14. The whole issue of homosexuality was constantly just beneath the surface, as many of the men accused by Garrison and his staff were part of New Orleans' large gay population. A lengthly article in a 1975 issue of the "Fag Rag," a Boston-based gay newspaper, is the only place where the sexual aspect of the assassination and its investigation is fully explored. The article concludes that Garrison's investigation was partly motivated by sexual attitudes. It was this sexual aspect of the assassination controversy which prompted Penn Jones to utter the immortal words, "I don't care how a man gets his orgasm, as long as he doesn't use that orgasm to destroy our democratic form of government."

New York Congressman Theodore Kupferman calling on the House of Representatives to review the Warren Commission findings was the first "legitimacy" the researchers' movement gained. Kupferman was virtually alone in Congress, however, and the resolution died.)

'They killed him! They've killed the president!"

—ABRAHAM ZAPRUDER

Dallas businessman while filming the event, November 22, 1963

While Jim Garrison was providing human and documentary evidence of the assassination conspiracy, the rest of the country was undergoing major shifts in other ways. Lyndon Johnson was ordering bombers to destroy Vietnam, dollars and soldiers were flowing nonstop into that country, the antiwar movement at home was rapidly growing, and civil rights activity was becoming increasingly militant. The political dynamics this created necessitated strong cultural support, and in 1966 the play *MacBird!* had its initial performances in Berkeley, California. *MacBird!* combined biting commentary on Lyndon Johnson, the assassination of John Kennedy, and the way power bloc politics works. Playwright Barbara Garson, using Shakespearean dialogue, had produced a work of art which gave both comfort and stimulation to those opposing the federal government. In the play Lyndon Johnson usurps power from John Kennedy and becomes locked in an untenable position on the assassination and the war. Recruiting the Earl of Warren to head a special commission, MacBird tells him:

MACBIRD: I'd like a full investigation,
                     Conducted by a man of such
                         repute
                     That we may put an end to
                         all these doubts.
                     That man is you.
EARL: Oh, cursed spite
                     That ever I was born to set
                         things right.
MACBIRD: I don't believe you understand the job.
                     I wouldn't say you're asked
                         to set things *right*.
                     I think you get the point.
EARL: Oh, whine and pout,
                     That ever I was born to bury
                         doubt.
MACBIRD: You get the picture now.[15]

Eventually *MacBird!* became a national hit, opening in New York in January 1967, with

---

15. *MacBird!* even alluded to the Robert Kennedy assassination two years early. After their brother has been shot, Ted and Robert discuss their plans. "What should we do?" Ted asks. Replies Robert:

This murderous gun that's shot
Is not yet empty, so our safest course
Is to avoid its aim.

stock companies playing throughout the country.[16]

On Broadway a play called *The Trial of Lee Harvey Oswald* opened in November 1967 while *MacBird!* was playing in Greenwich Village. (The same week, U.S. planes dropped bombs within three miles of Hanoi, and Defense Secretary Robert McNamara called up an additional 12,000 National Guardsmen for riot duty back home.) *The Trial of Lee Harvey Oswald*, evidently an underfinanced venture, depicted the courtroom drama which would have ensued had Ruby not killed Oswald. At the play's end, after Oswald maintained he was merely a dupe for a well-organized conspiracy, the audience was invited to be the jury.[17] Unfortunately, only a select few theatergoers became jurors, as the play closed in six days.[18] [19]

Other plays fared better. In Atlanta in April 1968, at one of the most extraordinary times

> *"Get a man on top of that triple underpass and see what happened up there!"*
> **—JESSE CURRY**
> speaking into his car's radio microphone to police department subordinates after hearing shots

in American history, theatergoers were treated to *Lee Harvey Oswald—A Far Mean Streak of Indepence Brought On By Negleck*.[20] The Garrison probe was going on at the time, Martin Luther King had been murdered a few weeks earlier in Memphis, and his killer had been traced as far as Atlanta.[21] The Poor People's March to Resurrection City at Washington, D.C., was about to pass through town. Georgia officials were chagrined when, that same week, demonstrators at the University of Georgia at Athens carried a coffin reading DEATH OF FREEDOM OF SPEECH AND ASSEMBLY. Emory University, normally a fairly sedate institution, was showing a movie about draft resisters, and *MacBird!* was playing to full houses elsewhere in town. Black uprisings in ghettos all across the country were just subsiding following the King assassination, and students at Columbia University and elsewhere were verbally

---

16. All quotes from *MacBird!* copyright 1966, 1967 by Barbara Garson.

17. This evidently did not sit well with *New York Times* critic Clive Barnes, who called the whole production "a perversion of democratic processes."

18. An effort to restage this particular drama for network television was underway in 1976.

19. During the week of previews and at the show's opening, a group calling for a reopening of the assassination investigation collected over a thousand signatures at a table in front of the theater. While it may convincingly be argued that one could collect a thousand signatures for *anything* at 52nd Street and Broadway in the course of a week, it does seem significant that it was done for this purpose at that time.

20. The title comes from Oswald writing in his diary, describing himself.

21. The week the Oswald play opened in Atlanta, newspapers headlined a possible link between the Kennedy and King murders.

and literally attacking their own colleges. Lester Maddox was governor, George Wallace was running for president, and Lyndon Johnson had abdicated only four weeks earlier. It was in this context that Michael Hasting's play about Oswald opened in Atlanta. The drama, which dwelled on the dynamics in Oswald's life, made use of the entire theater, as commentators roamed the audience speaking about Oswald and his relations with his wife, mother, and the rest of the world. Following the opening night performance, respected Warren Commission critic Josiah Thompson and commission staff attorney Alfredda Scobey debated facts and theories in the assassination investigation for the audience. The crowd supported Thompson. The Kennedy assassination had become a reference point not only in our personal and na-tional life, but a constant allusion on stage as well.[22]

In December 1973 The Invisible Theatre, a homegrown Tucson, Arizona, company performing original and creative drama, staged something called *Test Patterns*, a series of short skits depicting one day's television programming on a mythical station. One program was described as

7:00

5 PARANOIA PLAYHOUSE
"Jack Ruby—Private Eye"
(1963—***) Jack Ruby is offered a special assignment by Jackie Kennedy. Also featured in this tale of suspense and tangled emotions is Lee Harvey Oswald . . .

A free university course in San Francisco on political assassination presented its findings on Jack Ruby dramatically on stage in 1975.

There have been fewer movies on the Kennedy assassination. Other than the feature *Executive Action* released in November 1973, no full-length picture on the subject has appeared. While not a particularly well-produced film, the release of *Executive Action* was timed particularly well to coincide with the growing skepticism in the country caused in part by Watergate. Public dialogue on the

---

"In a crucial and astonishing breakdown in communications systems, the telephone system went out immediately after the shots were fired in Dallas, but the breakdown didn't occur in Dallas, it occurred in Washington, D.C."

—Executive Action movie fact sheet

"They [Senator Edward Kennedy and friend Claude Hooten] began to wonder whether the failure of the [telephone] system could be more than an accident."

—WILLIAM MANCHESTER
in *The Death of a President*

---

22. In the production notes to his 1968 drama "Little Murders," Jules Feiffer wrote "the play is a post-assassination play, but the era of gratuitous violence that Kennedy's death highlighted was, I think, coming into its own before November 22, 1963."

Can't Keep From Crying

TOPICAL BLUES ON THE DEATH OF PRESIDENT KENNEDY

Featuring Big Joe Williams, Johnny Young, James and Fannie Brewer, Otis Spann, Mary Ross, Avery Brady, John Lee Granderson, Jimmy Brown, Bill Jackson TESTAMENT RECORDS S-01

"Es una mala noticia."

—FIDEL CASTRO

to journalist Jean Daniel on learning of Kennedy's assassination, November 22, 1963

subject took a sharp upturn with the tenth anniversary of the assassination; old arguments were rehashed, and new ones slowly made their way into print.

In 1964 a movie entitled *The Trial of Lee Harvey Oswald* showed four times in Milwaukee, but never gained national distribution. Like the play of the same name, the movie attempted to show evidence that would have been presented at an Oswald trial. It was scheduled for rerelease in November 1976.[23]

The 1968 movie, *Greetings,* although not particularly concerned with the assassination *per se*, did make the buffs part of movie lore.

23. The new backers of the film claim the 1967 Broadway play was pirated from their film's brief 1964 showing. As the television version of the play was readied, a legal fight over the name appeared possible in late 1976.

One major role was that of an assassination buff consumed with the subject to the exclusion of everything else in his life. Robert De Niro was also in the movie. In 1976 De Niro played the lead role in *Taxi Driver,* which, along with the 1975 movie *Nashville,* reinforced the anticonspiracy idea of a lone-nut assassin.

Finally, *Rush to Judgment,* Mark Lane's media blitz, became a movie as well as a book and two records. The film effectively advocated conspiracy by demonstrating through interview and on-the-spot footage how it was impossible for one person to have killed John Kennedy. (Assisting Lane in his investigation were interested college students around the country. At Brandeis University aiding with the assassination research was budding actress Louise Lasser, who years later starred in the soap opera *Mary Hartman Mary Hartman.*)

Just as interesting as the plays and movies about the assassination is the recorded music. In popular music, this has taken different forms. Perhaps the best known line in rock & roll about the assassination is contained in the Rolling Stones' "Sympathy for the Devil," with Mick Jagger singing of collective guilt:

I shouted out 'who killed the Kennedys?'
When after all, it was you and me.[24]

The Byrds, in their highly acclaimed "Turn
Turn Turn" album took a traditional melody
for the song "He was a Friend of Mine" and
changed the words into a tribute to John
Kennedy.[25] Although lyricist Jim McGuinn
opted for the lone assassin theory ("from a
sixth floor window a gunner shot him
down"),[26] the song displays affection for
Kennedy on a level not found elsewhere.
Another emotional expression on the death
of John Kennedy was Phil Ochs' "That Was
the President," a folk-ballad of sorrow and respect.[27]

In the fall of 1968, on the fifth anniversary
of the Kennedy assassination, rock singer
Dion had a hit record with "Abraham, Martin
and John," a melancholy song of political
nostalgia. The verse about Kennedy goes:

*"We have just learned that the President of
the United States, the Vice-President, the
Governor of Texas, and a Secret Service man
have been murdered.*
*"We now continue with our matinee
feature."*
**—Manager of a Nevada movie house to
the theater audience**
November 22, 1963; quoted in *The Death of a
President*, by William Manchester

Has anybody here seen my old friend
    John?
Can you tell me where he's gone?
He freed a lot of people but it seems the
    good they die young.
I just looked around and he was gone.[28]

Country music has references to Kennedy's
death as well. Tommy Cash, a country singer
like his brother John, had a popular record in

*"They will pick up somebody within hours
afterwards, if anything like that [an assassination of Kennedy] would happen, just to
throw the public off."*
—J. A. MILTEER
National State Rights Party official, as taped
by the Miami Police, November 9, 1963

---

24. By Richard and Jagger, copyright Gideon Music
(BMI).

25. This is the same song which Dave Von Ronk performed with its more traditional lyrics at the April 1974
Madison Square Garden "Tribute to Salvador Allende"
benefit for Chilean refugees and again at the May 1976
memorial tribute to Phil Ochs.

26. Lyrics by J. McGuinn, copyright Tickson Music
Co. (BMI).

27. "My Marxist friends can't understand why I wrote
this song," wrote Ochs in 1964, "and that's probably
one of the reasons I'm not a Marxist."

28. By Dick Holler, copyright Roznique Music Inc.
—Sanphil Music (BMI).

1969 with "Six White Horses," a farewell to John and Robert Kennedy and Martin Luther King. The lines about John Kennedy go:

Some folks drink and some folks smoke
Some folks love and some folks don't
Some folks laugh and some folks frown
Some folks here that'll gun you down.
Goodby John
Six white horses come to take you home.
Goodby John
They took you away before you sang
    your song.[29]

Two obscure country songs about the Kennedy assassination are "The Tragedy of Kennedy" by the Justice Brothers[30] and "Memories of President Kennedy," sung by Bobby Atkins.[31] The first of these is a mournful country tune which ends with Kennedy in heaven ("Now he's resting in God's home, where there's no Berlin wall."). The Bobby Atkins tune, a bluegrass tearjerker, is one of the few songs available which expresses any doubt that Oswald was the assassin. It occurs in the fourth verse:

They say that Oswald was the one
And he paid for the crime they say he done.
Guilty or not, he did pay
For Jack Ruby took his life away.

29. By L. Murray, copyright 1969 Prodigal Son Music (BMI).

30. Del Ray Records (Harrington, Delaware) #214.

31. Stark Records (Mt. Airy, N.C.) #0018.

Other songs which propagate conspiracy views are Jack Kimbrough's "Does Anyone Remember Poor Old John," and Michael Danzig's "Who Killed JFK?," inspired by a slide show on the assassination. Both songs have limited distribution.

"I'm just a patsy . . . I didn't shoot anybody."
—LEE HARVEY OSWALD
November 22, 1963, quoted by reporter Seth Kantor in his Warren Commission testimony

---

One mode aptly suited for John Kennedy's death was the blues. Although far from the mainstream of American commercial music, mournful blues on Kennedy's death filtered through black communities in the months afterwards. Eleven of these songs were recorded on the album "Can't Keep from Crying: Topical Blues on the Death of President Kennedy."[32] The songs on the album are a remarkable representation of gospel blues evoking waves of sorrow and intimate personal confessions of love for Kennedy. As the album liner notes tell us, not since Franklin Roosevelt died in 1945 has such an outpouring of topical blues occurred. Big Joe Williams and Otis Spann are among the singers featured on the record.[33] A further example of this style appears on an album called "Negro

32. Testament Records #S-01.

33. Further details of this record are in *Sing Out!* magazine, September 1964, Vol. 14, No. 4.

Folklore from Texas State Prisons."[34] In mournful *a cappella* style, inmates of Unit #2 at the Ramsey Farm Unit of the Texas State Prison at Huntsville sing "Assassination of the President," featuring soloist Johnnie H. Robinson. Most recent of the black musicians expressing emotions on the death of Kennedy through song is Sleepy John Estes, whose tune "President Kennedy" appears on the Ry Cooder record, "Boomer's Story."[35]

"There was no doubt there—his head went forward with considerable violence."
—DAN RATHER
on the CBS Radio network after viewing the Zapruder film, November 23, 1963

Music about the assassination of presidents is not a recent phenomenon. It goes back to the Lincoln assassination and includes melodies about the Garfield and McKinley killings as well. It is a small but significant part of American folklore tradition. Enough songs in the field are known that the Library of Congress Music Division filled an entire side of a record with such tunes. The album, "Songs and Ballads of American History and of the Assassination of Presidents," features Bascom Lamar Lunsford of South Turkey Creek, North Carolina, singing and playing

banjo and fiddle. It was recorded in 1949.[36] Lincoln's death is represented by "Booth Killed Lincoln" (or, alternately, just "Booth"), an historical narrative ballad.[37]

The James Garfield assassination provided the best known of the pre-Kennedy songs, simply titled "Charles Guiteau."[38] The song is a traditional confessional, which alludes to the murder's national significance only casually. The other Garfield assassination song is called "Mr. Garfield," a half spoken and half sung narrative. McKinley's assassination by Leon Czolgosz is represented in song by "White House Blues," or alternately "Zolgotz." Different versions of the song exist, the most accessible one being the Library of Congress recording.[39]

In the ongoing movement to uncover facts about the assassination, there has been, until recently, a distinct lack of humor. With a few notable exceptions—Paul Krassner, John

---

34. Elektra Records #EKS 7296, no longer available.

35. Warner Bros. #MS 2117.

36. Library of Congress Music Division; Collection of the Archive of American Folk Song, record #L-29. Available from the Library of Congress, Washington, D. C.

37. Recorded as "Booth Shot Lincoln," this same tune is sung by Cisco Houston on the 1960 Folkways two-record set, "Songs of the Civil War."

38. It appears on the Library of Congress record, and on an album called "Sue Cow" sung by Tom Paley, Ango #ZFB3.

39. The Greenbriar Boys sing this (on "Ragged But Right," Vanguard Records, 1962); also Charlie Poole and His North Carolina Ramblers on "Old Time Songs Recorded from 1925-1930," County Records, #505.

"All the time we were talking I searched his eyes for any sign of guilt or whatever you call it. There was nothing there—no guilt, no shame, no nothing."

—ROBERT OSWALD

to the Warren Commission about his visit to his brother Lee on November 23, 1963

Henry Faulk, Mort Sahl, Dick Gregory (at times), and Lenny Bruce—the subject inspires little in the way of laughs. These five exceptions sense at once the intricate nature of conspiracy and the absurdist's view of the web of intrigue. In American assassination literature, no hoax has caused a greater stir than Paul Krassner's "Parts That Were Left Out of the Manchester Book." In the May 1967 issue of *The Realist*, a journal of believable satire and outrageous truths, Krassner published what he claimed were excerpts deleted from the William Manchester book, *The Death of a President*. Writing in a style modeled after Manchester, Krassner described the tension aboard Air Force One as it flew back to Washington from Dallas. In one particular scene, Jackie Kennedy goes back to her husband's casket, only to find newly sworn in President Johnson cackling astride the open casket, having sexual intercourse with the wound in his predecessor's throat.

Read a decade later, this seems hopelessly out of context, but in 1967 when Lyndon Johnson's barbarism allowed him to sleep well as Commander in Chief of the war against Vietnam, nothing was too incredible. A national controversy arose over the excerpts with numerous people willing to believe them. Oscillating between speculation and satire, Krassner proved his point well.[40]

Lenny Bruce also made allusion to the Kennedy assassination in the thirty-two months between Kennedy's death and his own. Referring to Jackie Kennedy's inexpli-

OSWALD: *I really don't know what the—what the situation is about. Nobody has told me anything, except that I'm accused of murdering a policeman. I know nothing more than that. I do request to someone to come forward to give me a legal assistance.*

REPORTER: *Did you kill the President?*

OSWALD: *No, I haven't been charged with that. In fact, nobody has said that to me yet. The first thing I heard about it was when the newspaper reporters in the hall asked me that question.*

—exchange in Dallas Police Department hallway

November 22, 1963

40. As Krassner relates it, friends gave him the germ of the idea, after which he spread it as a rumor to build up familiarity for when it appeared. Author Terry Southern, who got it from Krassner, used it in his essay, "The Blood of a Wig," which appeared in a collection of his stories (*Red Dirt Marijuana and Other Tastes*, New American Library, 1967). Southern played upon the sexual congress using the word "neckrophilia."

The propaganda begins.

New York Herald-Tribune

A black page in our history.

Tulsa World and Tribune

cable action crawling from the limousine's back seat onto the trunk of the car upon her husband's death, Bruce would tell audiences, "the moment her husband died, Jackie hauled ass."

In Texas, where one speaks quietly about the assassination even if one is serious, humorist John Henry Faulk, banned from radio and television in the fifties for attacking the blacklist, mixes assassination humor into after-dinner speeches. At a 1973 assassination conference in Washington, D.C., researchers who had worked on the case for years stared in

bewilderment as Faulk tossed out one-liners about the Warren Commission.

Mort Sahl is the one social humorist who has spent considerable time researching the case as well as commenting on it. Quite involved with the Garrison investigation, Sahl often had Mark Lane and other critics on his television show in Los Angeles to discuss the subject. This put him at odds with his station's management, which occasionally fired him for devoting so much time to the assassination. In his night club act, Sahl used the twenty-six volumes of Warren Commission testimony and evidence as a stage prop.[41]

Dick Gregory is a more complex case. His conspiracy humor is that of exaggeration, stretching government fables until they snap. Sometimes when he is serious Gregory is equally unbelievable. His serious advocacy of the theory that two of the three "tramps" picked up after the assassination in Dealey Plaza could possibly have been Frank Sturgis and E. Howard Hunt is as credible as his

---

" '*Everything ran true to form. I guess you thought I was kidding you when I said [JFK] would be killed from a window with a high-powered rifle.' [The following morning] Milteer advised that they did not have to worry about Lee Harvey Oswald getting caught because 'he doesn't know anything' and that 'the right-wing' is in the clear. Milteer further related that 'The patriots have outsmarted the Communists and had infiltrated the Communist group in order that they [the Communists] could carry out the plan without the right-wingers becoming involved.'*

—**Warren Commission Document No. 1347**

taken from an FBI report based on Miami, Florida, police intelligence reports regarding Joseph Adams Milteer, National States Rights Party official

---

41. Details of Sahl's involvement with the assassination controversy are spelled out in his book, *Heartland* (Harcourt, Brace, Jovanovich, 1976).

"Bobby Kennedy is just another lawyer now."

—**JIMMY HOFFA**

to a Nashville reporter, November 24, 1963; quoted in *The Fall and Rise of Jimmy Hoffa*, by Walter Sheridan

---

humor. When he told a crowd at Boston University in 1975 that the way to solve the Kennedy murder case was to fast—that's right, eat nothing—for ten days, no one was sure if it was sharp humor or serious beliefs.

Other humorous references to the Kennedy assassination are spotty. Occasionally K-SAN radio in San Francisco will play an ad for "Lee Harvey Oswald Savings and Loan." In typical commercial voice, listeners are told, "the loan nuts at Lee Harvey Oswald Savings and Loan are ready with the big payoff in handy untraceable cash!" *The National Lampoon* makes periodic reference to the assassination in its staff-written letters-to-the-editor page and the entire February 1977 issue was devoted to humorous speculation about the Kennedy dynasty had not the president been killed. Even the NBC "Saturday Night Live" program occasionally slips in allusions to the assassination. The Firesign Theater, originator of modern-day radio humor, got into the act in 1968 with its own assassination-related skit, "Profiles in Barbeque Sauce." One of the more noteworthy humorous events in assassination lore was a hotel room party during an early 1975 assassination researchers conference in Boston. After a particularly intense day of conspiracy theorizing, some thirty second-generation researchers broke the tension with a noisy hilarious gathering. Two people created a game show called "Name That Assassin!" in which contestants had thirty seconds to pick possible conspirators from a long list. Elsewhere, critics were holding a Jack Ruby look-alike contest while a visiting writer crooned the Al Martino song, "It was fascassination, I know . . . " A conference organizer picked up the phone. "Hello, room service? Could you send up a coroner?" Near the door others began a game of "conspiracy charade" in which your words or phrase had to relate to an assassination. ("Two words . . . first word: lone. Lone . . . lone . . . lone nut!") It became the only way critics could cope with the implications of their work. The alternative was to go off the deep end.

"The only good murderer is a dead murderer, and the only good Communist is a dead Communist."
—The New York Daily News
commenting on Lee Oswald's death

If the critics are to keep the initiative which the Congressional investigation, begun in 1976, has brought about, it would be wise for them to prepare books on the subject for the high school and elementary years. As it stands now, textbooks for those grades merely echo

"When patrons put their coins in the juke box, they did so in an almost mechanical manner."
—Billboard magazine
December 7, 1963, describing the days following the assassination

the conventional wisdom. Neither particularly good nor bad, the following is typical of the assassination story as presented to high school students:

In Dallas, Texas, at 13:30 P.M., November 22, 1963, a moment of madness occurred which changed the course of history. President Kennedy was assassinated. By 2 P.M. Dallas policemen had arrested a suspect, Lee Harvey Oswald. Before the facts could be determined, and in the midst of much confusion in the Dallas jail, another man, Jack Ruby, shot and killed Oswald.

A Commission headed by the Chief Justice of the Supreme Court, Earl Warren, spent months in careful examination of the evidence. This evidence revealed, almost beyond doubt, that Oswald had shot the President with a rifle.[42]

Like most other texts, that one makes minimal reference to the possiblilty that the assassin was not Lee Oswald, and totally omits mention of popular opinion on the subject.

42. From *United States History for High School*, p. 667. Reprinted by permission of Laidlaw Brothers, a division of Doubleday & Co., Inc.

After a quite informal survey of some fifteen history books covering the elementary years through high school, the following passage from an eleventh grade text seemed the very worst:

> . . . As the car carrying the President passed the Texas School Book Depository, a rifle fired several times. The President jerked forward and fell to the floor of the car, bleeding. He was rushed to a hospital but died very quickly . . .
>
> Most of the young people who, six years later, were radicals, hippies, and demonstrators in Chicago were high school students at the time of the assassination. With their parents they watched the murder, the funeral, and then Oswald's murder.[43]

The best way to think of that passage is as a panel on the back of a cereal box with the caption CAN YOU FIND THE MISTAKES HERE?[44]

The most aware reference to the assassination was also in a high school text:

> . . . Johnson appointed a Commission, headed by Chief Justice Earl Warren, to investigate the assassination. The Commission's report concluded that Oswald alone had planned and carried out the crime. Questions were soon raised, however, about the thoroughness of the Commission's investigation. Since a number of key witnesses died within a few years after the assassination and so could never be questioned, it seemed unlikely that the American people would ever know the full story of the tragedy.[45]

"It will require a lot of satanic and hell-manufactured lying to twist the truth in such a way as to make the world believe that the murder of the president by a Muscovite was a right-wing conspiracy of hate."

—GERALD SMITH
in the Christian Nationalist Crusade newsletter, December 27, 1963

"Few in America seem to believe it [the assassination] could be the act of a single person. They smell a conspiracy in which Oswald was the patsy and fall guy, the victim, like the president himself, of some strange and sinister disease newly injected into the national bloodstream. . . ."

—MIKE GOLD
in *The Worker* (Communist Party USA newspaper) quoted in *ADL Facts*, March 1964

---

43. From *Freedom and Crisis,* by Allen Weinstein and R. Jackson Wilson, p. 778. Copyright by Random House.

44. Those who have tried this count six factual errors in these five sentences.

45. From Wade, Wade and Wilder: *A History of the United States,* with Selected Readings, p. 663. Copyright © 1970 by Houghton Mifflin Company. Used by permission.

As the assassination controversy again takes a prominent position in the national news, it is becoming evident that younger teachers are opening up their classrooms to discussion of possible conspiracy in the case.

It was time to retrench after the Garrison investigation. Two years of noise from New Orleans produced one courtroom acquittal, the conventional wisdom said. Even though the Garrison probe had, in reality, advanced the field a great deal, there was little to show for it on paper. The amount of books and magazine articles on the assassination dropped significantly. As early as 1968, first-generation researchers were saying that the young newcomers to the field couldn't solve it. Perhaps, yes, if they had started a few years earlier, but not now. In the dry period following the Garrison investigation, long-time critics would wistfully resign themselves to not seeing the case solved in their lifetimes. And so, they passed the eternal flame on to the next generation of truth seekers.

The new generation was getting itself ready. In Cambridge, Massachusetts, a small group of young men was meeting informally to discuss and research the Kennedy assassination in the early 1970s. Unlike the first-generation researchers, their frame of reference was the Vietnam War and the policies which brought it about. Rather than divorce this from their investigations, it became inextricably involved. Dubbing themselves "The Grassy Knoll Debating Society," these critics saw no conflict between detailed library research and mass organizing. One of their number, Bob Katz, had been presenting a slide show on the assassination at colleges and churches, mainly in the New England area, with astounding reaction. He found a vast untapped curiosity on the subject, one which could best be met with lectures rather than books. Attending a two hour show was much easier than settling down to *Whitewash* or *Inquest*. People who had no previous exposure to the subject were packing auditoriums wherever Katz went, and soon a lecture agency, which booked speakers from Ted Mack to Sam Ervin, signed him up. Katz would be put on the road for weeks at a time,

---

"I know there are a few people who've written crazy articles, but so far as I know most people accept the Warren Report. . . . "
—HENRY WADE
Dallas County District Attorney at assassination time; quoted in *Fact* magazine, November/December 1966

"I've always had a gut feeling, which I still have, that someone—one or more persons—encouraged Oswald to shoot the president. There may have been an arrangement for someone to meet Oswald and get him out of Dallas."
—HENRY WADE
September 30, 1975

Courtesy Vanguard Records

speaking at colleges throughout the country on the subject "Who Killed JFK?"

Over the years, others had lectured on the assassination. Penn Jones had traveled widely talking on the subject. Manchester, Massachusetts, researcher Robert Cutler had spoken to groups; Mark Lane began virtually as Oswald was buried; and other critics and authors had appeared before groups spelling out the case for conspiracy.[46][47] What made Katz's presentation different was both politics and packaging. Politically, his lecture did not isolate the assassination as separate from either the suspects' ideology or shifts in domestic and foreign policies. While Katz's traveling conspiracy show was objective in that he discussed facts and avoided loose speculation, it presented the assassination and cover-up in a political context rather than as a distinct and lone episode in American his-

"I would say that the only ones who refuse to believe that a Communist by the name of Oswald killed President Kennedy are intentionally or unintentionally pro-Communist themselves. Only a diehard Communist or a stupid pro-Communist Leftist can ignore the facts that prove conclusively that (1) Oswald killed the president, and (2) Oswald was a Communist."

—BILLY JAMES HARGIS
leader of The Christian Crusade for many years; quoted in *Fact* magazine, November/December 1966

tory. The presentation was attractive as well. Using slides assembled from photo-analyst Richard C. Sprague, most of the lecture was a narration accompanying photos flashed on a screen. Step by step, the audience could actually see photographic evidence of conspiracy. It was dramatic and effective, with the Zapruder film of the actual assassination highlighting the show. There, in less than 400 frames, the audience viewed the most devastating piece of evidence, clear to the most cynical observer. One sees Kennedy slumping forward after a shot has pierced him from the rear. All of a sudden his entire body—head, shoulders, and torso—is thrust violently

46. The very first assassination lecturer on record, however, was John Surratt, at whose mother's rooming house it was alleged the conspiracy to assassinate Abraham Lincoln was hatched in 1865. Surratt was indicted in the assassination, went underground abroad, was captured, returned home for trial, and acquitted on a legal technicality. In December 1870 he gave a lecture at Rockville, Maryland, about his exploits as a Confederate spy in the Civil War, but most of his speech was devoted to the Lincoln assassination. Subsequently he gave more speeches for pay.

47. Buoyed by the mail he was receiving and under the delusion that he would soon be released, Jack Ruby, in the days following his murder of Lee Oswald, anticipated going on the lecture circuit. Jim Garrison's acquitted suspect, Clay Shaw, lectured at a few universities in 1970.

backwards and to the left, pressed up against the limousine's upholstery. The only plausible explanation is that a shot has come from in front of the car.[48] The film is shown again in slow motion,[49] and the mood of the crowd shifts dramatically. While at first it was skeptical and defensive, the audience is now willing—*anxious* to be told more about what happened and why it was covered up. One could literally hear minds being changed on the subject. By midway through the lecture, it seems the audience would accept that Farrah Fawcett-Majors acting in concert with Ronald McDonald murdered John Kennedy.

In the question-and-answer sessions, local buffs would make their presence felt. The lecture provided them with their first opportunity to publicly show off their knowledge and press the speakers for details. They would come clutching tattered copies of *Life*, books such as *Six Seconds in Dallas*, and note pads to record new data. The questions indicate extensive research by some, and gullibility by others. Why are certain frames missing from

---

"You ought to be as interested in this as I am, if you're really interested in law and order. There have been rumors circulating throughout the country for more than a decade now that all the major political assassinations in America—Malcolm X, the Kennedy brothers, Medgar Evers, King, Nixon, maybe even George Lincoln Rockwell—are the works of a single conspiratorial, violence-oriented right-wing organization, and that this organization has its base right here in Mad Dog. I came down to find out what I could about their group."

—GEORGE DORN
reporter, to local sheriff in the novel *Illuminatus*, by Wilson and Shea

---

48. A number of attempts have been made to explain how Kennedy's backward body motion would be consistent with a shot from the rear, where Oswald was positioned. None of these, including one by Itek Corp. laboratories conducted for CBS-TV in 1975, dispells the evidence convincingly. *Six Seconds in Dallas* best destroys the rear-shot-backward-movement theory.

49. There is an absolutely eerie sensation when the Zapruder film is rewound, showing the dead President coming alive once again—history reversed by an 8-millimeter projector.

"The fact that more than one person is engaged in an enterprise does not necessarily make it a conspiracy."

—HENRY FAIRLIE
commenting on assassination conspiracy theories; quoted in *The New York Times Magazine*, September 11, 1966

"Conspiracy: . . . 2: An evil, unlawful, treacherous, or surreptitious plan formulated in secret by two or more persons."

—Random House Dictionary of the English Language

the Zapruder film? Did Gerald Ford perjure himself in his vice-presidential hearings when he claimed not to have used classified Warren Commission material in his book *Portrait of the Assassin?* What were Jack Ruby's connections to the anti-Castro community? And the inevitable loonies: What about the possibility that Kennedy (a) is alive on Parkland Hospital's eighth floor; (b) a vegetable on the Greek island of Skorpios; (c) attended his own funeral in a wheelchair? These are the underground rumors nurtured by the supermarket tabloids gone berserk. Katz and his colleagues had a long way to go.[50]

It's a case of the chickens coming home to roost.... Hate, allowed to spread unchecked, finally has struck down this country's chief of state."
—MALCOLM X
on the death of John Kennedy, in *The Autobiography of Malcolm X*

Elsewhere, other critics of the newer breed had the same attitude about conspiracy research as the "Grassy Knoll Debating So-

---

50. Although campus reaction was overwhelmingly favorable, resistence came as well. When Katz was scheduled to speak at one southern school, a political science teacher angrily protested to the student activities office. The assassination lecture was nothing more than a freak show, he maintained. It would be more appropriate at a shopping center opening (a prospect Katz was not at all averse to).

" ...I certainly do think that our society was responsible for the assassination...."
—JOHN HOWARD GRIFFIN
writer, in *Fact* magazine, November/ December 1966

ciety." Their political outlook clashed with that of the first-generation researchers. The confrontation in style and method came on the tenth anniversary of the assassination. A Washington, D.C., group called "The Committee to Investigate Assassinations" held a two day conference at Georgetown University called "A Decade of Assassinations." Two hundred critics, lawyers, journalists, researchers, and others attended; few buffs were there. The sponsoring group, C.T.I.A., was founded by Washington attorney Bernard Fensterwald, Jr., at the end of 1968. Serving on his committee were a number of authors, private investigators, lawyers and first-generation critics.

It was an auspicious time for such a gathering. Watergate investigations had demonstrated links to the anti-Castro Cuban community in much the same manner as the assassination had. For many, looking down the elevator shaft at Watergate, Dealey Plaza appeared at the bottom. The meeting also came as *Executive Action* was released nationally, and Warren Commission attorney David Belin's *You Are the Jury*, the first major Warren Commission defense in years, was published. And, as on any assassination anniversary, newspapers were filled with stories reiterating arguments in the case.

The conference was organized as a series of panels covering old and new evidence, investigative techniques, and different cover-ups. Discussions on the evidence regarding Martin Luther King, John and Robert Kennedy, George Lincoln Rockwell, and George Wallace were sprinkled throughout the weekend. Norman Mailer delivered the keynote address. At the same time, activists from New York attending the meeting had scheduled a demonstration in front of the National Archives building downtown calling for all Warren Commission documents to be released. Advertised nationally for weeks in the underground press, the hastily assembled "Committee to Open the Archives" promised many speakers including west coast researcher Mae Brussell, Dick Gregory, and Mark Lane, none of whom showed. Other than brief remarks by Donald Freed, the gathering was most inauspicious. Speaking at length was Chicago researcher Sherman Skolnick, who could never be accused of erring on the side of caution. He blamed the malfunctioning speaker system on the CIA. Distressed at the low turnout—twenty-five

---

"Doc, how the hell can they believe I had anything to do with that conspiracy thing?"
—JACK RUBY
quoted in *Argosy*, September 1967

---

people at most, including press—they returned to the conference where Victor Marchetti, coauthor of *The CIA and The Cult of Intelligence,* was relating experiences from his years with the CIA. While he spoke, the back of the conference hall resembled a conspiracy swap-meet. Authors hawked assassination books, bootleg Zapruder films went for two dollars apiece; assassination bibliographies, magazine reprints, and envelopes with cancelled JFK stamps glued to them were handed out.

"If ten more wiretaps could have found the conspiracy [to assassinate John Kennedy] — uh, if it was a conspiracy—or the individual, then it would have been worth it."
—RICHARD NIXON
in a press conference, August 22, 1973

Throughout the weekend, the archives demonstrators and others raised the question of how the assassinations fit in with Watergate and other political crimes. They charged that conference organizer Fensterwald had hidden loyalties. He was just too smooth a Washington lawyer with many secretive connections, representing as he did Watergater James McCord. Finally, by the conference end, Fensterwald turned over the auditorium to the dissenters for their own meeting. Although little was learned at the rump session, it was significant as the first gathering of latter-day critics.

"If the bullet that wounded the president was not the same bullet that wounded John Connally, and I testified that it wasn't, and John Connally testified that it wasn't, then there would have had to be more than one assassin."
—**DAVID POWERS**
aide to President Kennedy and a Dallas motorcade passenger on WGBH-TV, Boston, May 13, 1976

Reaction to the C.T.I.A. conference within the critics movement was largely negative. "The goddamn country was kidnapped November 22, 1963, and they're playing lawn tennis with the footnotes," offered one dissenter. Fensterwald and other organizers were disappointed as well, feeling everything had been disrupted by the activists, who in turn were suspicious of the C.T.I.A.'s motives from the beginning.

The highlight of the conference was a midnight party at organizer Fensterwald's Alexandria, Virginia, townhouse. Here the elite of the conspiracy movement met for cocktails

"I don't doubt that there are a dozen people out there that are sure they are the ones who financed the Dallas job on Kennedy."
—**GERRY PATRICK HEMMING**
formerly a leading CIA paramilitary operative, in *Argosy*, April 1976

and gossip. Like any phenomenon in American society, the conspiracy researching movement is subject to class analysis. The "proletariat" in the field are those who keep up with the assassination through books, public lectures, magazine articles, and correspondence. The media refers to this group as buffs. They treat their collection of assassination material with the same respect and delicacy as they might an ivory chess set or glass menagerie. "The buffs," wrote Calvin Trillin, "toss around the names of witnesses and minor Dallas officials as casually as small boys discuss obscure baseball players."[51] Someone in this group may have solved the assassination years ago, but no one in the upper two classes would know it.[52] For new information, the "buffs" rely on the "petit bourgeoisie." This middle group has the information as well as the means to expose it to countless others. They are the critics, those who research the subject through the twenty-six volumes, interview knowledgeable sources, and spread the word. They write the books and magazine articles, file Freedom of Information actions, lecture on the subject, and agitate for an end

51. From *The New Yorker,* June 10, 1967, the first and one of the few well-balanced articles on the "buffs."

52. "From the beginning," the Louis Harris Survey stated in May 1967, "the group most prone to criticize the findings of the Warren Commission and to believe the assassination was part of a broader conspiracy has been the less well educated low income segment of the population. . . . People under thirty-five are more likely than their elders to suspect that Lee Harvey Oswald was not alone in the killing."

to the cover-up. They are constantly in touch with each other, and trade off information. The "elite" of the movement is all that and more. Not only are they knowledgeable in the field, but they share similar backgrounds with the intelligence operatives they are investigating. Many of them used to be in intelligence themselves. They make news as well as spread it. It was this group which filled Fensterwald's townhouse for the Committee to Investigate Assassinations' exclusive party. If the conference sponsoring group had a neon sign with its initials lit up outside, the T would have been blinking on and off.

The party was capped off by a private screening of Robert Groden's photo-optically enhanced Zapruder film. Not just your basic bootleg Z-film, mind you, but a clear first-generation print with special optical effects to make the key murder frames clearly stand out. Not a drink was stirred during the showing.

The Committee to Investigate Assassinations conference spelled out the difference between first-generation researchers, who methodically stick to legal documents, microscopic facts, footnotes, court cases, and the twenty-six volumes of Warren Commission testimony and exhibits, and the newer group of critics, which puts this information in its political context. In truth, the two complement each other well, but at times it has been difficult for the two to coexist in the conspiracy theorizing business.

One reason conspiracy theories abound is

that they are carefully built on supposition and fact, investigation and doubt, projected logic and fertile imagination. None have been proven absolutely true or false because that is the very nature of a conspiracy theory: You can't get to the bottom of it. When the John Kennedy assassination is finally solved, numerous leads uncovered since 1963 will prove irrelevant.

"Dallas, Oswald, Ruby, Watts, Whitman, Manson, Ray, Sirhan, Bremer, Viet Nam, Nixon, Watergate, FBI, CIA, Squeaky Fromme, Sara Moore—the list goes on and on. Who the hell wrote this script and where will it ever end?"
—GARY CARTRIGHT
in *Texas Monthly*, November 1975

It was shortly after the C.T.I.A. conference in Washington that the Grassy Knoll Debating Society in Cambridge, Massachusetts, legitimized itself. Feeling strength from its own politics and lectures, the group formed the Assassination Information Bureau (A.I.B), an organization which proved pivotal in the movement to reopen the assassination investigation. Bob Katz's presentation — historical, morbid, informative, and entertaining—was so successful that his booking agency arranged for a B-team to take the overflow dates. Politically, the A.I.B. put its facts in an overall context best articulated by A.I.B. member Carl Oglesby's "yankee-cowboy" theory of ruling class alignment. Reduced to its simplest form, the theory outlines a struggle through American history between two power elites, one representing the internationalism of east coast monied interests (yankees), and the other, the westward expansion of computer-aerospace-warfare-landboom-agribusiness interests (cowboys). The Kennedy assassination, the theory goes, was a coup by the cowboys seizing power from the yankees. Watergate exposure, then, was a counterattack by the yankees to wrest power back from the cowboys.[53]

In 1974 and 1975 presentations by the A.I.B. and other groups on the conspiracy to murder the thirty-fifth President of the United States were the most popular shows on the campus lecture circuit in the country.[54] [55]

---

53. Two books devote themselves to this theory: *The Yankee and Cowboy War: Conspiracies from Dallas to Watergate*, by Carl Oglesby (listed in Chapter 4), and Kirkpatrick Sale's *Power Shift—The Rise of the Southern Rim and Its Challenge to the Eastern Establishment*, Random House, 1975.

54. One evening in April 1975 in San Francisco there was a choice of no less than three different conspiracy lectures to attend.

55. Explaining why he is not asked to appear at universities, the redoubtable Penn Jones says, "I go too far to be on any college campus. I say who did it. I'd be delighted to be proven wrong, but it's too goddamn late to be still winkin' and saying 'ah well, we don't know.' If I'm wrong, fine, then make an ass out of me. But somebody's got to get off their ass and go to work on this and do it. And nobody's done that. *That's* the reason I don't get on campuses. The colleges get too much federal money to have a little sumvabitch like me on campus saying this is like Germany in 1934 and 1935."

"Just who the hell is this they *they keep referring to? Since November 22, 1963,* they *have been creeping around in and out of closets, bedrooms, onshore, and offshore, listening in on billions of inane conversations, slitting open envelopes like throats in the old days. They are in the White House, the Dallas police department, half the boardrooms, law offices, and newsrooms of the nation, and most of the bars, whorehouses, and prisons. They orchestrated Vietnam and Watergate from front to back. . . ."*

—ADAM KENNEDY
reviewing a new assassination novel in *Harper's Weekly,* August 23, 1976

Certainly, the logic went, if the government could lie to us against overwhelming evidence to the contrary about tens of thousands of Vietnamese and Americans killed in Asia, it could try to do the same about one death in Dallas.

A growing audience accepted this, and the result was more pressure on Congress to reopen the investigation. It had taken over ten years for evidence to accumulate in people's living rooms before a nationwide concerted push for a new investigation could come about. The watershed event in that drive was the "Politics of Conspiracy" conference at Boston University in early 1975.

The idea for the conference grew out of the response A.I.B. lecturers had been receiving on the road. Reaction to their presentations was so strong and favorable, it made sense to hold a national meeting, gathering together as many "experts" in the field as possible. While the microscopic material would not be ignored, political research would be in the forefront. Macroanalysis was the rule of the day. A.I.B. lecturers mentioned the conference at every whistlestop; the sleuth underground spread the word; notices were placed in the college; alternative and underground press and many radio stations plugged it. In anticipation of hundreds of people, a large hall at Boston University was rented for the weekend. When Mark Lane, who had been devoting his energies elsewhere in the preceding years, began his keynote address, more than a thousand people had shown up with more on the way.

The conference was a success beyond anyone's hopes. Serious political arguments were presented; loonies had their say and then kept quiet; invaluable contacts were made; and the prospect for mass organizing around the question "Who Killed JFK?" was endorsed. A significant number of long-time critics shared the stage with newer members

"The individualism of American assassins is what Europeans, and some Americans too, find hard to grasp. In other parts of the world, political assassination is usually the result of an elaborate plot. The object is to bring about a shift in power. No such plan appears to guide the American assassin."

—*Time* magazine
May 29, 1972

"I never believed that Oswald acted alone, although I can accept that he pulled the trigger. . . ."

—LYNDON JOHNSON
quoted in *Atlantic Monthly*, July 1973

of the clan. The loonies, the footnoters, and everyone in between tolerated each other for the weekend, which saw genuine advances in the fields of both political and scholarly conspiracy research.[56]

Among the more immediate results was the reformation of Mark Lane's "Citizens Commission of Inquiry" in Washington, D.C. Sensing a resurgence of interest in the field, Lane set about to lobby with Congress to have the assassination investigation reopened. Congressman Henry Gonzalez of Texas soon introduced a resolution calling for a new look at the John and Robert Kennedy assassinations, that of Martin Luther King, and the attempt on George Wallace. A bill covering just the John Kennedy assassination was similarly introduced by Virginia Congressman Thomas Downing.

"The president's orders to reduce the American military personnel in Vietnam by one thousand before the end of 1963 was still in effect on the day he went to Texas. A few days after his death, during the morning, the order was quietly rescinded."

—O'DONNELL and POWERS
in *Johnny We Hardly Knew Ye*

Momentum picked up across the country during the following eighteen months. In Il-

---

"The ST [Secret Team] struck quickly. While the echo of those shots in Dallas were still ringing, the ST moved to take over the whole direction of the [Vietnam] war and to dominate the activity of the United States of America. . . . Who could have expected a man who had been in the range of gunfire that ended the life of his predecessor, to make any moves in those critical days that would indicate he was not going to go along with the pressures which had surfaced so violently in Dallas? He knew exactly what had happened there in Dallas. He did not need to wait for the findings of the Warren Commission."

—L. FLETCHER PROUTY
former laison between the Pentagon and the CIA, in *The Secret Team*

---

linois, New Jersey, Massachusetts, Ohio, and California, state legislators introduced resolutions calling on Congress to reopen the investigation. Magazines flooded newsstands with articles on every aspect of the case.[57] Supermarket tabloids exploited every dribble of information. The initiative was with the critics, and the veneer of Warren Commission de-

---

56. "There are good scholars and bad scholars," respected critic Josiah Thompson said years earlier about the critics. "There are even analytical scholars and inductive scholars. But the marvelous thing about it is that there are no credentials. There's no Ph. D. in the assassination. You have to make your own credentials."

57. *Crawdaddy* magazine, one of the publications receptive to a conspiratorial overview of corporate-government politics, devoted the most space to conspiracy on a regular basis. They had a monthly column by William Burroughs called "Time of the Assassins," a regular feature by the Assassination Information Bureau, and a column by conspiracy *mavin* Paul Krassner. In a guide to mixed drinks, the magazine included a "Lee Harvey Wallbanger."

"Fortunately for the United States position in international relations, the various conspiracy theories about the Kennedy assassination have not been borne out by subsequent events; there has been no radical swing in American foreign or domestic policy to the left or to the right."
—The Washington Post
September 27, 1964

fense grew thinner by the month. The Rockefeller Commission investigating domestic CIA activities saw fit to glance at the assassination,[58] and a Senate committee found that evidence in the assassination investigation had been trampled by FBI and CIA footprints. Both the A.I.B. and Lane's C.C.I.

"The significance of the Dealey Plaza assassination was that the warfare sector of the government seized power from the president."
—JIM GARRISON
New Orleans Parish District Attorney, August 23, 1973

58. The Rockefeller Commission's staff director was none other than David Belin, a senior staff attorney with the Warren Commission. He concluded, on the basis of disproving the Dick Gregory tramps theory, that the CIA was not involved with the assassination. Still, the commission managed to grossly misrepresent statements by respected researchers Paul Hoch and Dr. Cyril Wecht.

sprouted chapters in cities and on campuses in most states. Conspiracy researching groups sprung up like grass on a downtown Dallas knoll.[59] Conferences on the subject took place in New England, California, Wisconsin, Michigan, Nebraska, and elsewhere. Teach-ins were organized. Geraldo Rivera put the Zapruder film on national television in March 1975 and received such a response that he played it again a few weeks later.[60] A November 1975 gathering at Seattle, with Josiah Thompson, Paul Hoch, and Mark Lane was taped and later used in local high schools. Three of the best books in the field came out, *The Assassinations: Dallas and Beyond,* along with *Accessories After the Fact* and *Six Seconds in Dallas* (both reissued from a decade earlier). So many people were giving presentations on the assassination that you could rate them by how they narrated the Za-

59. Typical of such groups was one at the University of South Florida, where the local free university, called the Common Learning Network, offered a course called Political Assassination in the United States. Taught by economics instructor Cliff Hawley, up to a dozen students attended each of the four quarters. The Zapruder film was screened for the public, petition drives to Congress were organized, and students studied the assassinations of Martin Luther King, Fred Hampton, and Mark Clark as well.

60. The following year in September, Rivera again devoted an hour to the assassination on his "Good Night America" program. Sloppy, filled with misinformation and degenerating into personality fights, Rivera's 1976 show exhibited the worst tendencies in popular media to portray the movement to reinvestigate the assassination.

pruder film and how they described the "bullet ballet."[61] Bootleg prints of the Zapruder film (technically copyright by Time, Inc., until they sold it back to the Abraham Zapruder estate for one dollar), once prized possessions, became so common that the researcher's status item soon became a Groden print of the Z-film.[62]

In Washington, D.C., the C.C.I. arranged screenings of the Zapruder film for members

---

"Then the other mystery is this other man—Ruby—who had no moral conditions . . . no political passions, becomes so enraged by Kennedy's assassination that he kills the assassin right in front of the police. It was incredible, inconceivable. That does not happen even in the most mediocre movies."
—FIDEL CASTRO
quoted in *With Fidel*, by Mankiewicz and Jones

---

61. The "bullet ballet" is the term given the flight of Commission Exhibit #399, a bullet which the Warren Commission theorized traversed Kennedy's body, exiting his neck, suspended momentarily in midair, angled into John Connally's body, exited his ribs, penetrated his wrist, and finally lodged in his thigh. After this miraculous flight, CE#399 was later found on an empty hospital stretcher in virtually pristine condition. To negate this flight path is to negate the lone assassin conclusion.

62. Tension and paranoia were so high at the 1975 Boston University conference for Robert Groden, who brought his original Zapruder film, that he actually kept it handcuffed to his wrist.

of Congress and organized petition drives out in the field. The A.I.B. continued its successful proselytizing, initiating thousands of new converts. The John Birch Society had a lecturer on the road speaking on political assassination.[63] Even Aleksandr Solzhenitsyn said the case was unresolved.[64] Information and new revelations on the assassination were coming at such a rapid rate, some suspected *that* was part of a government plot. Phil Ochs likened the steady output of information to a time-release cold capsule.

While the footnoters—researchers who never look outside solid documentation —continued with their work,[65] members of Congress were hearing from their constituents. The drive to reopen the assassination investigation drew from virtually every element of the country at all points along the political

63. Timothy Heinan, the Birch speaker, was an undercover cop infiltrating radical student groups for Milwaukee police when George Wallace's attempted assassin, Arthur Bremer, attended a few meetings. Heinan's lecture, presented to Birch chapters from town to town, outlined the possibility of conspiracy in the Wallace shooting and also covered possible conspiracy in the Kennedy case.

64. Kennedy's assassination was "all the worse," Solzhenitsyn wrote in the *New York Times*, December 1, 1975, "because of the inability or lack of desire by the American judicial authorities to uncover the assassins and to clear up the crime."

65. Best known of the footnoters is Harold Weisberg, author of the valuable *Whitewash* series, who takes the position that evidence is valid only if it has been notarized, originated with the government, comes out of a legal proceeding, or is lodged in the National Archives.

spectrum. Like *TV Guide*, the Pope, and Scotch tape, the Kennedy assassination mystery had crossed all class, racial, and ethnic lines.

"There's a fantastic way in which the assassination becomes a religious event," Josiah Thompson told *The New Yorker* in 1967. "There are relics and scriptures, and even a holy scene—the killing ground. People make pilgrimages to it."

That was still true ten years later. A trip to Dealey Plaza shows the area much as it was in 1963. The Texas School Book Depository

Postcards such as this sell well at the Dallas/Ft. Worth airport and area tourist traps.

stands at the corner of Houston and Elm, the subject of more snapshots than almost any privately owned building in the country. Now and then, its owner, a Col. Byrd, makes attempts to sell it. He found a purchaser once; in the early 1970s it was briefly owned by

Nashville music promoter Aubrey Mayhew, who wanted to open a museum there with his collection of Kennedy memorabilia.[66] In April 1972 Mayhew opened the lobby of the depository as a visitors' center, calling his group Friends of Kennedy Volunteers. He asked a dollar from every tourist to buy a square inch of the property upon which the building stood. Buyers would get a deed, suitable for framing, saying they owned ground on which stood the Texas School Book Depository. There was a small fire inside the depository not long thereafter (arson was the stated cause), and by the end of the year, May-

66. Two cars Kennedy once owned, a piece of John and Jacqueline's wedding cake, Kennedy letters purchased from autograph merchant Charles Hamilton, and PT Boat 59—the one that didn't sink—among other things.

hew had defaulted on his $650,000 purchase. Occasionally a city or county official will raise the question of buying the depository to keep it out of the hands of exploiters, but there is still official unease on the subject in Dallas.[67] [68]

Across from the depository on Elm Street is a private enterprise called The John F. Kennedy Museum. In the museum lobby is all the chintzy "Kennedyana" you would ever want to see—Kennedy ash trays, silverware emblazoned with likenesses of all the presidents, reproduced newspaper front pages from November 1963, Jack and Jackie chinaware, and Kennedy postcards. You can even get a plate which lists the "SIXTEEN AMAZING COINCIDENCES!" between the Kennedy and Lincoln assassinations.[69] As you wait for the $1.50 show inside the museum theater, you can hear "Greensleeves," "Where Have All the Flowers Gone?" and "Blowin' in the Wind" piped in like Muzak. The show, which lasts about fifteen minutes,

67. In 1970 assassination researcher Larry Harris wanted to see the inside of the building, and figured the only way was to apply for a job there. To his surprise he was hired and worked there two weeks.

68. "I'd like to kick the dogshit out of every yankee newspaperman, club the fuckers to the ground," former Dallas Assistant District Attorney Bill Alexander told *Texas Monthly* in 1975. "You can still see them, right up to this day, hanging around the Book Depository. Fatass yankees in shorts and cameras getting the roof of their mouths sunburned."

69. Kennedy is represented elsewhere on salt and pepper shakers, prayer rugs, and velvet art.

"I now believe McLuhan's theory about why Lee Harvey Oswald's police guards were so zombie-like while Jack Ruby was performing the second most suspicious assassination of the century. They were all so mesmerized by that giant TV eye watching them that they couldn't notice anything else. Ruby could have galloped in on an elephant and they still wouldn't have noticed anything but the camera until it was too late."

—ROBERT ANTON WILSON
in *The Berkeley Barb*, June 18, 1976

consists of a series of dotted electric lights running across a papier mache likeness of Dallas, prominently featuring the motorcade route taken by the Kennedy party. The narrator tells us about Kennedy and his wonderful trip to Texas until the lights reach Dealey Plaza, at which point three shots ring out and the lights speed off to Parkland Hospital. Slides flashed above the model city program comprise the visual effect. The narration, of

"Gentlemen, unless you get me to Washington, you can't get a fair shake out of me. . . . My life is in danger here."

—JACK RUBY
to Earl Warren, Gerald Ford, and Leon Jaworski (representing the State of Texas), during an interview in the Dallas County Jail, June 7, 1964

"Ruby [said] that the reason he went to the Dallas police department . . . was that he had received 'a phone call from Ft. Worth.' . . . He told [Loyola University psychiatry professor] Dr. Teuter that if he wanted to understand the Kennedy assassination he should read a book by Thomas Buchanan, Who Killed Kennedy?

"Buchanan's book . . . presented the theory that two assassins shot Kennedy . . . [Buchanan] also argued that Oswald's part in the plot was merely to smuggle one of the murder weapons into the book depository . . . and that Ruby was detailed to kill Oswald so that Oswald . . . could more easily be made the scapegoat."

—The Sunday London Times
August 25, 1974

---

course, presumes Oswald's guilt throughout. The museum is a big hit with tourists.

On any November 22 you can see school-children laying flowers in Dealey Plaza while television cameras passively record the event

---

"Well, you won't ever see me again. I tell you that. . . . A whole new form of government is going to take over the country, and I know I won't live to see you another time."

—JACK RUBY
to Earl Warren, Gerald Ford, and Leon Jaworski, as they departed the Dallas County Jail, June 7, 1964

---

for national news shows.[70] On a busy tourist day, you might catch Penn Jones handing out his leaflet on the assassination to tourists. If you are lucky, he will give you a guided tour to points of interest at Dealey Plaza, including a trip below street-level into a sewer with a clear view of the motorcade route. (Jones has been known to take entire tour buses on trips to all assassination-related sites in town.)

Other sites from the assassination are fading. There is a parking lot where Jack Ruby's Carousel Club stood atop the Real Pit Bar-B-Q; a Fotomat is in the center.[71] Posing as a homeless traveler, a west coast researcher visiting Dallas inquired at 1026 Beckley Street

70. On the tenth anniversary of the assassination, a number of conspiracy researchers and critics gathered at Dealey Plaza to commemorate the event as well as observe the countdown on the electronic clock adjoining the Hertz sign on top of the Texas School Book Depository for the precise moment at thirty minutes past the hour. The clock got as far as twenty-eight minutes after the hour, then inexplicably skipped backwards to twenty past the hour. A couple of minutes later, it jumped forward to thirty-four minutes past the hour, skipping the half-hour mark entirely. The Kennedy assassination missed its own 10th anniversary in Dealey Plaza.

71. In April 1972 remnants of the Carousel were auctioned off at a warehouse in Athens, Texas. The big attraction was to be the club safe, which, supposedly, had remained unopened since the assassination. Whoever got the safe was counting on a direct link with Jack Ruby himself. Two nights before the auction, the safe was stolen. It was never recovered and no arrests were ever made. No other items for auction were taken. (Jack Ruby's kitchen sink was sold for $22.50.)

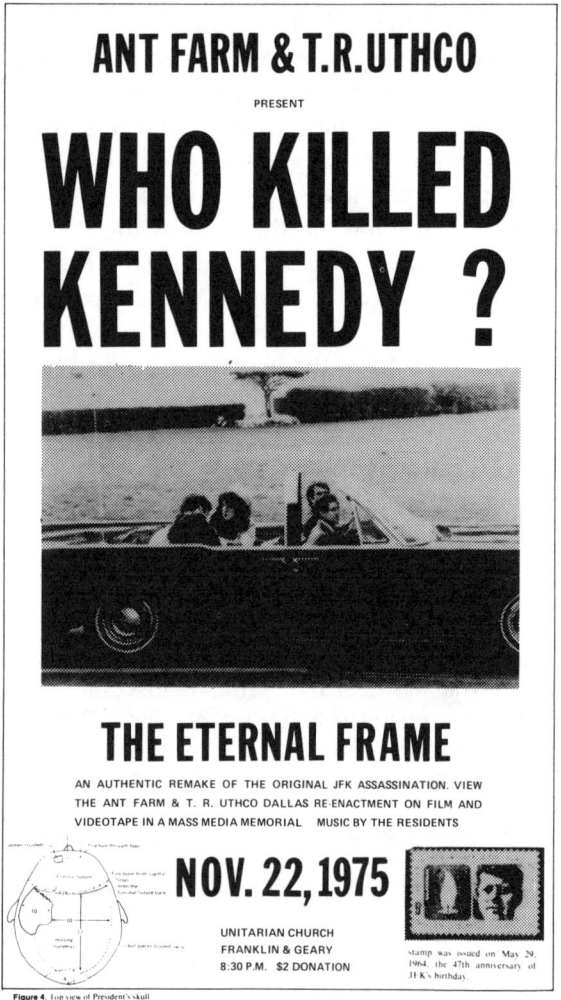

Assassination re-enactments began in 1975.

about a place to stay for a week. Lee Oswald's old room was not available. When writer Ovid Demaris inquired at the door if he could see Oswald's old room, the landlady told him for $300 he could look; with commentary, it would cost $500. Demaris declined.

In August 1975 an unusual group of vis-

itors invaded Dealey Plaza. They were members of two conceptual art collectives from San Francisco, T. R. Uthco and The Ant Farm. Equipped with a limousine like the one used November 22, 1963, the entourage set out to reenact the assassination. A man made up to resemble Jackie wore a pink dress and pillbox hat; other actors took the roles of John Kennedy, Governor and Mrs. Connally, and the Secret Service. It was a Sunday, and the group expected police to intercede. Instead, police stared, shrugged, and drove by.

As the group ran through the assassination, tourists gathered and stared. Some

---

*"You know we have our heroes
I mean Washington and Lincoln
Including Audie Murphy
Including old Jack Ruby
Wasn't Jack wonderful?
Oh, you know he certainly was"*
—LOUDON WAINRIGHT III
from his song "Bicentennial"*

---

laughed, some wept, and some pointed out to their children what was happening. ("You see? That's when he gets hit . . . ") Afterwards a few tourists commented how nice it was that the city of Dallas staged a reenactment for them.

The actors ran through the assassination twenty times, each time the president reacting as he did thirteen years earlier, each time Jackie climbing up on the trunk only to be pushed back by a Secret Service man, each time the limousine speeding off beneath the overpass. (They used a starter's gun for rifle sounds.) Finally, bored with the assassination, the troupe wandered over to the John F. Kennedy Museum where the manager

*© Copyright 1975, 1976, Snowden Music, Inc. All rights reserved.

"You got to be careful if you get an erection when you take penicillin; it fights off the penicillin."
—JACK RUBY
on his October 1963 gonorrhea case; as quoted in the *Texas Attorney General's Report*

---

promptly asked them to leave. In its final form, the videotape includes a speech by the "president" on the "President as Art" ("I am nothing more than another image on your television set, and that is all."). "The Eternal Frame," as it was called, took the Kennedy assassination, already ensconced in American culture, and elevated it beyond art to surrealism. It was shown in San Francisco on November 22, 1975.[72]

America changed when John Kennedy reached the presidency and is still changing by his leaving it. The years since that tragic event have seen one of the most remarkable movements in American history. The drive to

72. In what may be the start of a national trend of street truth-theater, a group in Madison, Wisconsin, also reenacted the Kennedy assassination in November 1975. Using a white limousine (no black ones were available), "assassins" in buildings near the state capitol fired blanks at the passing motorcade. The reenactment, sponsored by the Madison newspaper *Take Over*, was part of the "November 22 Coalition," a national effort to propagandize the politics of assassination. Other cities had rallies, speeches, conferences, teach-ins, petition drives, and Zapruder film screenings.

seek out the truth in the Kennedy assassination, to counter the conventional wisdom, has evolved from a few skeptics blindly grasping for information, to a congressional inquiry with subpoena power. The process has been difficult; at times it seemed hopeless. For a long period of time speculation about the assassination grew more and more convoluted because critical comments were, by and large, censored off the air. There was no voice of authority to back up the critics, so information traveled through word of mouth, the arts, the underground press, and talk shows. The public relied on private investigators and journalists for information because once the assassination was complete, all the evidence was behind closed doors. When the mystery of the John Kennedy assassination is finally solved, the skeptics and critics of the Warren Commission Report may well be shown as true heroes of contemporary history. Stalking the wild conspiracy, essentially an underground phenomenon at its inception, has at last come of age.

Newspoem

by Tuli Kupferberg

Who else died the day that Kennedy died?
A dumb Italian carpenter who tripped off the side
A stinking brown child, age of seven
Who dehydrated straight to hell: Bengali heaven

Nameless numberless
They did not make the news
Here's a tip of the hat to them
Or a dagger, if you choose

2
WHO KNOWS?

Paul Mavrides

Since the revival of interest in the Kennedy assassination, numerous groups have sprung up around the country to agitate for a reinvestigation, review government files, spread information on the subject, and focus on the government cover-up as a symptom of political expediency. Who benefits from a cover-up? Why are certain documents still classified? How did the assassination play a role in foreign policy? What was the power shift in the U.S. governing class which the assassination brought about? Who killed JFK and why?

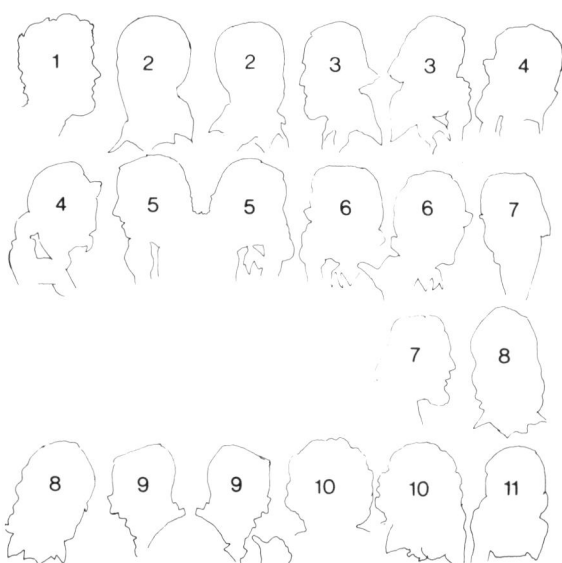

1. Mark Lane; 2. Dick Gregory; 3. Peter Dale Scott;
4. Sherman Skolnick; 5. Mae Brussell; 6. Penn Jones;
7. Richard Popkin; 8. Carl Oglesby; 9. Robert Cutler;
10. Sylvia Meagher; 11. The Accused.

These small groups, located in every section of the country, are speaking out on these questions. They have varying perspectives and levels of sophistication, but they all find that when they take their message to the public, it is well received. Some organizations operate on an academic calendar, while others are active year-round. It is estimated that well over a hundred such organizations exist in one form or another. Most of them operate on a low financial plane, and offer resources at cost. (Some lecturers find it necessary to establish an honorarium to cover their research expenses.)

The following is a sample listing. If there is no entry for your area, check your local college or write either of the two national groups. If you feel confident in your knowledge of the subject or want to know more, you might start a local group of your own. Both national organizations can help you begin.

In the following list a group may be listed in a region but strive for a national constituency (to send out a bibliography, for instance). It is advisable to read through the entire sampling before contacting any one person or organization. (When writing either national groups or anyone in the regional listings, *it is strongly suggested that you enclose a stamped self-adressed envelope to facilitate a reply.*)*

*Information about the various resource centers was supplied by the groups themselves.

National Organizations

*The Assassination Information Bureau
(A.I.B.)*
63 Inman Street
Cambridge, Mass. 02139
617/661-8411

1322 18th St., N.W.
Washington, D.C. 20036
202/857-0017
The A.I.B directs its efforts toward spreading information about the Kennedy assassination and the political context in which it rests. The group makes available speakers, films, videotapes, information sheets, sound tapes, photos, radio programs, and other modes of propaganda aimed at enlightening and agitating its national constituency. Efforts are primarily directed toward colleges; however, many presentations have been given to other community gatherings. Information kits include the Zapruder film and numerous slides with explanation. (Audiovisual material on "The Life and Times of the Mysterious Howard Hughes" is also available.) Major accomplishment: "Who Killed JFK?" conference at Boston University in early 1975. Write for details of available material; give specific interest if possible.

The Washington, D.C., office acts as a monitor of the congressional inquiry and serves as a briefing center for the media. Information for the general public is available from either A.I.B. office.

*The Citizen's Commission of Inquiry
(C.C.I.)*
103 2nd Street, N.E.
Washington, D.C. 20002
202/546-7500
The C.C.I. serves as a clearinghouse for information on the assassination, with a goal of provoking members of Congress to speak out and support the reopened investigation. C.C.I. director Mark Lane speaks extensively on the subject around the country. The group encourages local chapters to make public collected data on the assassination through films, speakers, and public relations. Petitions and kits for forming local chapters are available, as well as many other tools for popularizing legitimate criticism of the Warren Report. Major accomplishment: Translating constituent dissatisfaction with the Warren Report into congressional support for the reopened investigation.

South

Mark Biero
3008 Dewey
Tampa, Florida 33612
813/876-0528
Biero is the organizer of a course called Political Assassinations in the United States under the aegis of the Common Learning Network in the University of South Florida community.

"Ruby died six months ago of cancer, maintaining to the last that he was no conspirator. . . ."
—WALTER CRONKITE
CBS News Inquiry, June 27, 1967

"I do not want to die. But I am not insane. I was framed to kill Oswald."
—JACK RUBY
to psychiatrist Werner Teuter, shortly before death from cancer; quoted in *The London Sunday Times,* August 25, 1974

Cliff Hawley
1315 Morreena Rd., Apt. 12-E
Durham, North Carolina 27705
919/383-4039
Hawley is quite well-versed in the subject, and is available to speak to small and large groups concerning the JFK assassination and its political implications. His presentation includes the Zapruder film and other visual aids.

Wallace Milam
#30 Troy Road Apartments
Dyersburg, Tennessee 38024
901/285-8400
Milam presents a convincing show outlining "The Killing of John F. Kennedy and the Cover-Up," and reports audiences are quite receptive. He maintains an extensive library of research material, which he also uses in his

history class at Dyersburg High School. Interested parties may contact him at the above address.

C. C. I.—Northern Virginia Chapter
2923 Westcott Street
Falls Church, Virginia 22042
703/534-2424
Furnishes speakers for school, church, and civic groups in Northern Virginia; also can supply material from the nearby national office. Contact chapter director Andy Smith for further information.

Citizen's Committee for the Reinvestigation of the Assassination (CCRAP)
1806 N. Herndon Street
Arlington, Virginia 22201
703/243-5483
CCRAP presents a two-hour lecture using the normal visual aids (Zapruder film, slides) as well as a demonstration of a Mannlicher-Carcano rifle—the model the Warren Report says Oswald used to kill Kennedy. Further information on this group is available from

"A great and good president has suffered martyrdom as a result of the hatred and bitterness that has been injected into the life of our nation by bigots."
—EARL WARREN
immediately following the assassination, November 22, 1963

Robert F. Meunier at the above address (or 126 Old River Road, Lincoln, Rhode Island 02865).

C.C.I. Richmond Chapter
8600 Burgundy Road
Richmond, Virginia 23235
804/272-4568
This group makes available data on the assassination to the Richmond area with material primarily supplied by the Washington office; its members are available for speaking and bringing in outside speakers, as well as appearing on talk shows. Contact Kent Dyche at the above address for details.

"Marina Oswald has lied to the Secret Service, the FBI, and this commission repeatedly on matters which are of vital concern to the people of this country and the world."
—NORMAN REDLICH
Warren Commission counsel, in a memo to Chief Counsel J. Lee Rankin, February 28, 1964, discussing the commission's transcripts and files

---

The Grassy Knoll Gazette
903 W. Grace Street #2
Richmond, Virginia 23220
A quarterly publication, *The Grassy Knoll Gazette* had its first issue in March 1977. It covers information about political assassinations and the ongoing investigations to track down the guilty parties. Write J. W. Burke,

Jr., at the above address for subscription information.

© 1975 William Rice. Used by permission.

Michael L. Kurtz
University Station
Box 809
Hammond, Louisiana 70401
504/549-2103, 549-2109
An associate professor in the Department of History and Government at Southeastern Louisiana University, Kurtz maintains an extensive library of assassination data at SLU. He teaches a course on the subject for credit at the school, as well as a Continuing Education noncredit course. He is available for lectures in the area, and may be consulted regarding his resource collection.

Arkansas Assassination Information Bureau
P.O. Box 111
Knoxville, Arkansas 72845
501/885-3773
A.A.I.B. offers presentations to interested groups in the state, and comes equipped with slides and film as a visual aid. The group can

---

"But nobody reads. Don't believe people read in this country. There will be a few professors that will read the record . . . The public will read very little."
—ALLEN DULLES
Warren Commission member and former CIA Director at a commission meeting, July 9, 1964

---

also make Zapruder films available. A.A.I.B. has shown the Zapruder film at rural high schools in Arkansas with strong response. Write James E. Moore at the above address for details.

Robert C. Summer
307 W. Pasadena Avenue
Muscle Shoals, Alabama 35660
Summer is available to speak at local schools and community groups on the assassination, as well as talk with interested parties in the Muscle Shoals area about the subject. He is affiliated with the national C.C.I.

Tony Blumenberg
P.O. Box 1103
Summerville, South Carolina 29483
803/873-5458
Blumenberg can furnish a speaker on the assassination and its cover-up.

U.T.—C.C.I.
University of Tennessee Student Center
1601 West Cumberland Avenue
Knoxville, Tennessee 37916
Members of this group are knowledgeable about the Kennedy assassination, and welcome inquiries from others in the Knoxville area on the subject.

East

Assassination Conspiracy Resource List
P.O. Box 271
New Vernon, New Jersey 07976
201/538-6676
This is a well-balanced and provocative list of books, films, resource centers, and magazine articles on the assassination; updated periodically. Many documents/articles available at reprinting cost. Write Donelly/Colt at above address.

Terry M. Ripmaster
80 Lapton Lane #2-J
Haledon, New Jersey 07508
An assistant professor of History at William Patterson College, Ripmaster speaks often on the JFK murder. Parties interested in scheduling or attending a presentation should contact him at the above address or c/o William Patterson College in Wayne, N.J.

"People in the Pursuit of Truth"
815 Washington Street
Newtonville, Mass. 02139
A newsletter edited by Edmund C. Berkeley,

deals with assassination research and conspiracy links. *"People . . . "* is a continuation of a monthly series on the same subject in *Computers and People* (formerly *Computers and Automation*) magazine. Write above address for subscription rates. (Some back issues of *Computers and People* available.)

Connecticut Citizens Commission of Inquiry
122 Princeton Street
Bridgeport, Connecticut 06605
Like others, this group offers a slide and film lecture show. CCCI has an allied group called "Connecticut Citizens Against Assassinations." Parties interested in either organization may contact John J. Maher at the above address.

Committee to Open the Archives
6 Bleeker Street
New York, New York 10012
212/477-6243
C.O.A. conducts research into the CIA's links with organized crime, anti-Castro Cubans, and the Kennedy assassination, and maintains extensive files on those subjects. Its findings are periodically published in *Yipster Times,* a fairly outrageous journal of agitation and underground information. C.O.A., affiliated with the Youth International Party, has presented many of its findings in the book *Coup d'Etat in America,* whose coauthor A.J. Weberman coordinates C.O.A. activities. The group makes copies of its book and important documents available at cost, and can furnish speakers on the assassination.

(N.B. Many researchers consider some C.O.A. conclusions to be of dubious validity.)

Robert B. Cutler
Box 1465
Manchester, Mass. 01944
Cutler offers numerous precise drawings of people, bullet flight paths, and buildings in Dealey Plaza, both in his books and separately. He also presents a slide and lecture show in the New England area. Cutler, an architect by training, extracts theories from precise blueprint-style reconstructions.

Assassination Research Committee
Student Polity—State University
of New York
Stony Brook, New York 11794
516/246-6800
Funded by the SUNY student government, this campus group offers material on the assassination to the college community and elsewhere on Long Island. Speakers can be arranged on the subject.

Ralph Schoenman
c/o New Line Presentations
New York, New York
A long-time associate of the late British philosopher Bertrand Russell until their falling out, Schoenman was active in a number of international political movements, including the British "Who Killed Kennedy?" group. Schoenman, currently under contract to a lecture bureau, can speak on "Assassina-

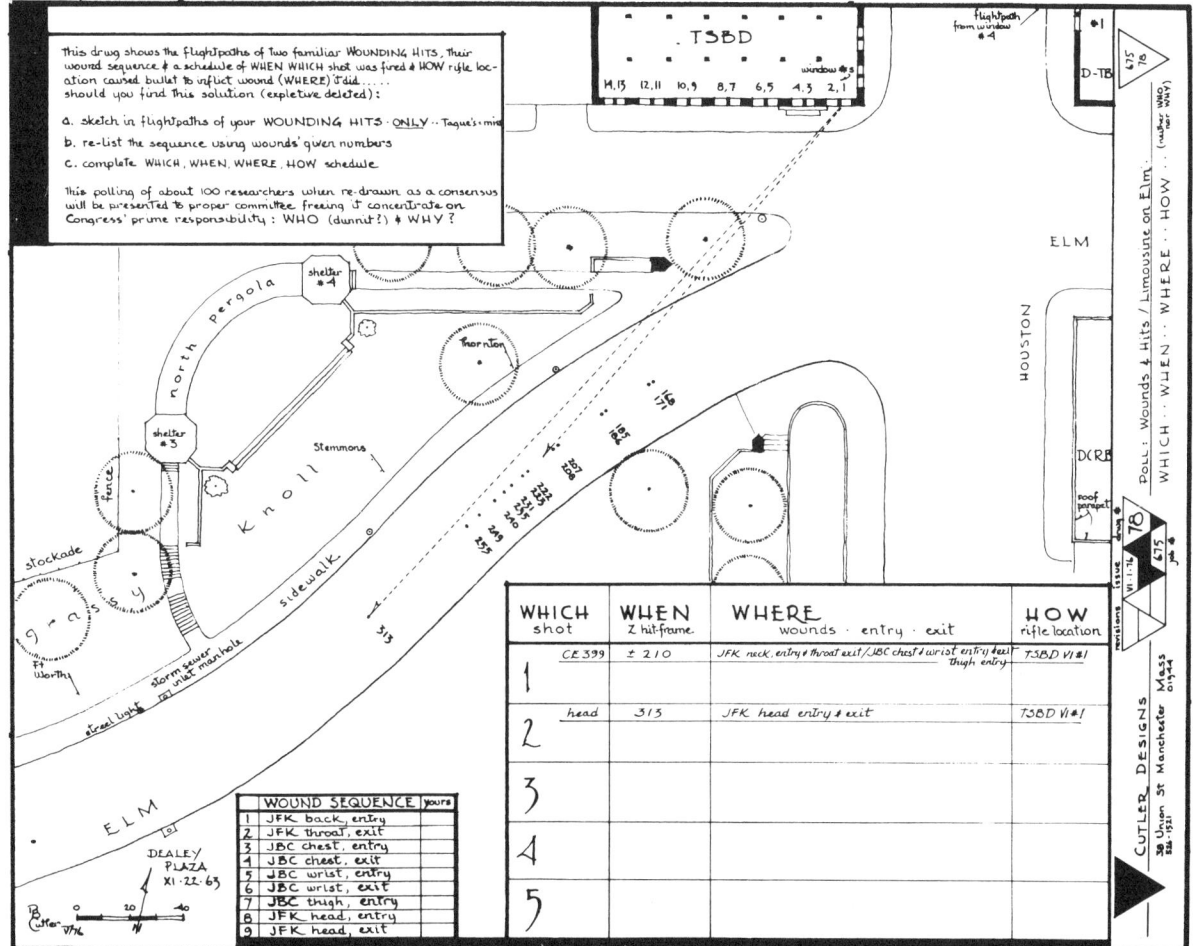

You get to play sleuth in Robert Cutler's sketch. Dotted lines are courtesy of the Warren Commission. You fill in the rest.

tion: Dallas to Watergate, Blood on Their Hands." Available through New Line Presentations, NYC. (N.B. Many of Schoenman's conclusions are considered somewhat speculative by other researchers.)

The Committee to Investigate Assassinations
c/o Fensterwald
1070 H Street, N.W., Suite 1005
Washington, D.C. 20002
The first of the latter-day organizations

(formed in late 1968), the C.T.I.A. maintains extensive files on political assassinations but does little public data dissemination except to distribute its bibliography. C.T.I.A. activities are confined to Freedom of Information requests and attempting to influence members of Congress. Bibliographies available from the above address.

"I heard one more than was fired."
　　—ROBERT EDWARDS, who was in Dealey Plaza,
replying to Warren Commission counsel David Belin's question, "How many shots did you hear?," April 9, 1964

Special Collections Division
Georgetown University Library
37th and O streets, N.W.
Washington, D.C. 20057
The GU library has the papers of researchers Robert Cutler and Richard E. Sprague, as well as those of the *Life* reporter who covered the Jim Garrison inquiry (including photographs). Also stored at the library are various books and periodicals on the assassination of John Kennedy, and a few papers of Charles Guiteau, the convicted assassin of President James Garfield. The library makes available tapes of the Committee to Investigate Assassinations conference held in Washington, November 1973. Researchers should contact George M. Barringer, Special Collections Librarian, for details. The collection is available to the general public.

Northern New Jersey C.C.I.
25 Carteret Street
West Orange, New Jersey 07052
This outlet furnishes material from the C.C.I. national office. Gary Meiseles can be consulted at the above address for Zapruder film screenings and arranging speakers.

Conspiracy!
6699 Springbank Lane
Philadelphia, Pa. 19119
215/844-7859
This outlet covers the entire spectrum of intelligence-related activities, all inextricably tied to the Kennedy assassination and its alleged sponsors. Occasional newsletter, voluminous research, and conclusions few others reach are all the work of John Judge at the above address.

Jim Pontarelli
35 Belvedere Blvd.
North Providence, R.I. 02911
Pontarelli can help correspondents with the intricacies of the Freedom of Information Act and how to pry documents out of the National Archives and other government agencies. He also makes available copies of the Schweiker Report and the Zapruder film.

Assassination Research Center
56 Spencer Court
Hartsdale, New York 10530
This group acts primarily as a clearinghouse for hard-to-find and out-of-print books and periodicals dealing with the assassination. They can give a presentation on the assassi-

JOHN J. MCCLOY: *I can't say that I have run into a fellow comparable to Oswald, but I have run into some very limited mentalities in the CIA and FBI.*
(laughter)
EARL WARREN: *... they and all the other agencies do employ undercover men who are of terrible character.*
—exchange at a Warren Commission meeting
January 27, 1964

nation, and also maintain a supply of films on the subject available to the public. A. R. C. buys and sells assassination literature; hence, it is advisable to write Marc Medoff, Director, first with specific needs.

"Reference is made to footnote 563, page 307 of chapter 6. The FBI was simply unable to get us [the document] in time. . . . I have inserted a phantom CE [Commission Exhibit] number which can be filled in with something. I believe I have fudged the text sufficiently so that almost anything can be fitted in [CE3074]."
—DAVID SLAWSON
Warren Commission attorney, in an interoffice memo to cocounsel Howard Willens, September 22, 1964

Inside, Straight
Blue Book Publishers
64 Prospect Street
White Plains, New York, 10606
This is an irregularly published newsletter which includes interesting and speculative information about clandestine power plays in American government; subjects from the JFK assassination to flying saucers are covered. Write Leon Davidson, editor, for a sample copy.

Midwest

Committee for Reinvestigation of Assassinations
1508 Barrington Road
Columbus, Ohio 43221
614/486-7802
Among this group's accomplishments is active encouragement of a resolution in the Ohio state legislature asking Congress to reopen the assassination investigation. CRA offers lectures and petitions and a bibliography to any interested parties. Details available from Christopher Compson at the above address.

Findlay (Ohio) Area C.C.I.
508 Trenton Avenue #34
Findlay, Ohio 45840
419/422-0916
This group's main organizer is a high school social studies teacher. Presentations are made in and out of schools and through local media. Members are available for further public

activity in the area. Contact Ron Fellows at the above address.

Project Alpha
Box 85
Warriner Hall
Central Michigan University
Mt. Pleasant, Michigan 48859
517/772-5001
Project Alpha ("American Legal, Political, and Historical Awareness") is an umbrella organization for a number of groups organizing around issues such as marijuana laws, civil liberties, government repression, the assassination of John Kennedy and the need to

Assassination sleuth Larry Harris surveys Dealey Plaza in his "WHO KILLED JFK?" shirt. Embroidery by Wanda Hughes.

Jeff Wallace

pursue its investigation. Interested parties in Central Michigan should contact project coordinator Gary Hatch.

C.C.I. Chicago Chapter
2143 N. Avers
Chicago, Illinois 60647
312/342-7035
This C.C.I. chapter offers the public films, a bibliography, and other related information. Further information is available from the head of the local chapter, Ted Kmiec, at the above address.

Sherman Skolnick
Citizen's Committee to Clean Up the Courts (CCCC)
9800 S. Oglesby
Chicago, Illinois 60617
312/375-5741, 787-8220
CCCC investigates conspiracy in government and mob-related activities, primarily as it relates to the Chicago area. In the course of this, CCCC has conducted considerable research into the attempt on JFK's life planned for early November 1963 and other examples of government conspiracy leading up through Watergate. Chairman Skolnick uses the scattershot approach to research; i.e. if you aim wide enough, you're bound to hit something. The organization maintains a twenty-four-hour dial-a-conspiracy at 312/731-1100. Write to the above address with specific inquiries. (N.B. Some of Skolnick's conclusions strain credulity even of true believing conspiracists.)

"The Commission's inquiry was at once monumental and meticulous."
— ***The New York Times***
following the release of 26 volumes of Warren Commission testimony and evidence, November 25, 1964

Ralph M. Singer
8715 N. Harding Avenue
Skokie, Illinois 60076
Singer, affiliated with the C.C.I., has spoken to school groups from junior high level through college. His presentation includes the Zapruder film. He is available for speaking engagements in the Skokie area.

Minnesota Action Council
1818 13th Avenue South
Minneapolis, Minnesota 55404
This group seeks to "bring about understanding of the political, social, and economic reasons for the major domestic political assassination of the last thirteen years so that citizens can begin to assert democratic control over the course of our society." Position papers will be issued periodically; contact secretary-treasurer Kerry Carlson at the above address for details.

David R. Wrone
History Department
University of Wisconsin/Stevens Point
Stevens Point, Wisconsin 54481
715/346-2334

Wrone, author of a well-reasoned annotated bibliography in the field, is active with a student group that discusses the assassination in public forums in the area. The UW/SP library maintains an extensive collection of books on the subject.

C.C.I. Milwaukee Chapter
3465 N. 76th Street
Milwaukee, Wisconsin 53222
This group can furnish talk-show guests to discuss the Kennedy murder and reasons for reopening the investigation as well as material from the national office. A local speaker for community groups is also available. Write Helen Swanson at the above address.

"Your commission, I know, has been guided throughout by a determination to tell the whole truth. . . .

"I have given instructions for the prompt publication of this report to the American people and to the world. . . . "
— **LYNDON JOHNSON**
in a letter to Earl Warren on receipt of the commission's report, September 24, 1964

Take Over
P.O. Box 706
Madison, Wisconsin 53701
608/256-8186
An underground newspaper, *Take Over* regularly prints articles on political conspiracy, with an emphasis on the Kennedy assassina-

tion. They cosponsored a significant conference in 1975 called "A Decade of CIA Involvement in U.S. Politics," and can supply a speaker on the subject equipped with film and slides.

Martin Shackelford
216 N. Webster Apt. #2
Saginaw, Michigan 48602
517/792-5488
Shackelford, a contributor to MacFarlane's *Proof of Conspiracy,* maintains an extensive slide collection as part of his presentation in political assassination going back through Lincoln. Small or large groups wishing to have Shackelford discuss the subject, as well as other researchers wanting to correspond, may contact him at the above address.

Horizone
Box 67
St. Charles, Mo. 63301
A newsletter service only, Horizone circulates information about "the grey zone where politics, crime, and government intersect," and as such, includes reference to the JFK assassination on occasion. Its analysis of trends in international violence and mercenary activity covers a wide range of material. Write to the above address for subscription information.

Southwest

Larry R. Harris
4129 Cole, #103
Dallas, Texas 75204
214/278-7862

"The Warren Commission! What the hell do they know? Did they learn anything you couldn't read in the papers the next day?"
—**JACK RUBY**
quoted in *Argosy,* September 1967

"When the Chief Justice [Warren] was asked if today's presentation [turning the completed report over to President Johnson] ended the commission's job, he answered an emphatic 'yes!'"
—**The New York Times**
September 25, 1964

Harris, coauthor of *Cover-Up,* presents a slide and film show on the "multiassassin ambush" of President Kennedy; also, if transportation provided, will conduct a tour of points of interest in the Dallas-Ft. Worth area connected with the assassination (Dealey Plaza, Tippit murder site, Oswald rooming house, etc.). Presentation is in simple and concise terms.

"The Continuing Inquiry"
Penn Jones, Jr.
P.O. Box 1140
Midlothian, Texas 76065
Jones is considered one of the great storytellers of the assassination researching business and knows his material backwards and forwards. Best known for his four-volume *Forgive My Grief* series, Jones also makes available many other hard-to-obtain research tools, including films of the assassination and

tapes of the Dallas police radio band during the hours following. His newsletter, "The Continuing Inquiry," published on the 22nd day of each month, carries information, speculation, and revelations. Jones is available for public speaking and meeting with serious researchers. Write to the above address for a list of available resources.

J. Gary Shaw
P.O. Box 722
Cleburne, Texas 76031
817/645-3908
The coauthor of *Cover-Up*, Shaw is available as a speaker on the assassination and its aftermath. He welcomes inquiries from the general public as well as other researchers.

Scott Sirota
P.O. Box 4157
Scottsdale, Arizona 85258
602/948-8685
Sirota is available to speak on the John Kennedy assassination in the Phoenix area and around the state. His presentation, which includes slides and film, has been well received at high schools and colleges. Interested parties should contact him at the above location.

John McClure
3015 Kearney
Denver, Colorado 80207
McClure, a former advertising man, is the artist who created an exact replica in three-dimension of Dealey Plaza at the precise moment of assassination. His study of the area

"The monumental record of the President's Commission will stand like a Gibraltar of factual literature through the ages to come."
—**GERALD FORD**
Warren Commission member and U.S. Congressman from Michigan in *Portrait of the Assassin* (coauthored with John Stiles)

John McClure's handcrafted reconstruction of the assassination scene.

led him to conclude that shots came from more than one gun, and he now presents lectures and college courses on the assassination. (His Dealey Plaza exhibit is displayed at the Movie Wax Museum in Estes Park, Colorado.)

Research Associates
3723 N.W. 13th
Oklahoma City, Oklahoma 73107
This group carries out research in a variety of fields, all interconnected, including the murder of John Kennedy. They can make available speakers and prepare a university course outline on the assassination, according to spokesman Anthony L. Kimery, who may be reached at the above address.

West

A.I.B.—Los Angeles
P.O. Box 327
Hollywood, California 90028

Affiliated with the national A.I.B., this regional office can present a slide show demonstrating a strong case for political conspiracy not just in JFK's killing, but in the larger framework of power dynamics in U.S. politics and foreign policy. Chapter director Jeff Cohen has appeared on numerous talk shows and debates and lectures in the West and Southwest both on and off campuses. Cohen is also an expert on the Martin Luther King assassination.

Mae Brussell
25620 Via Crotalo
Carmel, California 93921
408/624-9103
Voluminous research published in various magazines, in lectures, and on a weekly radio show called "Dialogue Conspiracy" links disparate events and personalities into a neat web of overbearing conspiracy. Individuals and radio stations write to above address for access to material and shows. (N.B. Some of

Brussell's conclusions are considered somewhat speculative by other researchers.)

Zodiac News Service
950 Howard Street
San Francisco, California 94103
415/956-3555
Written for radio stations and newspapers, Z. N. S. is a daily six-page print packet of general interest news in the fields of politics, youth, environment, music, conspiracy, and trends overlooked by mass media. It maintains extensive contacts among conspiracy researchers and often breaks national stories on the subject.

"Gerry Ford struck me as a very ambitious young man who saw his assignment on the commission as an opportunity to get some public attention. The way he walked, the way he talked, his entire manner. . . ."
—ROBERT OSWALD
in his book *Lee*

David Lifton
11818½ Dorothy Street
Los Angeles, California 90049
213/826-1610
An active researcher into the Kennedy assassination since 1966, Lifton is available to speak on the subject to interested groups. He is also interested in communicating with others doing serious research and maintains an extensive collection of documents in the assassination investigation.

"It is unlikely that the Warren Commission will quiet sensationalists who are bent upon exploiting the Kennedy assassination for their own ideological or monetary purposes."
—The Los Angeles Times
September 27, 1964

William R. Rice
P. O. Box 637
Orangevale, California 95662
Rice has an extensive library of material on the assassination of John Kennedy and shares his data with anyone having a genuine interest. His 1975 *John and Robert Kennedy Assassination Bibliography* includes privately published volumes on the subject, and is available from the above address. Rice lectures on both assassinations, and maintains an extensive photographic collection as well.

Josiah Thompson
P. O. Box 546
Bolinas, California 94624
415/868-1645
The author of *Six Seconds in Dallas,* Thompson has a commanding knowledge of the physical and eyewitness evidence from Dealey Plaza. His presentation includes photographic evidence on slides and film. (Thompson may also be reached c/o Haverford College, Haverford, Pa.)

Perry Adams and Fred T. Newcomb
P. O. Box 13390 U.C.S.B.
Santa Barbara, California 93107
805/968-2777
The authors of *Murder From Within,* Adams and Newcomb publish an investigative research newspaper called *Probe,* which occasionally carries material on the John Kennedy murder. The two make public presentations on the assassination at colleges, high schools, civic groups, and night schools. Further information is available from the above address.

International

Assassination Committee for the Truth (A.C.T.)
Hazel Hale
Breary Cottage
Arthington Road
Leeds, England LS16 8BD
Telephone: 097-335-2632

T. H. Irwin
32 Ravensdene Crescent
Ravenhill
Belfast, Ireland BT6 0DB
Telephone: 0232-642027

Mike Masterman
'Camelot' Rue de la Croute
St. Quen, Jersey
Channel Islands
Telephone: Central 82990

"The assassination was an attempted coup d'etat by the forces of political reaction, virulent racism, and unbridled militarism."
—SAM MARCY
Workers' World party chairman, September 28, 1964; quoted in *The New York Times*

Chris Scally
12 Woodfield
Parklands Estate
Wickford
Essex, England SS12 9BT

Brian Burden
300 Church Street
Bocking
Braintree
Essex, England CM7 5LQ

A.C.T. is a most active group, and started after the death of Europe's leading conspiracy researcher Joachim Joesten. They distribute a bibliography of English language books on the subject published outside the United States (available for $3.00 U.S. from Irwin) and have had some success bringing research data to light in the British media. Scally is best known for his research into the Zapruder film. Burden and Irwin publish a breezy monthly newsletter called "JFK Assassination Forum" ($12.00 U.S. annually includes airmail postage) and lectures on the subject. Hale is also active in the "Kennedy Society of Europe," an international group which

"We hear that the commission attorneys were too rushed to collect all the relevant evidence. But should you be interested in the condition of Jack Ruby's mother's teeth in the year 1938, you need merely turn to the page in the documents which publishes her full dental chart; which I suggest would not even be relevant if it were charged that Ruby bit Oswald to death."

—MARK LANE

in his lecture, 1965 to the present

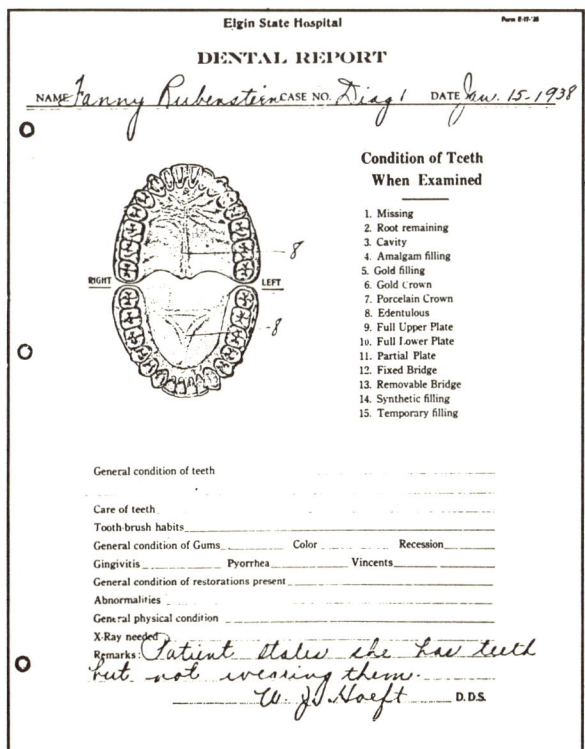

shares information about JFK's life (and, to a lesser extent, his death). A.C.T. relies on like-minded U.S. colleagues to furnish them with new developments, books, articles, etc. on the Kennedy assassination.

Ian MacFarlane
59 Talbot Crescent
Kooyong
Victoria
Australia 3144

MacFarlane has shown himself to be an expert on the subject from 9,000 miles away. His two books (especially *Proof of Conspiracy*) have been well-received in Australia, and he has been successful at having the Zapruder film broadcast on national television. In his two visits to the U.S. MacFarlane has filmed interviews on the assassination for airing back home. He may be consulted regarding specialized aspects of the Kennedy assassination at the above address.

"[David] Belin [Warren Commission counsel and chief counsel for the Rockefeller Commission's CIA investigation] is said to be exploring the theory that the compilation of dossiers, disruption of radical groups, wiretapping and interception of mail, and other illegal activities attributed to the CIA were all the acts of a single deranged individual acting alone . . . 'the lone character assassin.' "

—The National Lampoon

April 1975

The Australian Kennedy Society
137 Bell Street
East Preston 3072
Melbourne
Australia
According to A.K.S. president William Clyde, the group's purpose is to advocate Kennedy-like policies, examine the Kennedy legacy, and push for "justice in Dallas." A Sydney chapter is anticipated.

Justice Freedom and Knowledge Committee
77 Purnell Drive Unit 53
Hamilton, Ontario
Canada L9C 4Y4
416/383-5403
The "J.F.K. Committee" pursues leads in Canada as well as assembling the usual data on the Kennedy assassination. Among its efforts is to compel the Canadian government to declassify its file on Arthur Bremer, convicted of an attempt on George Wallace's life. Speakers can be arranged by the group, as well as talk show appearances. Contact national chairman Karen Walker at the above address for details.

The Collector's Archives
Box 114
Beaconsfield, Quebec
Canada H9W 5T6
Offers films (Zapruder, Nix), tapes, photos, bibliography, and other data on the assassination. Write Dave Hawkins for details.

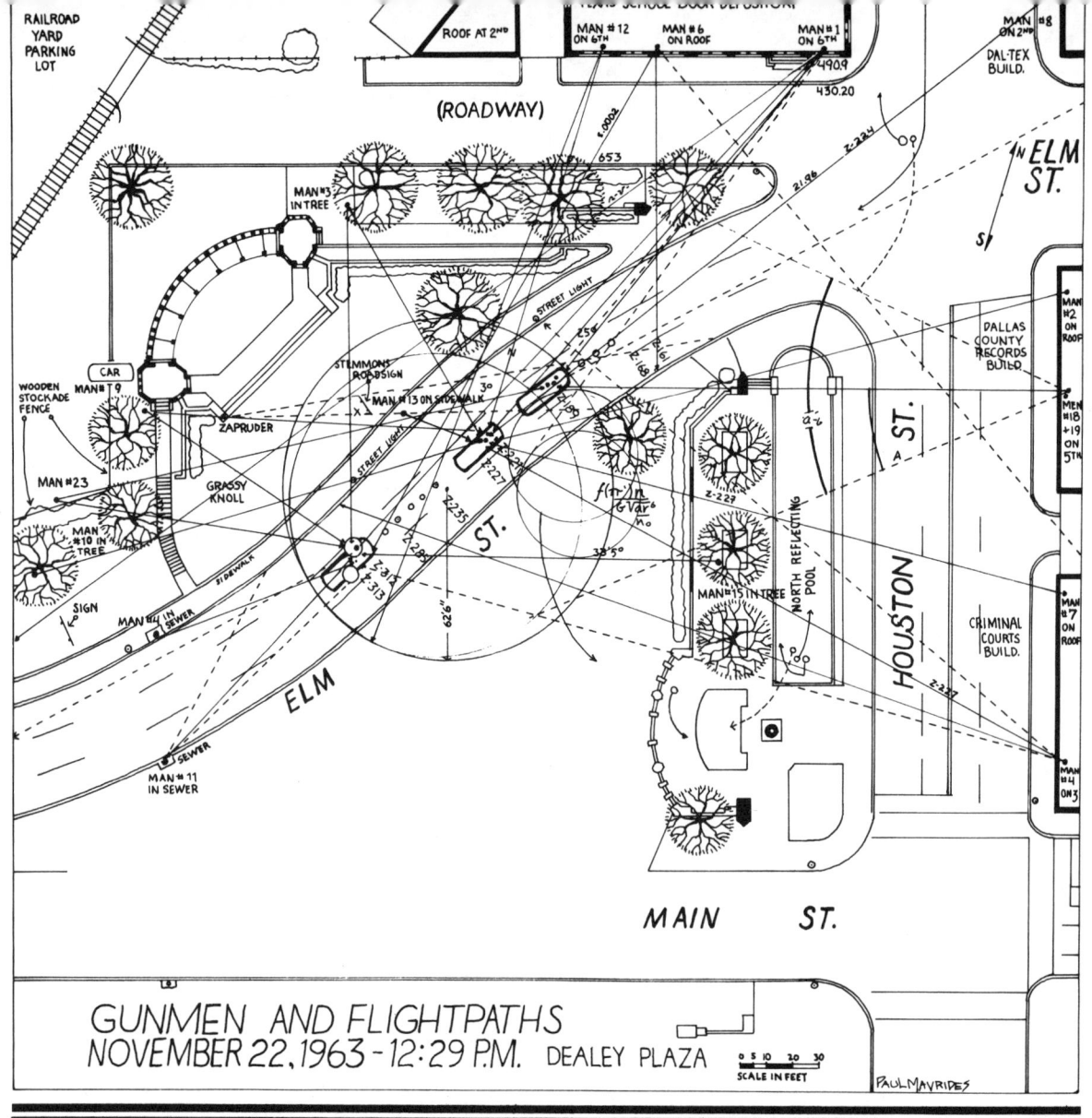

3 WHAT HAPPENED?

When the Warren Commission issued its twenty-six volumes of testimony, exhibits, and documents, only 8,000 sets were printed. The Government Printing Office, which determines book price by weight, sold complete sets for $76.00.[1] The twenty-six volumes of findings have become the major source of information and leads for researchers. They contain references to people and places which contradict some commission conclusions, and reveal others to be of dubious validity. Many potential areas of inquiry are hinted at and then never followed up. Some investigative and interrogative techniques are shown to be painfully lacking.

Additional basic source material is contained in documents stored at the National Archives in Washington, D.C. Much of this is declassified and available to the public. A lot of the material originally shielded from public eyes which later became declassified has led to further digging by researchers. Periodically the Justice Department or Central Intelligence Agency will review classified documents in the Warren Commission files and release some for public consumption. It is these government documents, published and unpublished, which comprise the bulk of resource material.[2] Unfortunately the truly

valuable documents were either not turned over to the commission staff to begin with or else require laborious legal maneuvering through the Freedom of Information Act to pry them loose.[3] Supposedly, the congressional investigation into assassinations has access to all the classified data.

From there, source material is where you find it. Newspaper articles, books, magazine pieces, television and radio interviews, court records, public speeches, private conversations, affidavits, and independent investigations all contribute to the body of knowledge. Like material in the twenty-six volumes, each assertion must be viewed in terms of its source, veracity, supporting data, and the motive for its publication. Occasionally facts which are valid by these criteria may still contradict each other.

In the following time-line, some of these contradictory assertions are included. Many are merely judgmental differences in the time of day or precise location of a witness; others are substantial contradictions, the most clear one being, perhaps, the Odio story. Mrs. Sylvia Odio, an articulate Cuban refugee living in Dallas, says that on or about September 26, 1963, three men from an anti-Castro group visited her home, one identified as "Leon Oswald." Mrs. Odio, whose testimony is firm and unshaken, says the man identified as "Leon Oswald" is the same man picked up for the murder of Officer Tippit and President

1. Many city and university libraries have sets.

2. Anyone contemplating using the twenty-six volumes should locate *Subject Index to the Warren Report and Hearings and Exhibits,* by Sylvia Meagher which is far more thorough than the commission's own index.

3. See *Whitewash IV,* pp. 166-214.

"[Earl Warren] has given us an immense and almost indisputable statement for the prosecution."

—MURRAY KEMPTON
in *The New Republic*, October 19, 1964

"There was never any substantial reason to congratulate the Warren Commission for its performance."

—MURRAY KEMPTON
from his introduction to *The Second Oswald*, 1966

Kennedy. In their visit the three men, who said they had just come from New Orleans, discussed anti-Castro activities. The next day one of the three telephoned, relating that "Leon Oswald" was an ex-Marine, a good shot, thought John Kennedy should have been killed following the Bay of Pigs because he had sold out the Cuban exiles, and was somewhat "loco." During this time, the Warren Commission painfully stretches documentation to show that Lee Oswald could not have been in Dallas at the time because he was en route to Mexico from New Orleans. If he was traveling straight to Mexico and Mrs. Odio's story is accurate, then an Oswald imposter, operating on some unknown party's behalf, was employed. On the other hand, if Lee Oswald was in Dallas as Mrs. Odio (and her sister, another witness) said, it would likewise be proof of conspiracy. Either way, the Warren Commission's conclusions are negated.[4]

4. A lucid and concise summary of the Odio story may be found in *Accessories After the Fact*, pp. 378-87.

The following time-line of events related to the assassination, alleged participants, and witnesses includes some contradictory evidence where it draws out vital differences. Most entries are followed by citations that can lead the reader to supportive material. Because the original investigation dwelled on Lee Oswald to such an overwhelming extent to the exclusion of others, there is more data on him than anyone else. Likewise, the Texas School Book Depository and its occupants are covered at length; much less so are other buildings facing Dealey Plaza or the area behind the grassy knoll and the railroad tracks. The available information—especially that which the Warren Commission collected—is equally informative for what it includes as for what is missing.

Explanation of sources cited: D.T.H. = Dallas Times Herald; D.M.N. = Dallas Morning News; N.Y.T. = New York Times; N.O.T.P. = New Orleans Times Picayune; N.O.S.I. = New Orleans States Item; W.P. = Washington Post; Cong. Rec. = Congressional Record; O.N.I. = Office of Naval Intelligence files. TAG refers to the *Files of Evidence Connected with the Investigation of the Assassination of President John F. Kennedy*, compiled by the Texas Attorney General's office. References to Warren Commission findings are as follows: volume number:page (11:372 is volume 11, page 372); Commission Document number:page (CD1553:3 is document #1553, page 3); Commission Exhibit number (CE1281:18 is exhibit #1281, page 18; some Commission Exhibits are physical objects or photos, and have no page numbers). Some Commission Documents are broken down further by including sources, such as CD349:SS974 (document #349 from the Secret Service, page 974).

Books cited just by name are listed in the bibliography (Chapter 4). Events without sources are either Historical Record (such as presidential speeches) or extrapolated from a number of different sources.

"You're going to introduce the Warren Report? You must be kidding!"
—BERNARD BAGERT
judge at the preliminary hearing for Clay Shaw (charged by New Orleans District Attorney Jim Garrison with conspiring to murder President Kennedy), ruling that the report was hearsay, March 14, 1967

1911
Jack Ruby is born in Chicago, Illinois. Eight different dates are offered in various sources. March 25 is the date most often used.

1917
MAY 29
John Kennedy is born in Brookline, Massachusetts (a Boston suburb).

1930
Jack Ruby serves thirty days in a Chicago jail for selling pirated sheet music. [TAG5:D26]

1930?/?1931
Jack Ruby is jailed for two days, the result of an altercation. [TAG5:D40]

"Don't believe the Warren Report. That was only put out to make me look innocent, so that it would throw Americans and all the European countries off guard."
—JACK RUBY
in a letter smuggled out of jail

1937
Jack Ruby begins periodic visits to Las Vegas. [CD1252:13, 17]

1939
OCTOBER 18
Lee Harvey Oswald born at French Hospital, New Orleans.

DECEMBER 8
Leon Cooke, attorney and president of waste handlers union local, is killed. Jack Ruby, union secretary, arrested and held overnight for questioning in the murder. Ruby starts using the middle name of "Leon." [CD351:2; TAG5:D26]

1939-1940
Jack Ruby says he leaves Chicago as a field organizer for Teamster Local #20467. [CD1254:8]

1940
AUGUST 3
Marguerite Oswald applies for Aid to Dependent Children in New Orleans. [CD906]

1940-1942
Jack Ruby is a traveling salesman in Ohio,

1941 *(cont.)*
New York, and New England. [CD1254:8; TAG5:D19, R9]

1941
Jack Ruby receives a concussion in a fight; spends five days at Edgewater Hospital. [TAG5:D40]

JULY 17
Marina Prusakova is born at Arkhangelo-blast, USSR.

1943
MAY 28
Jack Ruby enters the U.S. Air Corps for thirty-three months. [5:5]

JUNE 10
Jack Ruby is an M.P. at Kessler Field in Mississippi for twelve weeks. [CD856:83]

1945
Marguerite Oswald moves to Dallas with her son Lee. [1:255]

Lee Oswald is hospitalized for two weeks, and has a mastoidectomy. [19:592]

APRIL 17
Marguerite Oswald takes out $1,000 life insurance policy on her son Lee. [CD141:2]

1945-1946
Jack Ruby visits Dallas for the first time on a three-day pass from McDill Air Force Base. [CD1254:8]

1946
FEBRUARY 21
Jack Ruby is discharged from the Air Force. [CD5:5]

SUMMER-FALL
Lee Oswald spends his summer at Covington, La., and starts grammar school there that fall. [CD107:7, 9; CD860:16]

"Certainly you ought to have some confidence in a commission that is appointed by the president."

—EARL WARREN
to Marguerite Oswald, during her appearance before the commission, February 10, 1964

NOVEMBER
John Kennedy elected to the U.S. House of Representatives from the 11th Congressional District of Massachusetts.

1947
JANUARY 27
Lee Oswald attends first grade at Ridge West Elementary School in Ft. Worth. [CE1384]

MARCH 12
President Truman asks Congress to approve a proposed international intelligence gathering bureaucracy called the Central Intelligence Agency; Congress approves.

"It's, uh, very heavy."
—LYNDON JOHNSON
on receiving the first copy of the Warren Commission Report, September 24, 1964

SUMMER
Jack Ruby comes to Dallas and operates the Singapore (later the Silver Spur) Club. [26:560]

DECEMBER 30
Jack Rubenstein legally changes his name to Jack Ruby. [22:296]

1949
FEBRUARY 4
Dallas Police charge Jack Ruby with disturbing the peace. [26:560]

DECEMBER
Lee Oswald gives his fourth grade teacher a puppy for Christmas. [CD1103:1]

"At this stage, we are supposed to be closing doors, not opening them."
—J. LEE RANKIN
Warren Commission chief counsel, in response to counsel Wesley Liebler's suggestion that a conspiracy lead (the Odio story) be pursued; quoted in *Inquest* by Epstein, July 1964

1951
Lee Oswald sent to live with relatives in New Orleans from Ft. Worth for two weeks. [*A Mother in History*, p. 87]

Jack Ruby's left forefinger is bitten off in a barroom brawl. [TAG5:D40]

"The commission analyzed every issue in exhaustive, almost archeological detail. . . . The facts—extensively gathered, independently checked and cogently set forth —destroy the basis for conspiracy theories that have grown weedlike in this country and abroad."
—The New York Times
September 28, 1964

1952
Jack Ruby, while operating the Silver Spur nightclub, acquires interest in the Vegas Club; has financial difficulties and gives the Silver Spur away. Travels to Chicago and back. He also purchases the Bob Wills Ranch House, a mammoth dance hall which had featured western-swing great Bob Wills and his Texas Playboys. (Later this club becomes the Longhorn Ballroom.) [22:335; TAG5:D20, 42, 43; *San Antonio Rose—The Life and Music of Bob Wills*, by Charles R. Townsend, p. 270]

JULY 28
J. D. Tippit joins the Dallas Police force. [CD86:43]

1952 *(cont.)*

SEPTEMBER
Lee Oswald attends Trinity Evangelical Lutheran School, Bronx, N.Y., then changes to Junior High School· #117. [CD28:4; CD60:6]

NOVEMBER
John Kennedy elected to the U.S. Senate from Massachusetts.

1952-1954
Jack Ruby is involved in gunrunning out of

"The Warren Commission Report is like a house of cards. It's going to collapse."
—RICHARD SCHWEIKER
U.S. Senator from Pennsylvania, October 15, 1975

" . . . I have also viewed a detailed presentation of the Zapruder film here in Washington. Certainly no one would walk away from that presentation with much faith in the Warren Commission Report. . . . "
—MICHAEL HARRINGTON
U.S. Congressman from Massachusetts in a letter to a constituent, June 26, 1975

Miami, Fla., according to Atlantan Blaney Mack Johnson. [CD914:86-88]

1953
Fidel Castro and fellow guerrillas attack Batista forces at Fortress Moncada in Santiago and are defeated. Castro is jailed and deported following this first major battle of The Revolution.

MARCH 19
Lee Oswald arrested as a truant in New York; sent to Youth House for three weeks the following month. "An old lady," said Oswald later, "handed me a pamphlet about the Rosenbergs . . ." [CE1384; CD60:1; 8:214; 22:703]

JUNE 19
Ethel and Julius Rosenberg electrocuted.

JULY 26
Jack Ruby charged by Dallas Police Department with carrying a concealed weapon (.38 Smith & Wesson); charges later dropped. [TAG5:5; CD223:120]

1954
JANUARY
Lee Oswald moves to New Orleans with his mother; attends Beauregard Jr. High School. [CD205:554]

FEBRUARY 11
Jack Ruby, who has interest in Hernando's Hideaway bar, acquires full ownership of the Vegas Club. [22:336]

MAY 1
Jack Ruby arrested by Dallas police for carrying a concealed weapon. [TAG5:R5]

1955
FEBRUARY 5
Lee Oswald's first job is at the Dolly Shoe

"Not since the Pearl Harbor investigation of World War II has so sweeping and detailed an investigation been conducted by the government as that of the Warren commission into President Kennedy's assassination."
—The New York Times
September 28, 1964

"The Watergate investigation has been the most exhaustive, thorough, and complete investigation since the assassination of President Kennedy."
—RICHARD KLEINDIENST
U.S. Attorney General, March 1, 1973

Company; he earns $42.00 total. [CD6:4; CD7:356]

JULY
Lee Oswald starts reading about Marxism, enters the Civil Air Patrol in Louisiana. [*Lee*, p. 78; CD405:16]

OCTOBER
Expressing a desire to join the Marines, Lee Oswald quits high school. [CD1454:6]

1956
Jack Ruby sells the Silver Spur nightclub, also loses Hernando's Hideaway club. [CD1252:15; TAG5:R56]

Jack Ruby is sued by his brother Sam over a $4,400 loan. [CD1254:7, 8]

SPRING
Jack Ruby's face is mangled in a barroom brawl. [TAG5:G5]

JUNE
Sixteen-year-old Lee Oswald moves to Ft. Worth with his mother from New Orleans. [CD1066:89]

SEPTEMBER
Lee Oswald attends high school in Ft. Worth for twenty-three days; withdraws to join Marines. [CD205:3]

Lee Oswald enlists in the Marines at Dallas, Texas. He is stationed in San Diego until April 1957. [19:657; CD1:23]

"If you want Earl Warren, he'll do it."
—H. R. HALDEMAN
White House Chief of Staff in a discussion with John Erlichman (Assistant to the President for Domestic Affairs) and President Richard Nixon about who could head up a presidentially appointed panel to investigate Watergate, March 27, 1973

1956 *(cont.)*
OCTOBER 24
Lee Oswald is measured at 5'8" by the Marines within a month of entering the Corps. [19:615]

NOVEMBER
Fidel Castro leads fellow revolutionaries aboard the Granma from Tuxpan, Mexico, to Oriente Province, Cuba.

DECEMBER 21
Lee Oswald takes Marine rifle range exam; gets score of "sharpshooter" (medium). [CD1055]

1957
APRIL-MAY
Lee Oswald, U.S. Marine, stationed at Camp Pendleton (Calif.) and Jacksonville, Fla., in electronics school. [CD6:455; CD8:3]

MAY 3
Lee Oswald, U.S. Marine, stationed at Kessler Air Force Base, Biloxi, Miss.; authorized to handle material classified up to "confidential." [CD978]

JUNE 18
Lee Oswald, U.S. Marine, completes aircraft control school. [CD131:2]

JUNE-JULY-AUGUST
Lee Oswald, U.S. Marine, is stationed at Santa Ana, Calif. [CE1961:4]

U-2 (spy plane) base established at Atsugi, Japan, by U.S. military; used primarily for surveillance of Soviet Union. [*Operation Overflight* by Francis Gary Powers, p. 61]

SEPTEMBER 4
Soviet satellite Sputnik is launched.

SEPTEMBER
Lee Oswald, U.S. Marine, is assigned to a Marine Air Control Squadron at Atsugi, Japan radar unit.

1958
SPRING
Revolution in Cuba against military/imperialist rule, led by Fidel Castro, intensifies.

Rumor is circulated that Jack Ruby is in Miami, Fla., involved in smuggling to Cuba,

"Who controls the past controls the future."
—GEORGE ORWELL
in *1984*

along with some Eastern Airlines pilots. (At the time, David Ferrie, later implicated by New Orleans DA Jim Garrison in the Kennedy assassination, was an Eastern Airlines pilot.) [26:634-649]

APRIL 11
Lee Oswald, U.S. Marine, allegedly court martialed for illegal possession of a gun; gets 20-day confinement (suspended), partial forfeiture of pay, and is reduced to private. [CD324:1]

SEPTEMBER 14-OCTOBER 5
Lee Oswald is with a Marine unit for three weeks on Taiwan. [*The Assassination of John F. Kennedy: The Reasons Why*, p. 169]

DECEMBER 5
A box falls on the nose of Marguerite Oswald in a Ft. Worth department store. This bruise is later cited for Lee Oswald's discharge from the Marines. He gets one month leave from the Marines. [16:337]

1959
JANUARY 1
Fidel Castro and fellow revolutionaries are triumphant; Batista and many supporters rapidly depart Cuba.

JANUARY 7
Jack Ruby calls Castro friend Robert Ray McKeown in Houston to secure his help in getting three men out of Cuban jails. Ruby offers $5,000 per man. [CD441:1; *Kennedy Conspiracy*, p. 169]

JANUARY 9
Marguerite Oswald sees a Ft. Worth doctor for treatment of her 12-5-58 nose injury. The doctor "could not go along with alleged injury for compensation purposes." [CD5:298]

JANUARY 28
Jack Ruby sees Robert Ray McKeown in Houston about dealing some jeeps to Castro for a reported $25,000. [23:160]

Lewis McWillie, a Dallas gambler working in Havana at the Tropicana casino, asks Jack Ruby to ship him four pistols from Dallas. [5:202; 26:650]

"We had to lift the cloud of doubts that had been cast over American institutions."
—JOHN SHERMAN COOPER
U.S. Senator from Kentucky and Warren Commission member, in *Inquest*, by Edward Jay Epstein

FEBRUARY-MARCH
Lee Oswald, as a U.S. Marine, subscribes to the west coast Communist party newspaper *People's World*. [CD113:2]

FEBRUARY 25
Lee Oswald takes a Russian proficiency test in the Marines and fails it. [8:307]

Lee Oswald applies for admission to Albert Schweitzer College in Switzerland, express-

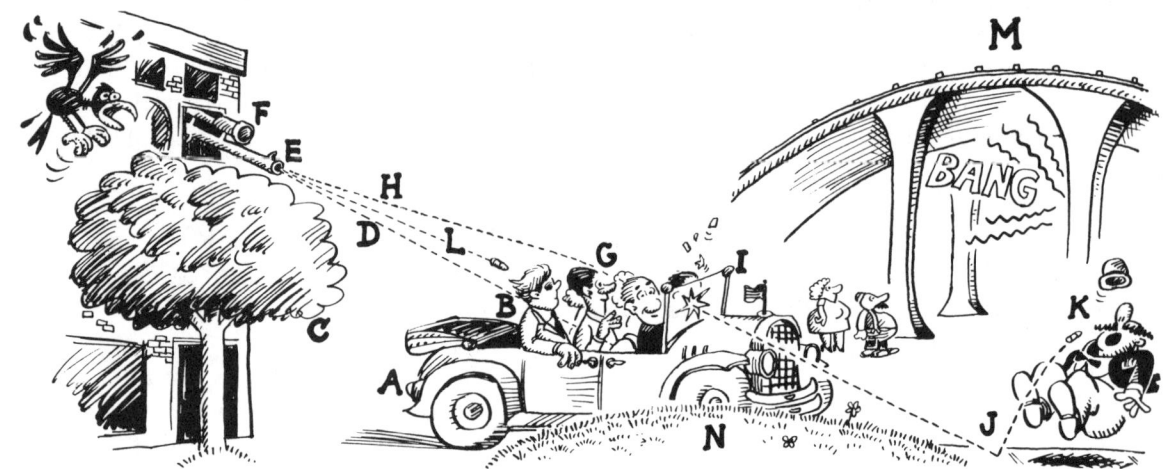

AS SOON AS LIMOUSINE (**A**) BEARING THE PRESIDENT (**B**) COMES INTO VIEW FROM BEHIND OAK TREE FOLIAGE (**C**), FIRST SHOT (**D**) IS FIRED FROM BOLT OPERATED ITALIAN RIFLE (**E**), WITH REPUTATION AS WORLD'S WORST SHOULDER WEAPON, EQUIPPED WITH TELESCOPIC SIGHT (**F**), WHICH HAS UNCORRECTABLE MECHANICAL DEFICIENCY. BULLET ENTERS BACK OF PRESIDENT'S NECK, EMERGES FROM THROAT, ENTERS GOVERNOR OF TEXAS' BACK (**G**), EMERGES FROM HIS CHEST, ENTERS HIS RIGHT WRIST, EXITS HIS RIGHT WRIST, AND ENTERS HIS LEFT THIGH.

SECOND SHOT (**H**) IS A WILD MISS THAT SMASHES LIMOUSINE WINDSHIELD (**I**), STRIKES CURB (**J**) 260 FEET IN FRONT OF LIMOUSINE, AND SLIGHTLY INJURES INNOCENT BYSTANDER (**K**). THIS SHOT THROWS OFF FBI, WHICH ANNOUNCES THAT SECOND SHOT (**H**) HIT GOVERNOR OF TEXAS (**G**), AN ASSERTION THAT COULD ONLY BE CORRECT IF ANOTHER GUNMAN IS INVOLVED — BECAUSE PRESIDENT AND GOVERNOR OF TEXAS ARE HIT LESS THAN 2.3 SECONDS APART AND RIFLE (**E**) REQUIRES 2.3 SECONDS BETWEEN SHOTS FOR BOLT OPERATION.

THIRD SHOT (**L**) ACTUALLY KILLS PRESIDENT. RIFLE (**E**) (REQUIRING 2.3 SECONDS BETWEEN SHOTS) HAS NOW FIRED 3 SHOTS IN 5.6 SECONDS.

ECHOS FROM RAILROAD BRIDGE (**M**) CONFUSE BYSTANDERS INTO THINKING SOME SHOTS CAME FROM GRASSY KNOLL (**N**).

How to Assassinate a President, after Rube Goldberg

1959 *(cont.)*

ing desire to enter in April 1960. He claims to have studied Russian for a year. [1:215; *Lee*, p. 92]

MARCH 9

Lee Oswald promoted to Pfc. in the Marines. [20:633]

MARCH 11

Jack Ruby is recruited by the FBI as an informant. [CD155-159; CD1052:1-3]

"[President Johnson's directive to have the Warren Report circulated world-wide immediately] seems to indicate that Mr. Johnson is eager to have this report read in Europe where fantastic versions of the Dallas tragedy were published and eventually believed by many."
—The Washington Post
September 25, 1964

APRIL

Fidel Castro visits the United States. [*Eye on Cuba,* by Edwin Tetlow]

APRIL 28

Jack Ruby is contacted by the FBI a second time for information. [CD732; Hoover letter to W.C. 4-7-64]

APRIL-MAY-JUNE

Lee Oswald meets fellow Marine Kerry W.

"One major hope—that the Warren Commission Report would minimize, if not end, the belief that is widespread in foreign countries that the full truth of the assassination has been withheld. . . ."
—The New York Times
September 25, 1964

Thornley, who the following year writes a novel based on Oswald. After the assassination Thornley testifies before the Warren Commission. [11:83-86, 113]

MAY 6

Lee Oswald scores a 191 on a Marine firing range, one point above minimum for rank of "marksman," Marine's lowest. [CD1055]

JUNE 5

Jack Ruby is again contacted by the FBI for information. [CD732; Hoover letter to W.C. 4-7-64]

JUNE 18

Jack Ruby contacted for more information by the FBI. [CD732]

JUNE 19

Oswald sends $25 enrollment deposit to Schweitzer College in Switzerland; the last time the school hears from him. [*Lee*, p. 93; 22:99]

1959 *(cont.)*

JUNE 20
Jack Ruby arrested by Dallas Police for dance hall violation at the Vegas Club. [22:343]

JULY
Lee Oswald, in the Marines, is told about his mother's 12-5-58 nose injury. [1:212]

JULY 7
Jack Ruby is contacted by the FBI for information for the fifth time. [CD732]

JULY 9
Dallas Police Department informs the FBI that Jack Ruby was among some Dallas gamblers arrested in Oklahoma City three months earlier. [23:166]

JULY 21
Jack Ruby is contacted by the FBI again for information. [CD732]

"An Associated Press survey of nine European countries today showed that leftist circles will take the lead in charging a whitewash if the Commission's report, to be made public Sunday, upholds the FBI's version of the Dallas killing."

—Associated Press dispatch
September 25, 1964

"There are still people who think Adolph Hitler is alive, people who think the so-called learned elders of Zion are engaged in a Jewish plot to control the world. The passage of years, the failure of anybody to come up with respectable evidence does not shake the people who cling to these illusions.

"And so, three and a half years later, there are people who still think some group of men are living somewhere, carrying in their breasts the most explosive secret conceivable, knowledge of a plot to kill Mr. Kennedy."

—ERIC SEVEREID
CBS News Inquiry, June 28, 1967

AUGUST 4
Industrial Accident Board awards Marguerite Oswald $934 for accident. [CD819]

AUGUST 5 AND 7
Jack Ruby is treated for gonorrhea. [TAG]

AUGUST 6
Jack Ruby is contacted by the FBI for more information. [CD732]

AUGUST 17
Lee Oswald requests a dependency discharge from the Marines because of his mother's injury nine months previous. [19:665]

Jack Ruby talks with the FBI for the eighth time. [CD732]

AUGUST 29

Lee Oswald is transferred out of his Marine unit to a more secretive one on Taiwan. [CE3099; 26:715]

SEPTEMBER (POSSIBLY AUGUST)

Jack Ruby travels to Havana to visit gambling friend Lewis McWillie. Ruby says he and McWillie spent the entire time trying to sell jeeps in Cuba. [CD1193:181; 5:201; D.M.N. 1-22-64]

SEPTEMBER 3

Lee Oswald's Marine records show his height as 5'11" on this date, a three inch jump from 10-24-56. [19:584]

SEPTEMBER 4

Lee Oswald receives word from the Marines that his discharge request has been approved and that he will be released 9-11-59. He immediately applies for a passport, stating plans for a four-month trip to include Schweitzer College in Switzerland, Cuba, Dominican

---

"The American people were denied the truth about the Vietnam war, the Cambodian bombing, and Watergate. I do not think we yet know the whole truth about the Kennedy assassination."

—RICHARD SCHWEIKER

June 23, 1976

Republic, England, France, Russia and elsewhere. [5:266]

SEPTEMBER 10

Oswald receives his passport in Louisiana. [5:266]

SEPTEMBER 11

Lee Oswald formally discharged from the Marines to care for his mother in Ft. Worth. Receives $219 severance and travel pay. [CD1:23]

"I had strong doubts about it [the single bullet theory]."

—HALE BOGGS

U.S. Congressman from Louisiana and Warren Commission member; quoted in *Inquest,* by Edward Jay Epstein

---

SEPTEMBER 12-14

Lee Oswald stays with his mother in Ft. Worth, mentioning that he may go to Cuba. [1:201, 326; CD1:24]

SEPTEMBER 12

Jack Ruby flies Pan Am flight #415 to Havana from Miami. [22:859]

SEPTEMBER 13

Jack Ruby flies Delta #750 from Havana to

1959 *(cont.)*

Miami. The Warren Commission says Ruby was a guest of "close friend and known gambler Lewis J. McWillie." The one day trip was called "purely social." [22:859]

SEPTEMBER 14

Lee Oswald withdraws the balance of his Ft. Worth bank account, $203. Gives his mother $100. [1:203; 22:180, 221; CD107:37]

SEPTEMBER 17

Lee Oswald books passage to London for $220 from New Orleans through Travel Consultants (the same agency used by Clay Shaw). [11:116; 23:747; N.O.S.I. 2-6-69]

SEPTEMBER 20

Lee Oswald leaves New Orleans aboard a ship. [11:116]

"It was important to show the world that America is not a banana republic, where a government can be changed by conspiracy."
—JOHN J. McCLOY
Warren Commission member; quoted in *Inquest*, by Edward Jay Epstein

OCTOBER 2

Jack Ruby is again contacted by the FBI. [CD732]

"Truth is the only client here."
—unofficial Warren Commission motto

OCTOBER 9

Lee Oswald's passport is stamped in London; he declares $700. [18:162; CD1:57]

OCTOBER 10

Lee Oswald arrives in Helsinki. (The CIA says the only direct London to Helsinki flight is Finn Air #852 arriving at Helsinki 11:33 P.M. This would not have allowed Oswald sufficient time to clear customs and check into his hotel within 27 minutes of arrival.) [26:32; CIA document CD1:57]

OCTOBER 10-15

Lee Oswald stays at the Torni and Klaus Kurki Hotel in Helsinki en route to Russia. [26:32]

OCTOBER 14

Lee Oswald secures a visa to visit the USSR. U.S. State Department official John A. McVickar, then stationed at the Embassy in Moscow, later says that only "knowledgeable" travelers to Russia come through Helsinki. [5:302, 322; 18:97]

OCTOBER 15

Lee Oswald's passport is stamped—departure from Finland. Arrives in Moscow later that day. [5:266; 18:163]

OCTOBER 15, 16
Lee Oswald requests Russian citizenship. [18:97, 98]

OCTOBER 18 OR 19
Lee Oswald makes anti-American radio broadcast within days of arrival in Moscow. [18:137-39; *The Assassination of John F. Kennedy: The Reasons Why*, p. 206]

OCTOBER 21
Lee Oswald "attempts suicide," is taken to the psychiatric ward of a hospital. [CD1:57]

OCTOBER 22
While in a hospital psychiatric ward, Lee Oswald's Soviet visa expires. [18:461; O.N.I. document:146]

OCTOBER 22
Jack Ruby is signed up in a YMCA membership drive by Judge Joe B. Brown (later the trial judge in the Ruby killing of Oswald). [*Jack Ruby: The Man Who Killed the Man Who Killed Kennedy*, p. 113]

OCTOBER 28
Lee Oswald is discharged from the hospital in Moscow. [18:461]

OCTOBER 31
Lee Oswald delivers a written statement to the U.S. Embassy informing them that he has applied for Soviet citizenship; gives up U.S. passport. According to U.S. Naval Intelligence, Oswald offers classified information to Soviet authorities. [CD1115; CD1122; 5:262, 265, 270; ONI document 146]

NOVEMBER 1
Aline Mosley, UPI correspondent, interviews Oswald in a Moscow hotel. In terminology uncharacteristic for a Marxist, Oswald says he "indoctrinated himself" in Marxism and that he sympathized "with niggers." [22:701]

NOVEMBER
Lee Oswald is granted resident alien status in Russia, but is denied Soviet citizenship [26:147]

"Give them a fall-guy and they'll stop there ....[The police prefer]an open and shut case. They like to keep it simple . . . they want to close the file."

—DASHIEL HAMMET

in *The Maltese Falcon*

NOVEMBER 15, 17
American journalist Priscilla Johnson interviews Lee Oswald at her Moscow hotel; Johnson's name later appears on a list of U.S. State Department employees. [11:446; CD49:24]

DECEMBER 7
Jack Ruby is listed as secretary-treasurer of the newly chartered Sovereign Club; his

1959 *(cont.)*

brother Earl is the vice-president. [22:340; CD302:66, 67]

DECEMBER 8

Lee Oswald's regular tour with the Marines would have ended this day. [*Look* 10-17-67, p. 72]

DECEMBER 11

Central Intelligence Agency Director Allen Dulles approves "thorough consideration be given to the elimination of Fidel Castro." [*Schweiker Report*, appendix C]

DECEMBER 29

Lee Oswald applies to the Moscow City Council for an I. D. card. [18:404]

1960
JANUARY 7

Lee Oswald arrives in Minsk, Russia, where the mayor welcomes him the following day. [CD1:57]

"The more I have learned, the more concerned I have become that the government was involved in the assassination of President John F. Kennedy."
—VICTOR MARCHETTI
former Executive Assistant to the Deputy Director of the CIA; in *True Magazine*, April 1975

JANUARY-MAY

Lee Oswald studies Russian with an Intourist teacher in Minsk. [16:340]

JANUARY 13

Lee Oswald begins work at a radio and TV factory in Minsk for 90 rubles ($80) per week; employed there for twenty-four months. [18:137]

"As early as Friday night [November 22, 1963] I heard some speculation about the possibility of a conspiracy behind the assassination. . . . On Saturday and Sunday there were rumors in Dallas that the 'conspiracy' might involve some government agency. By Sunday night I realized that the agency under the greatest suspicion was the FBI."
—ROBERT OSWALD

in *Lee*

JANUARY 14

Lee Oswald is issued a "stateless passport" by the Moscow City government. [18:137, 378]

JANUARY 19

Jack Ruby buys the Colt Cobra pistol with which he later shoots Oswald 11-24-63. A policeman accompanies him when he buys the weapon. [25:404; 26:499]

"They [the FBI] have tried the case and reached a verdict on every count."
—RICHARD B. RUSSELL
at a Warren Commission meeting, January 27, 1964

MARCH 6
Marguerite Oswald writes to Ft. Worth Congressman Jim Wright asking help in locating her son Lee. [22:118]

MARCH 17
Dwight Eisenhower authorizes training of Cuban refugees by U.S. "advisors." [*The Bay of Pigs: The Leaders Story of Brigade 2506*, p. 30]

APRIL
The national Fair Play for Cuba Committee is organized, advertised in a full page ad in the *New York Times.* [17:765]

APRIL 27
Robert Oswald, brother of Lee, is interviewed by FBI Special Agent Fain. [1:423]

APRIL 28
Marguerite Oswald is interviewed by the FBI. [26:92]

MAY 1
Francis Gary Powers shot down over Russia in a U-2 surveillance craft; says later that Oswald may have furnished information to the Soviets to shoot him down. [D.M.N. 4-20-70]

JUNE 3
J. Edgar Hoover writes a memo concerning the possibility that an imposter may be using Lee Oswald's birth certificate. [CD964B]

JUNE 22
The first group of anti-Castro Cubans are taken to a training camp in Guatemala from Florida at the behest of the CIA. [*Bay of Pigs,* p. 38]

JULY 14
The Democratic National Convention, meeting in Los Angeles, nominates John Kennedy as its presidential candidate. The following day Lyndon Johnson is nominated as his running mate.

JULY 29
Jack Ruby is treated for gonorrhea. [TAG5:G5]

JULY
William Julius McLaney, brother of Ruby gambling associate Mike McLaney, is run out of Cuba. (McLaney later is shown to be the owner of the cottage raided by federal authorities, under orders from Attorney General Robert Kennedy, in St. Tammany Parish, La., which housed CIA-equipped anti-Castroites and explosives.) [*Oswald in New Orleans,* p. 68; *The Kennedy Conspiracy,* p. 23]

1960 *(cont.)*

AUGUST
Guatemalan President Fuentes opens an air-strip at a CIA training base. [*The Invisible Government* by Ross and Wise, p. 28]

AUGUST
Francis Gary Powers goes on trial in Russia for espionage.

AUGUST, SEPTEMBER
Lee Oswald, writing in his diary, speaks of the disadvantages of life in Russia. [CD1:52]

AUGUST 20
Jack Ruby again arrested by Dallas Police, this time for dance hall violations at the Vegas Club. He is fined $25. [22:343; 26:560]

AUGUST 22
A paycheck stub dated this day issued to James A. Jackson is found on Oswald after his arrest, 11-22-63. [7:180; 22:178]

SEPTEMBER 13
Lee Oswald is issued an undesirable discharge from the Marine reserves. [17:663; 19:665]

LATE SEPTEMBER
A meeting between Robert Maheu, representing Howard Hughes interests, Johnny Roselli, organized crime figure, and CIA "support chief" is held to discuss assassination of Fidel Castro. [*Senate Report on Alleged As-*

"On two separate occasions . . . [FBI] Director Hoover asked for all derogatory material on Warren Commission members and staff contained in the FBI files."
—Senate Select Committee to Study Governmental Operations with Respect to Intelligence Activities
in *The Investigation of the Assassination of President John F. Kennedy: Performance of the Intelligence Agencies* (The Schweiker Report), June 23, 1976

sassination Plots Involving Foreign Leaders (issued 11-75), p. 76]

NOVEMBER 4
Lyndon Johnson, U.S. Senator and vice-presidential candidate, is hissed and spat upon at the Adolphus Hotel in Dallas following a Democratic party rally. He and running mate John Kennedy are elected to office over Richard Nixon and Henry Cabot Lodge.

DECEMBER 15
Seventy-three-year-old Richard P. Pavlick is arrested for planning to assassinate President-elect John Kennedy at Palm Beach, Fla. Equipment to manufacture bombs is found in his possession.

1961
JANUARY 3
The United States severs diplomatic relations with Cuba. [23:171]

JANUARY 26

Marguerite Oswald goes to the U.S. State Department in Washington, D.C., for help in locating her son Lee. [22:102, 118; 26:39, 40, 124]

JANUARY-MARCH

Jack Ruby changes over the private Sovereign Club (liquor allowed) into the Carousel Club, a public burlesque house (beer only). [14:340]

"The son of the late Congressman [and Warren Commission member] Hale Boggs, says that the FBI secretly gathered and disseminated information on the sex activities of the critics of the investigation of the assassination of President John Kennedy. . . .

"[Boggs'] son, Thomas, states that his father was encouraged by the FBI to release personal information and compromising photographs of the critics in an effect to stifle criticism of the Warren Commission Report.

"The younger Boggs says his father regarded the FBI's actions as 'Gestapo tactics.'

"The FBI has confirmed that it gathered information on Warren Commission critics. The Bureau states, however, that it does not know if this information or material was disseminated publicly."

—Zodiac News Service

February 4, 1975

FEBRUARY 5

Lee Oswald, in Minsk, writes to the U.S. Embassy in Moscow, requesting that his passport be returned. [16:685; 18:133]

MARCH 4

Lee Oswald meets 19-year-old Marina Prusakova, a Minsk pharmacist. He is, by this time, quite proficient in the Russian language. [22:31, 120; 22:748]

MARCH 11

Lee Oswald and Marina Prusakova go to a dance. [18:602; 22:748]

MARCH

John Kennedy raises the subject of assassinating Fidel Castro in discussion with Florida Senator George Smathers. Kennedy expresses disapproval. [*Schweiker Report*]

"They [U.S. intelligence agencies] could have conspired all together to try to conceal it [information] from us."

—J. LEE RANKIN

Warren Commission chief counsel, to Allen Stone; quoted on WRR radio, Dallas, May 1975

MARCH 30-APRIL 11

Records at Minsk show that Lee Oswald is hospitalized with an ear infection. Marina visits him several times. [18:450]

1961 *(cont.)*

APRIL 4

New Orleans organized crime leader Carlos Marcello is deported to Guatemala on orders from Attorney General Robert Kennedy. [*The Grim Reapers* by Reid, p. 150]

APRIL 15-17

With U.S. backing, supplies, money, and personnel, Cuba is invaded at the Bay of Pigs by forces hoping to depose Fidel Castro. The invasion fails. Many of those involved are later involved in various conspiracy theories surrounding the Kennedy assassination, and some of them are linked by evidence. Kennedy's half-hearted support of the invasion and subsequent shake-up at the CIA are often given as primary motives for the assassination.

"Not content to rely on secondhand reports, the Commission determined to investigate everything afresh."

—*Time* magazine

October 2, 1964

Cover-up Lowdown BY JAY KINNEY & PAUL MAVRIDES

© 1976 by Kinney & Mavrides

THE **MOORHOUSE** AND **NIX** FILMS OF JFK'S DEATH REVEAL A POSSIBLE GUNMAN ON THE **GRASSY KNOLL. 64** KNOWN WITNESSES INDICATED THAT SHOTS CAME FROM THAT AREA, BUT **VERY FEW** WERE ASKED TO TESTIFY BY THE WARREN COMMISSION!

APRIL 20

Lee and Marina apply for marriage license; permission granted in one week. [22:750]

APRIL 30

Lee Oswald and Marina Prusakova marry in Minsk on a Sunday. [1:95]

MAY 16

Lee Oswald writes to the U.S. Embassy in Moscow that Marina would like to accompany him back to the United States. [1:96; 22:120]

MAY 22

A memo from J. Edgar Hoover to Attorney General Robert F. Kennedy mentions that the CIA has used mobster Sam Giancanna in "clandestine affairs against Castro." [*Schweiker Report*, appendix C]

MAY 31

John Kennedy, riding in a Paris motorcade with French President Charles deGaulle, is the target of an assassination plot in which

"All of the records were in the hands of the two agencies [FBI and CIA] and, if they so desired, any information or files could have been destroyed or laundered prior to the time the Commission could get them."

—WAGGONER CARR

Texas Attorney General during the Warren Commission investigation, quoted in *The Houston Chronicle*, September 2, 1975

two Americans with apparent CIA connections hire Jose Luis Romero to carry out the murder. The plan is to make it appear deGaulle is the target and that Kennedy is accidentally hit. The assassin receives a $200,000 down payment and backs out of the deal. [*L'Aurore* (newspaper)]

JUNE

Gambler Lewis McWillie travels from Florida to Lake Tahoe to Dallas, staying overnight at Jack Ruby's apartment. [23:172]

JULY 8-10

Lee Oswald visits the U.S. Embassy in Moscow and applies for permission to return to the United States; his passport is marked valid for return to the U.S. only. [1:98; 5:281]

JULY-AUGUST

Lee and Marina Oswald complete necessary paperwork to travel to the United States (send marriage certificate to U.S. Embassy, apply for exit visa, etc.) [17:720; 18:405; 22:9, 87]

AUGUST

David Ferrie, a CIA anti-Castro operative, and two others steal explosives from a Louisiana munitions dump, Jim Garrison later charges. [D.M.N. 4-1-67]

AUGUST-NOVEMBER

Sometime in this four-month period, Nancy Perrin Rich, a former Carousel Club employee, says she and her husband attend meetings at which they are asked to pilot a boat carrying weapons to Cuba from the U.S., and return with refugees; for this they are offered up to $15,000. Jack Ruby attends one of these meetings as a key conspirator in this anti-Castro activity. Mr. and Mrs. Perrin back out of the deal. The Warren Commission chooses not to believe Nancy Perrin Rich. [14:345-53]

"It's been very rare in our history that any of these [intelligence] agencies have come forth and said 'we made a mistake.' "

—J. LEE RANKIN

to Allen Stone; quoted on WRR radio, Dallas, May 1975

SEPTEMBER 10

Oswald writes to his brother Robert from Minsk. Eight days later the FBI calls on Robert. [1:424; 16:838]

OCTOBER 1961-FEBRUARY 1962

The Cuban Revolutionary Council main-

1961 *(cont.)*

tains an office at 544 Camp Street in New Orleans. The group is militantly anti-Castro. [22:830]

NOVEMBER
Creation of Operation MONGOOSE, which was a massive covert U.S. effort based in Miami to support anti-Castro resistance inside Cuba leading to his overthrow. [*Senate Report on Alleged Assassination Plots Involving Foreign Leaders*, pp. 139-46]

NOVEMBER 29
John McCone succeeds Allen Dulles as CIA director. [*Schweiker Report*, p. 99]

1962
JANUARY 2
Lee Oswald writes his mother that he and Marina will get visas about 2-15-62 and that they need $800 for the trip home via New York and Washington, D.C., for sight-seeing. [16:554-56]

"I don't think some agencies were candid with us. I never thought the Dallas police were telling us the entire truth. Neither was the FBI."
—BURT W. GRIFFIN
Warren Commission cocounsel, in *Rolling Stone*, April 24, 1975

" . . . assume that every government is run by liars, until proven otherwise."
—I. F. STONE

JANUARY 4
Lee Oswald is issued a new passport by Soviets for "foreigners residing in the Soviet Union" superseding his previous status of "resident alien." [26:119]

JANUARY
Lee Oswald writes to Texas Senator John Tower for help in returning to the U.S. Letter is forwarded to the State Department. [18:272; 22:5]

JANUARY 15
U.S. Consul Wise at Embassy in Moscow writes to Lee Oswald in Minsk that the Embassy will discuss a loan for the return trip when he comes to Moscow. [22:10]

JANUARY 29
An Internal Revenue Service agent talks over the phone with Jack Ruby; Ruby owes IRS $20,676. [23:312]

JANUARY 30
Lee Oswald writes to former Navy Secretary John Connally from Minsk protesting his undesirable discharge from the Marine reserves. [16:736; 19:713]

FEBRUARY
Kerry Thornley, Lee Oswald's Marine buddy, finishes a 250-page novel called *The Idle Warrior*, with Oswald as the main character.[11:113]

FEBRUARY 15
Lee and Marina have their first child, June Lee, born in Minsk. [1:95; 16:567]

"I think it's solved now. And I don't know of any connection with any conspiracy."
—CLARENCE KELLEY
FBI director; quoted in Hearst Newspapers, June 20, 1976

FEBRUARY 23
John Connally writes Lee Oswald that his letter has been turned over to the current Navy Secretary Fred Korth. [19:711]

APRIL
U.S. government continues its efforts to kill Fidel Castro; a CIA official gives poison pills to Johnny Roselli for eventual ingestion by Castro. (See late September 1960.) [*Senate Report on Alleged Assassination Plots Involving Foreign Leaders*]

APRIL 10
New York attorney Mark Lane honored for civil rights work at a testimonial dinner at the Astor Hotel. [26:305]

MAY 7
Attorney General Robert Kennedy learns of pre-Bay of Pigs underworld assassination plot on Castro in briefing by CIA General Counsel Lawrence Houston and Security Director Sheffield Edwards. [*Senate Report on Alleged Assassination Plots Involving Foreign Leaders*, pp. 124-39]

MAY 18
Teamsters Union president Jimmy Hoffa indicted for taking payoffs from trucking companies. [*The Fall and Rise of Jimmy Hoffa*, by Walter Sheridan]

MAY 24
Lee Oswald's passport is renewed in Moscow; amended to include new-born daughter. [18:164, 167; 22:22]

MAY 30
Lee Oswald writes his mother from Moscow that "we shall leave Holland for the USA on June 4." [16:578]

JUNE 1
Lee Oswald signs a note for $435.71 loan from the State Department for his return trip by rail and steamship. [22:47]

JUNE 2-4
Lee and Marina and their daughter travel through Russia, Poland, Germany, and the

"Washington, D.C.—An agent who investigated the assassination of President Kennedy testified today that he flushed down the drain a note that Lee Harvey Oswald had delivered to the Dallas office of the Federal Bureau of Investigation."

—Associated Press dispatch
December 12, 1975

1962 *(cont.)*

Netherlands, staying in a private apartment en route for a couple of days. [18:165-69]

JUNE 4
Steamship tickets are delivered to the Oswalds in Rotterdam. [16:619, 620]

JUNE 5
Department of Health, Education and Welfare notifies the New York Traveler's Aid Society that the Oswalds will be arriving soon. [26:8]

JUNE 13
The Oswald family lands at Hoboken, New Jersey, at 1:00 P.M. Oswald has $63 with him. [22:204]

JUNE 13
Traveler's Aid representative Spas T. Raiken greets the Oswald family on their arrival in New York. Raiken is also secretary general of the Friends of the Anti-Bolshevik Bloc of Na-

tions, a group which has numerous direct connections with right-wing and intelligence organizations internationally. Raiken's report says that Oswald was "with the Marine Corps, stationed with the U.S. Embassy in Moscow." [*The Assassinations—Dallas and Beyond,* pp. 366-67; 26:8, 10]

JUNE 14
Lee Oswald's brother Robert wires him $200 for the trip to Texas. [8:327]

JUNE 14
The Oswalds fly Delta to Dallas and are greeted by Lee's brother Robert at Love Field. Marina later tells the Secret Service that they arrived by air in New York and took a train to Texas; she repeats this a number of times. [1:4; 23:407]

JUNE
Wally Weston begins as an MC at the Carousel Club; stays on through 9-15-63. Claims that Oswald was an acquaintance of Jack Ruby's, and that Lee came to the club once and heckled him (Weston), saying, "You're a Communist." [13:369; 19:37; *N.Y. Daily News* 7-76]

JUNE 15
Marguerite Oswald is told by Lee that "not even Marina knows why I came home." [1:233]

JUNE
Dallas resident Mrs. Voshinin wonders why

"The FBI is being badly shaken by the revelation that its former leaders withheld evidence from the Warren Commission during the investigation of the assassination of President Kennedy."

—*Time* magazine

November 3, 1975

Lee Oswald does not lecture on his Russian experiences for money. [8:436]

JUNE-JULY
Bill de Mar (aka William D. Crowe), an entertainer, works at the Carousel Club for three weeks. He later testifies that Oswald visited Ruby at the club. [15:98]

JUNE 18
Lee Oswald applies for a review of his undesirable discharge. [17:651]

JUNE 26
FBI Special Agent Fain interviews Lee Oswald in Ft. Worth. [17:728]

JULY 16
Lee Oswald finds employment at Leslie Welding as a metal worker. He receives $1.25 per hour. He pays $59 cash for house rent; has no known funds of his own. [1:134; 20:19]

JULY
Lee Oswald subscribes to *Time* magazine. [CD1231]

JULY 20-AUGUST 15
Lee Oswald writes to the Soviet Embassy in Washington, D.C., asking how to subscribe to Russian periodicals. [18:486]

"[Schweiker] believes Hoover may have been lying when he told the Commission that the FBI had rejected Oswald's offer to work as an informer in 1962 and 1963."

—*Time* magazine

November 3, 1975

1962 *(cont.)*

AUGUST 5
Lee Oswald sends $2 to the Communist party paper *The Worker* for a subscription. On his return from the Soviet Union, however, Oswald sharply criticizes Russian society. [16:106-22; 22:271]

AUGUST 7
Lee Oswald starts repaying the State Department for his travel loan with a $10 cash payment. [18:316]

AUGUST
Robert Oswald returns Lee's Imperial Reflex camera that Lee had bought in 1957 and left with Robert in 1959. It is this camera which was allegedly used to photograph Lee holding "the murder weapon" and leftist newspapers. [CE2083]

AUGUST 12
Lee Oswald writes the Socialist Workers party, a rival of the Communist party, inquiring of their aims. [19:575]

AUGUST 16
Special Agent Fain of the FBI talks with Lee Oswald in his car in front of the latter's residence. [1:20, 430]

AUGUST 25-SEPTEMBER
The Oswalds meet various members of the Russian community in Dallas, including George and Jeanne de Mohrenschildt, a

> *"If we cannot trust the FBI, the CIA, and Earl Warren, then God pity us!"*
> **—MELVIN BELLI**
> attorney for Jack Ruby; quoted in *The People's World,* October 17, 1964

wealthy and cultured couple whose previous travels put them in locations where the CIA had been particularly active at the time of their visits. [CD541:10; 8:377; 9:101, 165, 214, 216; *Heritage of Stone*]

SEPTEMBER 1
Lee Oswald sends the State Department another $10, in partial repayment for the travel loan. Ten more dollars go out five weeks later. [18:316]

OCTOBER 8
Lee Oswald quits job as metal worker because his hours are reduced. Total income from the job at Leslie Welding is $500. [10:166]

OCTOBER 8
Jeanne de Mohrenschildt takes Marina to the dentist; another member of the Russian community pays for it. [8:373; 9:228]

OCTOBER 8
The Oswald family moves in with Mrs. Elana Hall, a member of the Ft. Worth Russian community. [9:77; 10:230]

OCTOBER 9
Lee Oswald rents a Dallas post office box, #2915. [7:295]

"So much possible evidence was beyond our reach."

—RICHARD B. RUSSELL
in *The Atlanta Constitution*, September 29, 1964

OCTOBER 10, 11
Texas Employment Commission gives Lee Oswald an aptitude test. Conclusion: He is bright enough for college. [10:122, 124]

OCTOBER 12
The Jaggers-Chiles-Stovall photo-lithography firm hires Lee Oswald at $1.25 per hour. [10:198; 22:161]

OCTOBER 22-28
"Cuban Missile Crisis"

OCTOBER 30
Lee Oswald applies for membership in the Socialist Workers party. [19:576]

NOVEMBER 3
Lee Oswald rents an apartment at 604 Elsbeth in Dallas; pays $68 per month. [26:539, 540]

NOVEMBER 8
Marina Oswald says that husband Lee beats her; the de Mohrenschildts come and take her, daughter June Lee, and some baby things from the apartment. Lee fails to reconcile their differences in a meeting three days later. [2:299, 304; 5:418; 23:392, 475]

NOVEMBER 14
Lee Oswald continues to repay his loan from the State Department; reduces balance by another $10. [18:316]

NOVEMBER 18
Lee and Marina make up. [8:416]

1962 *(cont.)*

NOVEMBER 22
Lee and Marina have Thanksgiving dinner at Robert Oswald's home. Marguerite is not invited. Lee and Marina buy the soundtrack to "Exodus." It is the last Robert sees of his brother for a year and a day. [1:387; 2:343; *Lee*]

NOVEMBER
Operation MONGOOSE ends (see 11-61). [*Schweiker Report*]

DECEMBER
Jimmy Hoffa's trial for receiving kickbacks from trucking companies ends in a hung jury. [*The Fall and Rise of Jimmy Hoffa*, by Sheridan]

DECEMBER 7
Lee Oswald gets a Dallas public library card, valid for three years. [CE2650]

DECEMBER 15
Lee Oswald sends in $1 for a subscription to

"There is no longer any reason to have faith in its [the Warren Commission's] picture of the Kennedy assassination. . . . Had Oswald been convicted twelve years ago, he would be entitled to a new trial today based upon the FBI and CIA cover-up."
—RICHARD SCHWEIKER
June 23, 1976

---

the Socialist Workers party newspaper, *The Militant.* It is this paper that appears in the questionable photo of Lee on the cover of *Life.* [19:567]

DECEMBER
Captured invaders from the Bay of Pigs are returned to the United States in return for farm and medical supplies. [*Schweiker Report*]

1963
JANUARY 5
Lee Oswald reduces his State Department loan by $100, leaving a balance of $106, which is paid twenty days later. [18:316]

JANUARY
The February issue of the *American Rifleman* comes out, containing the coupon which Lee Oswald fills out in ordering the alleged assassination rifle. [7:367]

JANUARY 27
Lee Oswald first uses the pseudonym "A. J. Hidell" filling out a mail order form of Seaport Traders. [16:511]

JANUARY 28
Lee Oswald begins a two month, three nights a week typing course, which he regularly attends. Cost: $9. [CE1130]

JANUARY 31
Jack Ruby borrows $1375 from a bank. [14:614, 617]

"The FBI withheld from the Warren Commission hundreds of documents about the John F. Kennedy assassination."
—JACK ANDERSON
October 28, 1975

FEBRUARY
Marina says later that Lee tells her that she must return to Russia. [1:35]

FEBRUARY 12
Jack Ruby gets into a fight; his opponent is asked by a Dallas Police detective to drop charges against Jack. [25:715; 26:560]

FEBRUARY 14
Jack Ruby is told by the Carousel Club landlord that he owes $1650 back rent. [23:144]

FEBRUARY 17
Marina Oswald writes to the Soviet Embassy in Washington that she wants to return to Russia but that her husband would remain in the U.S. [1:35; 16:10]

FEBRUARY 20
Lee Oswald writes the Communist party office in New York for information, whether for himself or for someone else is not known. [22:163, 165]

FEBRUARY 27
Jack Ruby is found not guilty of assault in the fight at the club two weeks earlier. [12:64; 23:18]

"A twenty-one-year veteran FBI agent says that the Federal Bureau of Investigation intentionally and consistently avoided leads when investigating possible conspiracies behind the murders of President John Kennedy and Dr. Martin Luther King, Jr.

"Former agent Arthur Murtaugh, a Special Agent in the FBI's Atlanta bureau for 21 years, says that he participated in the Kennedy and King investigations and that he personally saw 'leads being washed out.' The 52-year-old Murtaugh recalls that he was assigned to investigate the activities in Atlanta of Jack Ruby. . . . According to Murtaugh, he uncovered evidence in Atlanta which directly linked Ruby to right-wing members of the Cuban community.

"As Murtaugh tells it, after his reports were submitted, they were screened and rewritten—and in the final versions, all references to Ruby's Cuban connections were deleted. . . .

"Murtaugh says he believes a full-scale public investigation into the John Kennedy and Martin Luther King cases would uncover right-wing conspiracies behind both of them."
—Zodiac News Service
August 24, 1974

"It was a cheap old weapon."
—SEBASTION LATONA
FBI weapons expert on the alleged Oswald rifle

1963 *(cont.)*

FEBRUARY 28
Lee Oswald renews his subscription to *Time* for thirty-nine weeks. [22:270]

MARCH 2
Lee Oswald moves into a duplex apartment at 214 W. Neely; pays $60 monthly. [CE1144:8]

MARCH 5
Robert Oswald moves from Ft. Worth to Arkansas. [1:310, 391]

MARCH 7
The 3-11-63 issue of *The Militant,* a Socialist Workers party newspaper, is mailed to subscribers from New York. It is this issue along with the 3-24-63 issue of *The Worker,* a Communist party newspaper, which Oswald is holding in the questionable *Life* cover photo of him with a rifle. [22:789]

MARCH 10
Lee Oswald allegedly takes photos of Major General Edwin Walker's home. (In the photos published in the Warren Commission volumes, the license plate number of a 1957 Chevrolet in the photo is obliterated; however in Dallas Police Chief Curry's *JFK Assassination File,* it is not obliterated.) [1:14, 38; 5:537; *JFK Assassination File*]

MARCH 11 OR 12
Lee Oswald receives a receipt from the State Department confirming that his loan has been repaid; he may now apply for another passport. [24:341]

MARCH 12
Lee Oswald allegedly mails off for a Mannlicher-Carcano rifle under the name "A. J. Hidell." On 11-23-63 Oswald denies this. [7:295, 366; 17:635, 677; 24:19]

MARCH 13
Klein's in Chicago receives the Hidell rifle order; a telescopic sight for a left-handed person is mounted. (Oswald is right-handed.) [7:295; 25:799]

MARCH 13
The Internal Revenue Service files liens against Jack Ruby totalling $20,880 which re-

---

REPORTER: *What about the ballistics test, Chief?*
JESSE CURRY: *The ballistics test—we haven't had a final report, but it is—I understand it will be favorable."*
—at a news conference in Dallas Police Headquarters
November 22, 1963

> *"We know with as much certainty as you can have that he [Oswald] fired the rifle, but we don't know if he did it with the encouragement or knowledge of anyone else."*
> —**RICHARD B. RUSSELL**
> Warren Commission member and U.S. Senator from Georgia; quoted in *The Atlanta Constitution,* September 29, 1964

main forever uncollected. [D.M.N. 12-4, 6-63]

MARCH 17
Marina Oswald fills out a questionnaire sent by the Soviet Embassy in Washington dealing with her request to return home. [16:13-20; 18:506]

MARCH 20
Klein's ships the Mannlicher-Carcano rifle to "A. J. Hidell" at Lee Oswald's post office box. (The gun, an Italian model vintage World War II, had the nickname "the humanitarian rifle" because it never hurt anyone on purpose. The particular gun sent by Klein's was later called "a cheap old weapon" by an FBI weapons expert.) [7:365, 369; 25:797]

MARCH 26
Cuban raiders based in Florida attack a Soviet ship off the coast of Cuba. The action by the anti-Castro "Alpha-66" provokes John Kennedy to order a crackdown on such activities. [*Schweiker Report*]

MARCH 26
Lee Oswald given termination notice by Jaggars-Chiles-Stovall. [22:161; 24:872]

MARCH 28
Jack Ruby, in conversation with a Dallas Internal Revenue Service agent, learns that he owes $39,000 to the government for the last thirty month period. [23:299; 314]

MARCH 31
Marina later says she took two photos with the Imperial Reflex camera of Lee holding the rifle and copies of *The Militant* and *The Worker* in their backyard on this date. Although this day was rainy and overcast, Marina's photos show it to be sunny. Transcript of interview with Marina shows evidence of coaxing by the questioner. Later, four such photos appear to have been taken rather than two. The photos themselves show signs that they are doctored, possibly superimposing

> *"We have a sure case."*
> —**JESSE CURRY**
> November 22, 1963

> *"We don't have any proof that Oswald fired the rifle. No one has been able to put him in that building with a gun in his hand."*
> —**JESSE CURRY**
> quoted in a United Press dispatch, November 5, 1969

1963 *(cont.)*

Lee Oswald's face onto the body of another person. [1:48; 23:400; 7:410-18; *New Times* 3-19-76; *They've Killed the President!*, pp. 78-80]

APRIL 2

Lee and Marina Oswald have dinner in Irving, Tex. (Dallas suburb), with Ruth and Michael Paine. Lee and Michael discuss Gen. Edwin Walker (ret.), a well-known right-wing militarist. [26:543]

APRIL 3

One week before a shot is fired at Gen. Walker's home, a Walker neighbor sees the same black-and-white Chevrolet parked in the lot which he sees again on the day of the shooting. [23:764; 26:61]

APRIL 6

Lee Oswald is laid off his job. From 10-17-62 to 4-10-63 he has earned $1,520 from the photo-lithographer firm. [19:192]

" . . . It seems reasonable to say that an expert could fire that rifle in five seconds. It seems equally reasonable to say that Oswald, under normal circumstances, would take longer. But the circumstances were not normal. He was shooting at a President."
—WALTER CRONKITE
CBS News Inquiry, June 25, 1967

APRIL 9

Jose Miro Cardona resigns as head of the militant anti-Castro Cuban Revolutionary Council (supported by the CIA) because John Kennedy refused to give $50 million for another invasion army. Cardona charges that Kennedy has broken his promise for a new invasion and instead opted for "peaceful co-existence" with Cuba. [*Schweiker Report*]

" . . . the best evidence that Oswald could fire his rifle as fast as he did and hit the target is the fact that he did so."
—WESLEY J. LIEBLER
Warren Commission counsel, in an internal memo, September 6, 1964

APRIL 10

Major General Edwin Walker is fired upon at his Dallas home from forty yards; the bullet misses entirely. Marina Oswald's testimony following the Kennedy assassination implicates her late husband. The bullet fired at Walker is identified as a 30.06 size, but following the Kennedy assassination is identified as a 6.5 mm. cartridge. Witnesses see two men leave from the alley behind the Walker residence following the 9 P.M. shooting; Lee Oswald did not know how to drive at the time. Walker's first reaction is that Black Muslims were behind the shooting. [1:36; 22:756; 24:40; 26:328, 339; *The Dallas Conspiracy*]

APRIL 12

Lee Oswald files for unemployment compensation at the Texas Employment Commission. [Cunningham Exhibits 1 and 2]

APRIL 15

Lee Oswald reportedly passes out Fair Play for Cuba Committee literature on Main St. in Dallas, wearing a "viva Castro" sign around his neck. [22:796; 23:477; D. T. H. 12-9-63]

APRIL 15

George de Mohrenschildt visits the Oswalds and sees a newly purchased rifle. George asks Lee if he shot at Walker, and how could he miss. According to later testimony, Oswald says that although he did not like Walker, he was not the assailant. [1:18; 9:248, 314, 315; 22:777]

APRIL 16

Lee Oswald writes the Fair Play for Cuba Committee in New York that he has passed out literature; he requests more be sent him. [10:87; 20:511]

"I think it was a conspiracy. I mean, there was more than one gun. There was a pathologist in here today, and he said the base of the bullets was different; one was squarish and the other two were round—or is it the other way around?"

—receptionist at the National Archives November 1973

"The [JFK] autopsy was incomplete, incompetent, and superficial."

—CYRIL WECHT
Allegheny County (Pa.) Coroner and leading forensic pathologist, University of Arizona symposium, January 14, 1974

APRIL 19

The New York Fair Play for Cuba Committee sends literature to Oswald. [10:87]

APRIL 24

Ruth Paine and Marina escort Lee to the bus station where he departs for New Orleans. [2:457, 459, 462, 467]

APRIL 24-29

Lee Oswald's whereabouts and associates unknown except for a 4-26-63 visit to the New Orleans unemployment office. [25:626]

"I, James J. Humes, certify that I have destroyed by burning certain preliminary draft notes relating to the Naval Medical School autopsy report A63-272 [JFK autopsy]."
—JAMES J. HUMES
admitting he set fire to Kennedy autopsy material, November 24, 1963

1963 *(cont.)*

APRIL 29
Lee Oswald files a claim for unemployment compensation; looks for a job. [8:137; 10:158]

MAY
A Dallas office of JURE (anti-Castro *Ju*nta *Re*volutionary) is set up; among the Dallas members is Mrs. Sylvia Odio, a Cuban exile (see 9-25-63). [11:375; 26:349, 401]

MAY 8
Jack Ruby, in Houston, rents a car to visit stripper Candy Barr (Juanita Slusher) in Edna, Tex. [CE1652]

MAY 9
Jimmy Hoffa is indicted in Nashville for jury tampering. Attorney General Robert Kennedy supervises Justice Department handling of Hoffa case. [*The Fall and Rise of Jimmy Hoffa,* by Sheridan]

MAY 9
Lee Oswald finds work at the Reilly Coffee Company, the owner of which is a former CIA agent, through an employment agency. [24:903]

"Selecting a hospital pathologist to perform a medico-legal autopsy . . . and evaluate gunshot wounds is like sending a seven-year-old boy who has taken three lessons on the violin over to the New York Philharmonic and expecting him to perform a Tchaikovsky symphony. He knows how to hold the violin and the bow, but he has a long way to go before he can make music."
—MILTON HELPERN
New York City Chief Medical Examiner, on the JFK autopsy, in *Where Death Delights*

Cover-up Lowdown BY JAY KINNEY & PAUL MAVRIDES

WELL MAYBE THEY JUST GOT UP AND LEFT BY THEMSELVES... HA HA.

JFK'S PRESERVED **BRAIN** AND RELATED **SLIDES**, IMPORTANT FOR FIXING THE TRUE FLIGHT PATH OF THE FATAL SHOT, WERE DISCOVERED **MISSING** FROM THE **NAT'L. ARCHIVES** IN '72. THERE'S STILL NO CLUE TO WHO TOOK THEM OR WHERE THEY ARE.

MAY 9

Lee Oswald rents a room at 4907 Magazine Street, New Orleans, for $65 a month; enters change of address from Dallas P.O. box. He moves in the following day. [10:265; 22:159; 24:870, 879]

MAY 10

Jack Ruby orders a .38 Smith & Wesson pistol from Ray Brantley, a Dallas gun dealer, asking that it be sent to L. J. McWillie, organized crime/gambling figure, in Las Vegas. McWillie returns the gun to Brantley soon after receiving it. (In early 1959 McWillie had asked Ruby to have Brantley ship him "four little cobras" [pistols] to Havana.) [26:499]

MAY 24

Lee Oswald renews his subscription to *The Militant* at his New Orleans address. [19:567]

MAY 26

Lee Oswald sends five dollars to the national Fair Play for Cuba Committee office in New York for membership. [V. T. Lee Exhibit 3]

MAY 29

Lee Oswald orders 1,000 Fair Play for Cuba Committee handbills from the Jones Printing Co.; also, using the name Lee Osborne, buys a rubber stamp kit for the committee the same day. Handbills picked up six days later for $9.60. [22:797; 25:58, 773]

JUNE-JULY

New Orleans lawyer Dean Andrews says that

"M-G-M contacted me about taking Portrait *[of the Assassin, about Oswald, co-authored by John Stiles] and making a documentary of it. [White House counsel] Buchen turned them down. Then M-G-M contacted Jack [Stiles] and he went to California for a day or so. They want to make three 2-hour documentaries, using* Portrait *as a theme. . . . Simon & Schuster's thinking of republishing it. Jack wants to find out how the radio and television rights stand."*

—GERALD FORD

quoted in *The New York Times Magazine,* April 20, 1975

Lee Oswald comes to see him three times relative to his U.S. Marine discharge, his citizenship status, and his wife's citizenship status. Oswald is accompanied by five persons, all homosexuals from the Gaslight Bar, Andrews says. [11:325-99; 26:704]

JUNE 3

Lee Oswald orders 500 Fair Play for Cuba Committee membership application forms; uses the name Lee Osborne; picks them up

"We have not been told the truth about Oswald."

—RICHARD B. RUSSELL

quoted in *Whitewash IV,* by Harold Weisberg

"One of his [Lee's] favorite radio programs was 'Let's Pretend,' a Saturday morning show that popularized fairy tales."
—ROBERT OSWALD
in *Lee*

1963 *(cont.)*

two days later, paying $9.34. [22:800; 25:770, 773]

JUNE 3

Lee Oswald rents a box at the Lafayette Station post office. [CE158]

JUNE 4

Teamsters Union president Jimmy Hoffa indicted by a federal grand jury for pension fund fraud in Chicago. [N.Y.T. 6-5-63]

JUNE 5-10

Lee Oswald writes the Fair Play for Cuba Committee in New York giving his new P.O. box number, enclosing samples of his newly printed application forms, and mentioning his newly rented office in New Orleans. [20:517-18; 25:771]

JUNE 5-13

Jack Ruby drives to New Orleans, ostensibly looking for showgirls for the Carousel Club. [14:150; 23:13, 14, 49]

JUNE 5

John Kennedy, in El Paso, meets with Lyndon Johnson, Governor Connally, Johnson aide Cliff Carter, and Navy Secretary Fred Korth; discussions include possible political trip to Texas, including Dallas. No public statement is released. [7:475; 17:574]

JUNE 8

Lee and Marina Oswald apply at New Orleans Charity Hospital for prenatal care for Marina; they are denied services because they have not been Louisiana residents long enough. [26:772]

JUNE 9

Dallas Police Department informers say that a Cosa Nostra meeting is going on in Dallas, primarily of Chicago mafia figures. [D.M.N. 1-7-64]

JUNE 10

Lee Oswald sends his Fair Play for Cuba Committee handbill and application card to the *Worker* newspaper, and requests literature. [17:753; 20:257]

JUNE 10

John Kennedy delivers a major foreign policy address at American University in Washington, D.C., with a proposal for a nuclear test ban treaty.

"He [Lee] loved to play monopoly."
—MARGUERITE OSWALD
CBS News Special, September 27, 1964

JUNE 15

Lee Oswald's Fair Play for Cuba Committee Card is dated this day, signed by "Hidell" in Marina's hand. [24:17; 25:681; 26:105]

JUNE 15

Lee Oswald hands out Fair Play for Cuba Committee literature at the dock of the U.S.S. Wasp in New Orleans. [22:806]

JUNE 17

The Dallas office of the FBI receives a query from the New Orleans FBI office regarding Oswald. [4:443]

"One of his [Lee's] favorite [television] programs was 'I Led Three Lives,' the story of Herbert Philbrick, the FBI informant who posed as a Communist spy."
—ROBERT OSWALD
in *Lee*

JUNE 24

Lee Oswald applies for a new U.S. passport at New Orleans, states he intends to leave between September and December, 1963, to visit Europe and the Soviet Union. [22:12; 24:509]

JUNE 26

The New Orleans FBI office is notified that Oswald had contacted the *Worker* newspaper as recently as June 10, 1963. [26:94]

"I was convinced all along that Lee Harvey Oswald had acted alone. Now I don't even know who's buried in Oswald's grave. I think there should be an exhumation of the body."
—BILL ALEXANDER
former Assistant Dallas County District Attorney, November 24, 1975

JULY 1-2

John Kennedy is in Italy.

JULY

An office at 544 Camp Street, New Orleans, is rented for night Spanish classes by a man (not Oswald); Oswald writes the Fair Play for Cuba Committee that he has rented an office. The building's second floor has a private detective agency run by Guy Bannister, a former FBI agent in charge of the Chicago office, and head of the "Anti-Communism League of the Carribean" and "Friends of Democratic Cuba." He and his employees, including David Ferrie, have many ties to the CIA and ultra-rightist organizations. [20:518; 25:771; N.Y.T. 12-9-63; *Ramparts,* 1-68]

JULY 1

Lee Oswald checks out *Portrait of a President* by Manchester from the public library. [25:929; 930]

JULY 1

Lee and Marina write the Soviet Embassy in

1963 *(cont.)*

Washington that they both want to return to Russia. A week later Marina writes again urging them to rush the visas. [16:32; 18:527]

JULY 3

John Kennedy returns from a highly successful European trip.

JULY 11

Mrs. Ruth Paine, a liberal Quaker woman interested in international affairs, invites Marina to live with her in Dallas. [2:492; 19:102]

JULY 19

Lee Oswald is fired from the Reilly Coffee Company. [17:754; 19:213]

JULY 23

FBI informant known as "T-1" says that Lee Oswald has rented a post office box (#30061) in New Orleans 6-3-63. Lee Oswald is checked upon four or five times while in New

---

"Oswald was following the pattern of behavior in which he had been tutored by person or persons unknown . . . that he had been in contact with others before or during his Marine Corps tour who had guided him and encouraged him in his actions."
—JOHN A. McVICKAR
Assistant Counsel, U.S. Embassy, in Moscow, commenting on Oswald's visit there

---

"I was under, uh, the protection of the, uh—of the, uh—that is to say, I was not under the protection of the, uh—American government. But that is I was at all times considered an American citizen."
—LEE HARVEY OSWALD
concerning his stay in the Soviet Union, on WDSU radio, New Orleans, August 21, 1963

Orleans. It is never ascertained whether "T-1" is Oswald or someone else. [CD12:2; CD372]

JULY 24

Lee Oswald contacts the Cuban president of the Modern Language Institute regarding Spanish. [24:659; CD4:819]

JULY 24

Ten Cuban exiles arrive in New Orleans from Miami and join a covert "training camp" north of New Orleans. [*Schweiker Report*]

JULY 25

The U.S. Navy writes Lee Oswald that there will be no change in his undesirable discharge from the Marine reserves. [CE2016]

JULY 26

The name "Lee H. Oswald" is signed in the guest register at the Atomic Energy Museum at Oak Ridge, Tenn. [CD1066:612; CD897:506]

JULY 26

Fidel Castro makes a lengthy analytical speech celebrating the 10th anniversary of the Moncado Barracks raid.

JULY 27

Lee Oswald, traveling with relatives, visits the Jesuit Seminary at Mobile, Ala., where his cousin attends. Oswald speaks to some seminarians and is critical of communism. [FBI to Warren Commission 2-11-64]

JULY 31

The FBI seizes more than a ton of dynamite, 20 bomb casings, napalm material, and other "devices" at a home in the New Orleans area; material was evidently stockpiled for anti-Castroite terrorist activity, such as bombing an oil refinery in Havana. Eleven are arrested. The land is owned by the brother of Mike McLaney, Havana gambling casino operator and friend of Jack Ruby. [CD984b; N.O.T.P. 8-1, 2, 4-63; *Schweiker Report,* appendix C]

JULY 31

Lee Oswald asks Texas Governor Connally's office to have his undesirable discharge from the Marine Reserves changed. [24:733]

"Mr. O. was with the Marine Corps, stationed with the U.S. Embassy in Moscow."
—SPAS T. RAIKEN
Travelers' Aid Society case record fact sheet on Lee Oswald, June 1962

"I have and allways[sic] had the full sanction of the U.S. Embassy, Moscow, USSR, and hence the U.S. government...."
—LEE HARVEY OSWALD
in a letter from Russia to Senator John Tower of Texas, January 30, 1962

AUGUST 1

Lee Oswald writes the national Fair Play for Cuba Committee office in New York claiming that he had rented office space for his New Orleans FPCC chapter but had been evicted three days later. [20:524, 533]

AUGUST 3-8

Jack Ruby leaves Dallas briefly; goes to Edna, Tex., to visit stripper Candy Barr, then Houston, possibly New Orleans, back to Dallas, then New York by plane, on to Chicago, and returns to Dallas. [vols. 22, 23]

AUGUST

New Orleans attorney Wray Gill hires David Ferrie as an investigator in preparing Carlos Marcello's defense in the deportation case. [CD75:287]

AUGUST 5

Nuclear test ban treaty signed in Moscow by the U.S., Great Britain, and the USSR. Military spokesmen vehemently attacked Kennedy before a Senate committee for his support of the treaty.

1963 *(cont.)*

AUGUST 5

Lee Oswald goes to the Casa Roca store in New Orleans owned by Carlos Bringuier, a fanatical anti-Castroite with CIA connections. Oswald offers to help the anti-Castro Cuban Student Directorate, which Bringuier heads, and help fight Castro. [10:35, 76; 19:240; 25:773]

AUGUST 6

Lee Oswald once again visits Casa Roca, store owned by Carlos Bringuier. [10:37; 26:768]

AUGUST 7

Lee Oswald tells the FBI (later, during a jail interview three days later) that "A. J. Hidell" asked him on this day to distribute Fair Play for Cuba Committee literature. Oswald told New Orleans attorney Dean Andrews that someone paid him $25 to distribute the handbills. [11:328; 17:760]

AUGUST 7, 8 OR 9

Lee Oswald is seen with a Latino at the Ha-

"Now I don't know who killed cock robin, but we do know Oswald had intelligence connections. Everywhere you look with him, there're fingerprints of intelligence."
    —RICHARD SCHWEIKER
quoted in *The Village Voice,* December 15, 1975

"I love Lee. Lee good man. He didn't do anything."
    —MARINA OSWALD
shortly after her husband was charged with killing Kennedy and Officer Tippit; quoted in *LIFE,* November 29, 1963

"All this blood. All this dying. Did Lee bring this down on America?"
    —MARINA OSWALD PORTER
quoted in *People* magazine, Premier issue, February 1974

---

bana Bar at 3:00 A.M.; the bar is owned by Orest Peña, a former FBI informer. The Habana is on the same block as Carlos Bringuier's store. Peña later tells CBS News that he saw Oswald with FBI agent Warren Debrueys on many occasions. [11:343, 356; 25:671; 26:358; CBS News Special 11-75]

AUGUST 9

Lee Oswald goes to the 700 block of Canal Street and starts distributing Fair Play for Cuba Committee literature in front of the International Trade Mart. At approximately 2 P.M. Carlos Bringuier and two other anti-Castroites get in a fight with Oswald; all four are arrested for disturbing the peace. Bar owner Orest Peña posts bond for Bringuier. Court records have Oswald listed as a Cuban. [11:358; 25:90, 773; 26:348, 578, 768; CD6:223]

AUGUST 9

Lee Oswald tells New Orleans police that the Fair Play for Cuba Committee chapter in New Orleans has 35 members, 5 of whom attend meetings regularly. [25:773]

AUGUST 9

Lee Oswald spends the night in a New Orleans jail, and is listed as 5'9" by police—a drop of two inches from 9-3-59. [CE826; *They've Killed the President!* p. 209]

AUGUST 10

Lee Oswald asks to see an FBI agent while he is being held in the New Orleans jail. [26:95, 96]

AUGUST 10

Emile Bruneau, a friend of Lee Oswald's relatives, bails him out of jail. [8:175]

AUGUST 10

Lee Oswald visits the New Orleans newspapers seeking to get some pro-Castro material printed. [21:626]

AUGUST 12

Lee Oswald goes to New Orleans court and sits on the "colored" side. He pleads guilty and pays a $10 fine. [CD114:VI29:26; 10:38; 16:342]

AUGUST 13

Lee Oswald writes to Arnold Johnson of the Communist party in New York, enclosing a clipping of his arrest. [10:99; 20:261]

AUGUST 13

New York radio personality Long John Nebel says that Lee Oswald calls him on this date from Louisiana and offers to appear on his show at his own expense. [*Were We Controlled?,* p. 66]

AUGUST 16

Lee Oswald and a companion, unknown, go to the International Trade Mart on Camp Street in New Orleans to distribute Fair Play for Cuba Committee literature. Oswald hires a couple of men at $2 apiece to help. WDSU-TV is tipped off by CIA contract employee Carlos Bringuier to film the leafletting. Oswald leaves as soon as TV cameras disappear. Leafletting reported to the FBI. [10:41, 61, 68; 16:342; 25:771; Zodiac News Service 7-2-76; CD206:216-17; CD1114:VI-29; CD75:69-70]

"To one kind of intellectual, a mysterious assassination, such as that of President Kennedy, provides an irresistible urge to play 'private eye.' "

—HENRY FAIRLIE

in *The New York Times Magazine,* September 11, 1966

AUGUST 17

WDSU radio interviewer Bill Stuckey visits Lee Oswald at home; Oswald agrees to appear on a "Latin Listening Post" interview show broadcast at 7:30 that evening. Oswald

"One of the things that keeps [assassination researchers] going is the puzzle. You never start with the intention of going all the way—at least I never did—but you keep finding pieces and putting them together, you make progress all the time."
—JOSIAH THOMPSON
author of *Six Seconds in Dallas;* quoted in *The New Yorker,* June 10, 1967

1963 *(cont.)*

inflates the size of his one-man Fair Play for Cuba Committee. [10:49; 11:160, 162, 163, 166, 172]

AUGUST 19
Jack Ruby calls the Thunderbird Hotel in Las Vegas; one of many calls to Las Vegas by Ruby. [25:253]

AUGUST 20
WDSU interviewer Bill Stuckey gives the FBI a complete tape of the first Oswald interview, only part of which had been aired. [11:165]

AUGUST 21
Carlos Bringuier asks for a congressional investigation of Lee Oswald. [19:175]

AUGUST 21
Lee Oswald, on a panel at WDSU in New Orleans, discusses Cuban-American relations with moderator Bill Stuckey, Carlos Brin-

guier, anti-Communist propagandist Ed Butler, and Bill Slatter of WDSU. Confronted about his defection to the Soviet Union, Oswalds slips and indicates he was protected by the U.S. government while he was there. [10:42; 11:171, 172; 17:763]

AUGUST 21
The FBI instructs field offices in New Orleans and Dallas to conduct further investigation of Lee Oswald. [CE843#47]

AUGUST 22
WDSU radio in New Orleans makes available a transcript of the second Oswald interview to the FBI. [CD12:11]

AUGUST 26
Lee Oswald is reportedly seen by several witnesses in the company of David Ferrie and Clay Shaw in Clinton, La. Shaw had taken the day off for "personal" reasons. [from the Garrison investigation]

AUGUST 26
Anti-Castro forces land near Mayari, Cuba, in

"The Americans butcher and kill their presidents. Why don't you go ask them to allow an investigation?"
—IDI AMIN
March 8, 1977, replying to a suggestion that he permit an international commission to investigate atrocities in Uganda.

Orienté Province near the Guantanamo Naval Station. [*Red Friday,* p. 6]

AUGUST 27

The FBI checks the court records in New Orleans for mention of Lee Oswald. [CD12:11; CD114:VI-29:25]

AUGUST 29

Bill Stuckey of WDSU in New Orleans again makes a transcript of his broadcast with Lee Oswald available to the FBI, and talks with them the next day. [CE826; CD897:540]

AUGUST 30

"Hot line" between Washington and Moscow opens.

AUGUST-SEPTEMBER

Jack Ruby places an ad in the *Dallas Morning News* offering a nightclub for sale. [23:117]

SEPTEMBER-NOVEMBER

Eva Grant, Jack Ruby's sister, says that Carousel Club employee Leo Tort recalls seeing Officer J. D. Tippit of the Dallas Police at Ruby's Vegas Club during this time period. [14:486]

SEPTEMBER

Lee and Marina write out Russian-Spanish exercises. [1:51; 6:36]

SEPTEMBER

Attorney General Robert F. Kennedy tells the McClellan Committee (Senate group looking into organized crime) that he is expanding his war on organized crime. Privately, Robert Kennedy has singled out Jimmy Hoffa, Sam Giancanna, and Carlos Marcello as his chief targets. (Privately Marcello often threatened Kennedy's life.) [*The Grim Reapers,* by Reid, p. 159]

SEPTEMBER

Talks between the Cuban delegate to the U.N., La Chuga, and a U.S. delegate, William Attwood, are proposed by the Cubans. [*Schweiker Report,* appendix C]

1963 *(cont.)*

SEPTEMBER 12

Cuban Co-ordinating Committee meets in Washington to review government Cuban "contingency plans." Agreement among those present that Castro might retaliate for rash of U.S. backed covert activity in Cuba; however an attack on U.S. officials within the U.S. is considered unlikely. [*Schweiker Report*]

SEPTEMBER 13

The *Dallas Times Herald* announces an upcoming Kennedy trip to Dallas; no specific date is given.

SEPTEMBER 15

Six active anti-Castroites are warned by the Justice Department in Miami about raids on Cuba. The six include Frank Fiorini (aka Frank Sturgis) and Alexander Rorke, who dies several days later in a plane crash. The six were told that there was "evidence which strongly indicated that you may be engaged in activities in violation of the provisions of

---

"Mark Lane, by the questions he raised here and abroad, seemed to be trying to give the appearance that the Commission was sweeping something under the rug."
—GERALD FORD and JOHN STILES
in *Portrait of the Assassin*

"Do you have any plans to put all your information together and take it to the, uh, government or the FBI—who would you take it to?
—reporter for WBIR-TV, Knoxville
to assassination lecturer Bob Katz, Autumn 1973

---

the munitions control laws of the United States." [N.Y.T. 9-16-63]

SEPTEMBER 17

Lee Oswald gets a fifteen day tourist visa for Mexico at the New Orleans consulate. [24:549, 685; 25:17, 811]

"I am no more an expert on that [Kennedy] assassination than anybody else. . . ."
—RICHARD NIXON
in a press conference, August 22, 1973

SEPTEMBER (3RD WEEK)

David Ferrie is in Laredo, Tex., just prior to Lee Oswald's trip to Mexico City. Ferrie purchases a Mannlicher-Carcano rifle. [*The Councilor*, a White Citizens Council newspaper, 11-30-67]

SEPTEMBER 19

John Kennedy attends a private dinner party

at the residence of former Ambassador to Cuba Earl T. Smith. Several young people throw paint at the president's car as it travels through New York streets. [*Red Friday*, p. 7]

SEPTEMBER 19
Lee Oswald checks more books out of the New Orleans public library, including books by Ian Fleming and Aldous Huxley. [22:83; 23:388]

SEPTEMBER 20
The FBI questions Oswald's relatives about Lee and Marina. [8:146]

SEPTEMBER 20
Richard C. Nagell, a CIA contract agent, fires a shot in an El Paso bank and is arrested. Later he says he wanted to be in federal custody during the upcoming presidential assassination of which he claimed prior knowledge. Nagell related that the assassination attempt would be in Washington 9-26-63. [CD253:3]

SEPTEMBER 20
John Kennedy addresses the United Nations General Assembly, criticizes the Cuban government.

SEPTEMBER
Jack Ruby is treated again for gonorrhea. [TAG5:J5]

SEPTEMBER
Jack Ruby is warned by a parking lot attendant that a short, stocky, 30-year-old Jewish man said he was going to kill Jack. Jack pistol-whips the man. [CD1254:33; 13:254]

SEPTEMBER 23
Marina Oswald is invited to live at the home of Ruth Paine in Irving, Tex., until one month after the expected baby is born. [1:23, 37; 3:8-10; 9:360]

SEPTEMBER 24
Ruth Paine and Marina Oswald arrive in Irving, Tex., from New Orleans. [2:415, 418; 24:220]

SEPTEMBER 25
Juan D. Bosch is deposed in a military coup in the Dominican Republic; the CIA supported the coup plotters.

SEPTEMBER 25
Lee Oswald calls Mrs. Horace Twifold in Houston, whose husband is a Socialist Labor party official; tells her he is flying to Mexico City in a few hours, asks her about the Fair Play for Cuba Committee. [11:179, 180; 24:726; 25:114, 299]

SEPTEMBER 25
Lee Oswald travels from New Orleans to Houston; route and method not ascertained by Warren Commission.

SEPTEMBER 25, 26, OR 27
Sylvia Odio, a Cuban exile from a wealthy family, is visited by three men at her Dallas

1963 *(cont.)*

home who bring information about her father in a Cuban jail. One of the three men is introduced as "Leon Oswald" who repeats his name twice. A day later "Oswald" is explained to Mrs. Odio as a crazy guy who thinks Cuban exiles are cowards for not having killed John Kennedy over the Bay of Pigs defeat. [11:327; 386; 26:362, 472; *Accessories After the Fact*, pp. 378-87]

SEPTEMBER 26

The FBI calls on Lee Oswald's New Orleans landlord; it is the 4th or 5th time they have done so. [22:190; CD325:4]

SEPTEMBER 26

Lee Oswald travels Trailways from Houston to Laredo; tells fellow passengers that he is en route to Cuba. [11:214]

SEPTEMBER 26

Lee Oswald crosses the border into Nuevo Laredo between 6 A.M. and 2 P.M.; says he is a photographer. [22:159; 24:549, 567, 571, 574, 665]

SEPTEMBER 26

First public announcement of John Kennedy's November 21-22 trip to Dallas-Ft. Worth. [4:348; 22:619]

SEPTEMBER 27

Lee Oswald arrives at 10 A.M. in Mexico City and registers at the Hotel Comercio, a "meeting place for anti-Castro exiles." [25:37, 39,

"Lee Harvey Oswald wasn't available Thursday to receive a package addressed to him at the Texas School Book Depository.

"The package, mailed from Los Angeles, drew the shocked attention of United Parcel Service employes who quickly notified Dallas police and the FBI, who feared it might be a bomb. FBI agents and Dallas bomb squad officers examined the cigar-box sized parcel at the UPS truck depot, 10155 Monroe in North Dallas, shortly after sundown.

"The bomb squad officers carefully opened the package and found it filled with styrofoam 'peanuts.'

" 'It was somebody's idea of a joke,' an FBI spokesman said."

—Dallas Morning News
February 4, 1977

633, 819; *They've Killed the President!*, p. 251]

SEPTEMBER 27

Lee Oswald visits Cuban consulate in Mexico City and asks for transit for himself so he may visit Cuba for two weeks en route to Moscow. Oswald has heated argument with Cuban consul over Cuba's refusal to grant him a visa immediately. Visit monitored by David Phillips, CIA agent attached to the U. S. Embassy. [25:586, 634; 16:33; 24:590; Phillips speech to National Military Intelligence Association 6-76]

SEPTEMBER 28
Lee Oswald applies for a visa at the Soviet Embassy in Mexico City; visits again three days later. [17:811, 812]

SEPTEMBER 28
John Kennedy is in California and Nevada.

SEPTEMBER 30
Lee Oswald, using the name "O. H. Lee," buys a ticket to Laredo, Tex., from Mexico City. [22:233; 24:603]

LATE SEPTEMBER-EARLY OCTOBER
Planned Parenthood pays a call on Marina Oswald. [CD524:27]

OCTOBER (FIRST WEEK)
New Orleans Police Department vice squad detective believes he sees Jack Ruby in New Orleans with Frank Caracci and Nick Kovans, both reputed organized crime figures. [CD75:491]

OCTOBER 1
Lee Oswald contacts the Soviet and Cuban embassies in Mexico City again. [17:811]

OCTOBER 1
The CIA takes photos of a man they call "Oswald" in front of the Soviet Embassy in Mexico City. The man is stocky, crew-cut, blond, and 35 years old. [16:638; CE237]

OCTOBER 2
Jack Ruby tells Nathan Wyll, an ex-night club reporter now in the travel business, that he is interested in a Caribbean cruise. [25:317, 325]

OCTOBER 2
After meeting with Defense Secretary McNamara and General Maxwell Taylor, John Kennedy says that "1,000 U. S. military personnel assigned to South Vietnam" can be withdrawn "by the end of 1963."

OCTOBER 2
Lee Oswald leaves the Hotel Comercio in the

"The sleuths worked for the sheer joy of it; in return one was expected to exhibit consummate interest in the details of their handiwork, which at times was a high price to pay. I was forever being stopped in a hallway, or cornered in the office bistro to be subjected to minutiae of Oswald's alleged love affair with Jack Ruby. One of the most horrific experiences of my life was when a dogged female sleuth trapped me in the men's room . . . [and] lounged against the urinal, lecturing me for a half an hour through the stall door about the conspiratorial significance of Oswald's having shaved off all his pubic hair."
—WARREN HINCKLE
former *Ramparts* editor, from his memoir *If You Have a Lemon, Make Lemonade* (Chapter 6: "Give Us This Day Our Daily Paranoia")

1963 *(cont.)*

early morning, and using a ticket bought two days earlier, travels as "O. H. Lee" to Laredo, Tex., via Monterrey, Mex. [24:598, 603; 25:608, 738, 767]

OCTOBER 3

Dallas FBI agent James Hosty searches for Lee Oswald. [*Assassination of the President*]

OCTOBER 3

Jack Ruby calls an Internal Revenue Service agent regarding his huge debt. [23:303, 383]

OCTOBER 3

Lee Oswald crosses the border back into the United States in the early hours of the morning. Total expenses for the Mexican trip estimated at $27.32. [24:549, 569, 571]

OCTOBER 3

Still traveling as "O. H. Lee," Lee Oswald takes a Greyhound from Laredo to Dallas. Later he denies the Mexican trip entirely to

---

BELUSHI: *If you could be any animal in the world, what would you like to be?*
GARRISON: *Vice-president.*
—Conversation between actor John Belushi and former New Orleans District Attorney Jim Garrison
quoted in *Rolling Stone* magazine, January 13, 1977

"We must find the existential truth between paranoia and naivete."
—DONALD FREED
speaking at the "Committee to Investigate Assassinations" conference at Georgetown University, November 24, 1973

Dallas Police Captain Will Fritz. [4:210; 22:234, 706, 707; 25:650, 763, 764]

OCTOBER 3

On return from Mexico, Lee Oswald checks into the Dallas YMCA and gives El Toro, Calif. (first Marine duty station four years earlier), as his address. He does not contact Marina. [10:281, 283, 285; 11:478; 22:159, 207; 24:702; *Ft. Worth Star Telegram* 12-5-63]

OCTOBER 3

John Kennedy, at the Arkansas Fair Grounds, pays tribute to then-powerful Congressman Wilbur Mills.

OCTOBER 3

Lee Oswald goes to the unemployment office and files for the balance of his benefits—$6. He gives the Paine address where his wife and daughter live. Between 5-21-63 and this date, Oswald collects $402 in unemployment benefits. [10:152; 19:193, 399, 404]

OCTOBER 4-16

The FBI visits the Paine residence looking for

Lee Oswald; Mrs. Paine says she doesn't know where he lives or where he works. [23:508; D. M. N. 12-7-63]

OCTOBER 4
Former Oswald employer Mr. Stovall of Jaggers, Childs and Stovall, tells prospective Oswald employer that Lee might be a Communist and is definitely a troublemaker. [10:170; 22:478; 20:3]

OCTOBER 4
Texas Governor John Connally sees John Kennedy in Washington; the upcoming Texas trip is discussed, and the Dallas visit is firmed up. [*Life* 11-24-67]

OCTOBER 4
Lee Oswald checks out of the YMCA and calls Marina; gets a ride to the Paine house in Irving and tells Mrs. Paine he has been in Houston. [23:509; 24:702]

OCTOBER 4
According to intelligence reports, Lee Oswald has subscriptions to a Minsk (USSR) newspaper, *Krokadil* (Soviet humor maga-

---

"If we're not paranoid, we're crazy!"
—SHERMAN SKOLNICK
conspiracy researcher at the "Assassination Information Bureau" conference at Boston University, January 31, 1975

---

zine), *Time,* and *The Militant,* among other publications. [3:1117]

OCTOBER 4
Lee Oswald hunts for work at an employment agency; lists George de Mohrenschildt as his "closest friend." [23:752; CD534:16; CD734:19]

"Out of the Files and Into the Streets"
—headline of the *Village Voice* article about the Assassination Information Bureau conference
February 10, 1975

OCTOBER 6
Three men, driving a 1957 black-and-white Chevrolet, practice shooting in the field of Mrs. Lovell T. Penn, who lives 20 miles from Dallas. Later Mrs. Penn claims one of the men was definitely Lee Oswald, who objected when she insisted they leave her property. A 6.5 mm cartridge is found. [25:588; 26:406, 601]

OCTOBER 7
John Kennedy signs the Nuclear Test Ban Treaty.

OCTOBER 7
Lee calls Marina to say he has a room in the

"It takes a very accommodating gullet to swallow the conspiracy theory whole, and my present inclination is to stick with the Warren Report."
—JAMES J. KILPATRICK
syndicated columnist, May 27, 1975

1963 *(cont.)*

Oak Cliff section of Dallas, a middle class area, at 621 N. Marsalis. [23:390; 26:538]

OCTOBER 9
John Kennedy holds a televised press conference from the State Department auditorium—speaks well of Barry Goldwater; says he will wait until 1964 to announce for re-election; and replies to a question that a special congressional "watchdog" committee to oversee the CIA is not necessary.

OCTOBER 9
The New Orleans public library acknowledges a gift from Lee Oswald. [25:8]

OCTOBER 8-10
The FBI gets information about Lee Oswald —evidently from having his mail watched. [25:578; CD2444; CD206]

OCTOBER 10
The CIA tells the FBI, State Department, and U.S. Navy about a visit 9-28-63 by Lee Oswald to the Soviet Embassy in Mexico City. [11:482; 17:811]

OCTOBER 11-18
David Ferrie goes to Guatemala from New Orleans regarding the Carlos Marcello deportation case. Marcello is a top mobster in the New Orleans area. [*Plot or Politics?*, p. 45]

John Kennedy addresses the Commission on the Status of Women, saying, "there used to be an old story that a civilization could be judged on how it treats its elderly people. But I think it can also be judged on its opportunities for women."

OCTOBER 11
A State Department officer inspects the Lee Oswald file. [CD1082]

OCTOBER 12
Jack Ruby distributes Carousel Club cards at the University of Texas-Oklahoma game at the Cotton Bowl. (Texas wins, 28-7.) [25:336]

OCTOBER 13
Major General Edwin Walker attends a Dallas meeting of the Cuban Student Directorate. CIA contract agent Carlos Bringuier is the head of the New Orleans chapter of this group, which Oswald had volunteered to help 8-5-63. There is a possibility Oswald attends this meeting. [CD246:19-24; 11:425]

OCTOBER 13
Ruth Paine gives Lee Oswald a driving lesson; he is eager to learn. [2:505; N.O.T.P. 2-23-69]

*" . . . You don't have to be a third-order con-
spiracist to understand that the [JFK] investigation has to be reopened."*
         —WILLIAM RASPBERRY
syndicated columnist, in *The Washington
Post*, September 15, 1975

OCTOBER 14

Lee Oswald, using the name "O. H. Lee"
rents a room at 1026 N. Beckley; also applies
for a job at the Weiner Lumber Co., saying he
has an automobile. [4:211]

OCTOBER 14

Ruth Paine, Marina Oswald's landlady,
learns of a job opening at the Texas School
Book Depository in downtown Dallas from a
neighbor, Linnie Mae Randle, whose brother
Wesley Frazier works there. Ruth Paine telephones Roy Truly, depository superintendent, who tells her to send Lee in to fill out an
application. [CD5:325; 3:34-36, 121]

OCTOBER 15

Lee Oswald is hired at the Texas School Book
Depository. [3:121, 212]

OCTOBER 15

The Cuban Foreign Ministry tells its Mexico
City Consulate to have Oswald cable when he
has his Russian visa. [25:817]

OCTOBER 16

Lee Oswald begins work at the School Book
Depository at $1.25 an hour. He meets Wesley
Frazier, brother of the Paine neighbor, who
offers him a ride to Irving, Tex. Frazier later
says that Oswald would ride with him every
Friday to Irving and every Monday back in to
work. [24:209]

OCTOBER 17

Yugoslav President Tito visits John Kennedy
at the White House.

OCTOBER 18

Larry Crafard begins work at the Carousel
Club, sleeping in Ruby's office. [13:421;
19:353]

*"Don't you know that Mark Lane has friends
who want to overthrow the government?"*
         —FBI agent, New Orleans office
in a debate with Warren Commission critic
Don Redmann, June 1967

OCTOBER 18

Lee Oswald's 24th birthday. He rides to Irving with Wesley Frazier and spends the weekend at Ruth Paine's with his wife and daughter. [1:53; 3:40; 17:189]

OCTOBER 19

John Kennedy makes a political trip to New
England.

"They [Warren Commission critics] are more talmudic scholars than private detectives."
—ROBERT SAM ANSON
in *They've Killed the President!*

1963 *(cont.)*

OCTOBER
Defense Secretary Robert McNamara announces that all American personnel will be out of Vietnam by 1965.

OCTOBER 22
The Dallas FBI office tells headquarters in Washington that the Dallas Immigration and Naturalization Service office has received a report from the CIA about Lee Oswald's visit to the Russian Embassy in Mexico. [17:811]

OCTOBER 23
General Edwin Walker holds a "USA Day" rally at Memorial Auditorium; Lee Oswald is in attendance. [D. M. N. 10-24-63]

OCTOBER 24
Adlai Stevenson speaks at Memorial Auditorium for "UN Day," and is spat upon and struck with picket signs by angry protesters. Michael Paine says Lee Oswald might have attended. [2:412; *Newsweek* 12-9-63]

OCTOBER 24
French journalist Jean Daniel conducts a brief interview with John Kennedy before leaving for Cuba, where he acts as informal and temporary representative of the Kennedy administration in an attempt to thaw relations. [*Schweiker Report; New Republic*, 12-14-63]

OCTOBER 25
In a letter to South Vietnamese President Ngo Diem, John Kennedy offers "best wishes to the Republic of Viet-Nam on its 8th anniversary."

OCTOBER 25
Lee Oswald and Michael Paine attend an American Civil Liberties Union meeting at Southern Methodist Univerity. [20:407]

OCTOBER 28
A gunsmith in Irving fixes the sight on a rifle belonging to a "Lee Oswald"; a subsequent Secret Service investigation says Oswald is at a rifle range on this day. [D. T. H. 11-28-63; 23:403]

OCTOBER 29
FBI agent Hosty goes to see Lee Oswald's landlady Mrs. Roberts to check on Mrs. Paine and the Oswalds' presence. There are also reports of Lee Oswald receiving $10-$20 by wire

"Whatever Mark Lane's motives, he succeeded in injecting a new element of confusion in the public mind."
—FORD and STILES
in *Portrait of the Assassin*

"Assassination researcher Harold Weisberg filed an affidavit in a Washington federal court this week accusing the FBI of committing perjury by withholding evidence related to the 1963 assassination of President John Kennedy.

"Weisberg's affidavit charges that the FBI is continuing to withhold scientific evidence from the public which he believes would prove that at least two assassins fired at the presidential motorcade.

"Weisberg recently filed suit against the government under the Freedom of Information Act; as a result of that suit, he was given a series of test results which had been locked up by the FBI for the previous eleven years.

"The FBI stated in court recently that it has given Weisberg all of the results of tests conducted on the various bullets related to the assassination. Weisberg, however, claims that the documents he has obtained thus far refer to still other tests which have not been given to him. His affidavit specifically refers to scientific analysis of President Kennedy's clothing and of a curbstone which was struck by an assassin's bullet in Dealey Plaza.

"Weisberg, a Maryland private investigator, says 'if they ever produce a full scientific analysis, there will be nothing left of the Warren Report.' "

—Zodiac News Service

June 4, 1975

from out of town sources. [1:55; 4:448; *Accessories After the Fact,* p. 366]

OCTOBER 31

John Kennedy holds a press conference televised from the State Department auditorium. He pokes fun at Barry Goldwater; reiterates plans to withdraw troops from Vietnam; says that Russian troops are being reduced in Cuba; discusses civil rights; and says that Lyndon Johnson will be on his 1964 reelection ticket.

OCTOBER 31

TV commentator Lisa Howard talks with Castro aide Dr. Rene Vallejo and learns that Fidel would like a U.S. official to come visit him. Earlier, Vallejo had told Howard that Castro wanted "to talk personally to us about improving relations and was pleased to find out we were ready to listen." [*The Reds and the Blacks,* by William Attwood, p. 143; *The Dallas Conspiracy*]

NOVEMBER 1-15

Irving Sports Shop gun repairman Ryder gets a rifle scope mounting job; the order ticket says "Oswald" but the Warren Commission doubts his story. [11:225; 23:499]

"We articulate the unthinkable!"
—SHERMAN SKOLNICK
November 25, 1973

1963 *(cont.)*

NOVEMBER 1
FBI agent James Hosty, Jr., goes to the home of Ruth Paine; Marina claims to record his auto license number. [1:18, 57]

NOVEMBER 1
Jack Ruby gets a new roommate named George Senator. [23:460; 24:225]

NOVEMBER 1
Lee Oswald rents a post office box (#6225) at the Terminal Annex post office building a block from Dealey Plaza; uses correct name. He authorizes the following to enter the box: The Fair Play for Cuba Committee, the American Civil Liberties Union, and A. Hidell. As his home address, he gives 3610 N. Beckley Street (no such address; Oswald rents a room at 1026 N. Beckley). [22:717]

NOVEMBER 1
Ruth Paine gives Lee Oswald driving lessons. [3:41; 24:694]

NOVEMBER 1
Diem is assassinated as top official in Vietnam; U.S. says it welcomes the coup but denies active role in it—later concedes that U.S. policy helped bring it about. [N.Y.T. 11-2-63].

NOVEMBER 2
Lee Oswald is said to be at a rifle range with a bearded man. [23:403; 26:350]

"He [Lane] was once struck by a beer can at an East Harlem political rally. It was never determined whether its trajectory originated from the left front or the right rear."
—RICHARD LEWIS and LAWRENCE SCHILLER
in *The Scavengers*

NOVEMBER 2
A plot to kill John Kennedy this day in Chicago is investigated, resulting in the arrest of lithographer Thomas Arthur Vallee who, like Oswald, had been in the Marines and assigned to a U-2 base. When Secret Service agent Abraham Boulden attempted to talk with the Warren Commission about it, the Justice Department brought unrelated bribery charges against him and gained a conviction. [*Chicago Independent* 11-75]

NOVEMBER 4-14
Lee Oswald takes a rifle to the Irving Sports Shop to have a scope mounted. On 11-28-63

"My feeling about the conspiracy theory is this: that if after the statute of limitations is up, somebody doesn't write a book for a million dollars, then there was no conspiracy."
—SEYMOUR HERSH
New York Times reporter, in *Rolling Stone* magazine, April 24, 1975

repairman discovers a $4.50 ticket with the name "Oswald." [7:225; 24:328]

NOVEMBER 5
FBI agents James Hosty, Jr., and Gary Wilson visit Ruth Paine. [1:56; 3:15]

NOVEMBER 6
Lee Oswald goes by the FBI office to drop off a note. (This is the famous "threatening" note left for agent Hosty and later destroyed at the direction of top FBI officials.) [2:18]

NOVEMBER 7
Jack Ruby rents a post office box (#5475) at the Terminal Annex post office building a block from Dealey Plaza. [7:30; 20:175]

"The first indication of her [Marguerite Oswald's] emotional instability was the retaining of a lawyer [Mark Lane] whom anyone would not have retained if they were really serious in trying to get down to the facts."
—J. EDGAR HOOVER
quoted on Mark Lane's promotional brochure

NOVEMBER 8
Lee Oswald presents a personal check in the amount of $189 made out to him for cashing at Hutch's Grocery (in Irving); cashier refuses to cash it. [10:334; 22:155]

"I think that people are always willing to listen to all sorts of attacks on the Establishment, to listen to outrageous gossip. Good God, there's always been a market for that. And nowadays the surest way to make a buck is to attack the Warren Report."
—AL CAPP
cartoonist; quoted in *Fact* magazine, November/December 1966

NOVEMBER 8
A note is allegedly sent to a Mr. Hunt (H. L.? E. Howard?) in the handwriting style of Lee Harvey Oswald. It reads: "Dear Mr. Hunt, i would like information concerning my position. I am asking only for information. i am suggesting that we discuss the matter fully before any steps are taken by me or anyone else. Thank You. /s/ Lee Harvey Oswald."
"The Oswald note" becomes public years later via Texas researcher Penn Jones, who received it from a source with an accompanying letter in Spanish from Mexico City. [*New York Daily News* 3-2-77]

NOVEMBER 8
Marina Oswald sees her husband's rifle in a blanket in the Paine garage. [24:219]

NOVEMBER 8
State Department Intelligence receives a report from October 25 and October 31 on Oswald. [11:482]

"I've scrupulously avoided the assassination stories. I think it's probably saved me about 35,000 years."

—SEYMOUR HERSH
in *Rolling Stone* magazine, April 24, 1975

1963 *(cont.)*

NOVEMBER 9

A man identifying himself as "Oswald" goes to Downtown Lincoln-Mercury and test-drives a car on the Stemmons Freeway going at a reckless and high speed. He tells the salesman, Bogard, he will have plenty of cash in two to three weeks. When he is told he has no credit, "Oswald" becomes angry and remarks that he may go back to Russia to buy a car. Salesman Bogard passes a lie detector test on this, with story verified by other employees. [26:450-52, 577]

NOVEMBER 9

A threat is made in Florida against John Kennedy by National States Rights Party officer J. A. Milteer. Milteer states that Kennedy will be killed by a high-powered rifle from a window, that a patsy would be picked up to throw off the police, and the Communists would be blamed and the right-wing in the clear. Miami police take this threat seriously; FBI less so. [CD1347]

NOVEMBER 9-10

Lee Oswald is reportedly at the Sportsdrome rifle range. [10:357, 373; 24:304]

NOVEMBER 12

Secret Service agent Lawson and White House official Jack Puterbaugh arrive in Dallas to make preparations for the upcoming

"Why are we obsessed with assassination? We find we are continually confronting a question for which there are no satisfactory answers; or perhaps the worst obsession of all, when we are confronted with not one possible answer, but two wholly opposing answers—both equally plausible."

—NORMAN MAILER
in his keynote speech to the "Committee to Investigate Assassinations" conference, November 24, 1973

visit by John Kennedy. The following day they officially advise the Dallas Police of the pending trip. [20:453; 21:546, 562]

NOVEMBER 14
The State Department reviews Lee Oswald's Office of Security file after receiving FBI reports from October. [CD1082]

NOVEMBER 14
Leaflets to be distributed upon Kennedy's visit, entitled "Wanted for Treason," are taken by a Mr. Surrey to Monk Brothers for printing. [25:659]

NOVEMBER 14
Secret Service agent Lawson meets with Police Chief Curry and tells him that final parade route has not been chosen. [21:546, 563]

NOVEMBER 14
The Dallas Trade Mart is selected as the site for the Kennedy luncheon on 11-22-63. [18:715; 22:613]

NOVEMBER 14
A meeting is alleged to take place this day at the Carousel Club between Jack Ruby, policeman J. D. Tippit, and Bernard Weissman (who puts the right-wing anti-Kennedy ad in the D. M. N. 11-22-63). Club employee Billy De Mar (aka William D. Crowe) says that Lee Oswald comes to the club this day and the following three days. Other Carousel Club employees and customers recall seeing Oswald

"Hard core assassination buffs don't like me because I'm strictly in it for the money . . . a really super new angle could bring in as much as $20,000. Just a good mood piece with a catchy slant could mean several thousand [dollars].

—BRYAN SMYTHE
British free-lance writer; quoted in *The Dallas Morning News*, June 1, 1975

in the club around this time period. [2:58; 5:521; 14:106; 15:112, 620; 25:349; 26:728; D. T. H. 11-25-63]

NOVEMBER 15
Paul Rowland Jones, identified as a member of the Chicago syndicate in 1947, visits Jack Ruby. [22:297]

NOVEMBER 16
The *Dallas Morning News* outlines the motorcade route which does not go by the School Book Depository, but rather straight onto the Stemmons Freeway from Main Street.

"When other researchers come up with new information or new theories, they expect everyone else to swallow it hook, line, and sinker."

—ROBERT SMITH
assassination researcher, March 1974

1963 *(cont.)*

NOVEMBER 16

A Dr. Wood and his son are at the Sports-drome Gun Range from 3:00-4:00 P.M. at booth #4; a person identifying himself as "Oswald" is in booth #5; "Oswald" tells the younger Wood that he is firing a 6.5mm Italian made carbine with a 4-power scope. (This is one of many instances where a double appears to have been employed to set up the real Oswald.) [10:386; 23:403]

NOVEMBER 17

Marina Oswald says that Ruth Paine telephones Lee at his rooming house and is told there is no one there by the name "Lee Oswald." The following day Lee calls Marina from work, and she asks why he gave them a phone number when he is living there under an assumed name which she does not know. Lee tells her it is none of her business and they quarrel. [23:392]

NOVEMBER 17

Jack Ruby is reported to be in Las Vegas. [23:74, 82]

NOVEMBER 17 (APPROX.)

Salesman Pizzo at Downtown Lincoln-Mercury says that Lee Oswald spends two hours there after dark on a weekday toward the weekend; says Oswald tells him that he will have $200-$300 in two to three weeks. [10:344]

"I don't care how a man achieves his orgasm, as long as he doesn't use that orgasm to destroy our democratic form of government!"
—PENN JONES, JR.
conspiracy researcher, commenting on the preponderance of gays among the New Orleans conspiracy suspects of Jim Garrison's probe, February 1, 1975

NOVEMBER 17

New Orleans FBI clerk William Walter receives a PBX message from Washington FBI office warning of an attempt to be made on John Kennedy's life during the upcoming Dallas visit. [*Kennedy Conspiracy*, p. 274]

NOVEMBER 18

Dallas Police and Secret Service representatives drive over the motorcade route. [21:547]

NOVEMBER 18

Rose Cheramie, who says the purpose of her Miami to Dallas trip is to smuggle narcotics for Jack Ruby, is thrown from a moving vehicle near Eunice, La. During hospitalization, she tells attending physician that she has learned in the car with two associates of Jack Ruby that John Kennedy is to be killed when he comes to Dallas. [*Playboy* 10-67, pp. 174, 175]

NOVEMBER 18

John F. Kennedy is in Florida, speaks out in

vague terms against Castro, makes obligatory reference to Cuban community in Florida regaining its homeland.

NOVEMBER 18

On or about this date, U.S. Treasury agent Ellsworth arrests (and releases) an Oswald look-alike ("an absolute dead-ringer," he later says) in Dallas on a firearms violation. The Oswald double, according to Ellsworth, was a right-wing Minuteman, an associate of anti-Castro exiles, had traveled in and out of Mexico, and had often practiced at a Dallas rifle range where witnesses had mistaken him for Oswald. [*Village Voice*, 8-23-76]

NOVEMBER 20

Warren Carter, an employee of Southwestern Publishing Co. (which occupies the southwest corner of the School Book Depository Building second floor) shows a Mauser rifle and a .22 caliber rifle to building superintendent Roy Truly and foreman Bill Shelley. On 11-22-63 TSBD employee Geneva Hine tries unsuccessfully to get to the window of

---

"Theories about second assassins and missing bullets, which were once the exclusive property of idiots, are now debated seriously by responsible people."
—MARIANNE MEANS
columnist, in *The San Francisco Chronicle*, Spring 1975

"Paranoia is a little like dog shit. Once you step in it, you can never be sure it is not still with you."
—WARREN HINCKLE
from *If You Have a Lemon, Make Lemonade*

Southwestern Publishing Co. to determine what has happened to the motorcade. Although someone is in the office, the door is locked. [6:396; 7:381]

"It's too hard to accept Oswald as the only assassin. It's such a fantasy. After reading all these things, I find it too hard to believe."
—ANDY WARHOL
artist; quoted in *Fact* magazine, November/December 1966

NOVEMBER 20

A work crew begins laying a new floor on the sixth floor of the Texas School Book Depository. [3:163]

NOVEMBER 20

A man identified as "Oswald" eats breakfast at the Dobbs House, 1221 N. Beckley, not far from Lee Oswald's rooming house. Officer J.D. Tippit is in the restaurant at the same time but does not see "Oswald." [26:516]

> *"J. Edgar Hoover sent a memorandum to the State Department in 1960 raising the possibility that an imposter might be using the credentials of an American defector named Lee Harvey Oswald, who was then in the Soviet Union."*
>
> **—The New York Times**
>
> February 23, 1975

1963 *(cont.)*

NOVEMBER 19-22

French journalist Jean Daniel and Fidel Castro confer in Cuba about reducing tension between the U.S. and Cuba; Castro comments that Kennedy could become a greater leader than Lincoln and that Kennedy has learned much in recent months. [*New Republic* 12-63]

ALL TIMES GIVEN IN THE FOLLOWING DAYS ARE C.S.T., INCLUDING EVENTS CLOCKED IN OTHER TIME ZONES.

NOVEMBER 21

Lee Oswald rides to Irving, Tex., with co-worker Frazier; the first time he has gone on a weekday. [22:161; 24:209, 695]

NOVEMBER 21

While John Kennedy is in Houston, Jack Ruby is seen there as well by three different people who spot him at mid-afternoon alternately looking for a pool hall and a night club. One of the three witnesses, a deputy sheriff, says Ruby is dressed as an oil field worker. [25:378]

NOVEMBER 21
10:05 A.M.

Air Force One, the presidential plane, leaves Andrews Air Force Base for San Antonio with John Kennedy aboard. [*The Death of a President*, p. 655]

NOVEMBER 21
1:30 P.M.

Air Force One arrives in San Antonio. [*The Death of a President*, p. 655]

> *"He [Oswald] was playing ball, writing letters to both elements of the Communist parties. I mean, he was playing ball with the Trotskyites and with the others. This was a strange circumstance to me."*
>
> **—GERALD FORD**
>
> commenting on Oswald's possible link to the FBI, Warren Commission meeting, January 22, 1964

NOVEMBER 21
3:15 P.M.

In an unprecedented trip, six Cabinet members, Dean Rusk, Douglas Dillon, Orville Freeman, Luther Hodges, Willard Wirtz, Stuart Udall, and White House press secretary Pierre Salinger depart California for meetings in Japan. [*The Death of a President*, pp. 139, 655]

NOVEMBER 21
3:52 P.M.

John Kennedy, aboard Air Force One, departs San Antonio for Houston; arrives 1:17 later. [*The Death of a President,* p. 655]

NOVEMBER 21

Lee Oswald uncharacteristically spends a Thursday night at the Paine residence in Irving with his wife Marina. [24:209, 695]

NOVEMBER 21
11:07 P.M.

John Kennedy arrives aboard Air Force One in Ft. Worth. [*The Death of a President,* p. 655]

NOVEMBER 22
12:30 A.M.

Presidential party arrives at the Texas Hotel in Ft. Worth for the night. [*National Observer* 11-25-63]

NOVEMBER 22
2:00 A.M.

Jack Ruby closes the Carousel Club for the night; fires stripper Tammi True (who had

---

"Lee Harvey Oswald, the man who shot President Kennedy: Did he ever have contact with E. Howard Hunt or Gordon Liddy or any of the others in that mysterious and dangerous crew convicted in the Watergate Crime . . . ?"
—DAN RATHER
CBS First Line Report, August 10, 1973

---

quit two days earlier) and goes to his Ewing Street apartment. [5:183; 13:209; 25:185, 198]

NOVEMBER 22
2:30 A.M.

Jack Ruby goes to the Vegas Club to pick up Larry Crafard; they go to the Lucas B&B Coffee Shop. [19:356; 25:173, 322]

NOVEMBER 22
EARLY MORNING

Secret Service agents go to the "Cellar," an after-hours drinking club in Ft. Worth. [CD71:33]

NOVEMBER 22
3:00 A.M.

A waitress at the Lucas B&B Coffee Shop claims that Jack Ruby and Lee Oswald are there together. [5:234]

NOVEMBER 22

Jack Ruby's roommate George Senator says he and Jack discuss the Kennedy visit; Senator sees Ruby's pistol for the last time. [14:216, 427]

NOVEMBER 22
EARLY MORNING

Jack Ruby goes to local newspapers to place the weekend ads for his clubs. [20:10; 15:566]

NOVEMBER 22

The *Dallas Morning News* publishes a strong anti-Kennedy advertisement paid for by Bernard Weissman. [CD989]

1963 *(cont.)*

NOVEMBER 22

Neither the Secret Service nor the FBI gives the Dallas Police Department leads on any possible assassins to watch, according to Police Chief Curry. [*JFK Assassination File*, p. 17]

NOVEMBER 22
6:40 A.M.

The Oswalds' alarm goes off; Marina feeds the baby and wakes Lee up at 7:00. (Testimony later contradicted by Mrs. Paine and at the Shaw trial in 1969.) [22:747; 23:412]

NOVEMBER 22
7:00 A.M.

Lee Oswald leaves Mrs. Paine's residence earlier than his usual time. [*Time* 2-14-64, p. 19]

NOVEMBER 22
7:00 A.M.

Dallas Police Department starts posting "no parking" signs along the motorcade route. [*JFK Assassination File*]

NOVEMBER 22

Marina Oswald says Lee has a small package with his lunch when he leaves Mrs. Paine's residence; contradicts herself at the Clay Shaw trial saying she does not see Lee leave her home. [1:73; N.O.T.P. 2-22-69]

NOVEMBER 22
7:10-7:15 A.M.

Mrs. Randle, Wesley Frazier's sister, sees Lee Oswald approach her residence for the ride

---

"There are things about Lee that only a mother could know."
—MARGUERITE OSWALD
December 1974

---

into town. Lee is wearing a light brown or tan shirt, she says, and carrying a long package which at various times she describes as twenty-seven inches long, and three feet by six feet. [CD5:320; 24:223, 408]

NOVEMBER 22
7:20 A.M.

Lee Oswald puts a package of what he calls curtain rods on the backseat of Frazier's 1954 black four-door Chevrolet sedan. [24:209; 26:385; CD5:316-17]

NOVEMBER 22
7:25 A.M.

Lee Oswald and Frazier leave for work; Oswald does not bring his lunch, telling Frazier he'll buy it. The next day in a jail interview he insists that lunch was the only package he brought. [24:209, 223, 293, 482]

NOVEMBER 22
EN ROUTE TO WORK

Lee Oswald tells Frazier he will not be riding with him back to Irving that afternoon. [26:385; W.P. 12-1-63]

NOVEMBER 22
7:55 A.M.

Frazier and Lee Oswald arrive at the Texas

School Book Depository for work. Lee Oswald goes from Depository parking lot to the building carrying the long package in his right hand, with the other end in his armpit. [24:409; CD897:23, 24]

NOVEMBER 22
Bonnie Ray Williams says that many TSBD employees are planning to watch the motorcade from the sixth floor. [3:169]

NOVEMBER 22
8:00 A.M.
TSBD employee Jack Dougherty sees Lee Oswald enter the building without a package. [6:376; CD206:11]

NOVEMBER 22
8:45 A.M.
Officers in motorcade route have a detail meeting in the City Hall basement for fifteen minutes. [22:599]

NOVEMBER 22
8:50 A.M.
White House security and communications staff is at the Trade Mart. [CD3]

NOVEMBER 22
9:00 A.M.
Abraham Zapruder goes home to retrieve his movie camera. [*The Death of a President*, p. 656]

NOVEMBER 22
9:05 A.M.
Richard Nixon departs from Dallas's Love Field aboard American Airlines flight #*82* for New York. [*The Death of a President*, p. 656]

NOVEMBER 22
9:30 A.M.
Jack Ruby gets up at his Ewing Street apartment (contradicted elsewhere—he was at his sister Eva Grant's place). [14:433; 20:49]

NOVEMBER 22
9:30-10:00 A.M.
Lee Oswald asks James Junior Jarman, a fellow employee, about the presidential motorcade route. [3:200; 24:213; CD334]

NOVEMBER 22
9:45 A.M.
Close to 200 city and county officers gather at the Trade Mart for the day's detail. Sheriff Bill Decker instructs his deputy sheriffs to be spectators along the motorcade route and to "take no part in security." [*JFK Assassination File*, p. 23; *Two Men In Dallas* (film)]

NOVEMBER 22
10:00 A.M.
Lee Oswald fills book orders to be shipped. [*Life* 2-21-64]

NOVEMBER 22
10:00 A.M.
Jack Ruby goes to the *Morning News* and eats breakfast there. [5:183; 25:281, 563, 858]

NOVEMBER 22
10:15 A.M.
Hank Norman, TSBD employee, sees Lee Oswald looking out the Elm Street first floor

"If Oswald was indeed a madman acting alone, what justification is there for keeping these documents classified? The most probable explanation is that they link Oswald or Ruby or both to U.S. intelligence agencies."
—RICHARD SCHWEIKER
September 8, 1975

1963 *(cont.)*

window, a view which is obstructed by concrete panelling.

NOVEMBER 22
11:00 A.M.

Lee Oswald is seen on the first floor by Frazier and on the sixth floor by Danny Arce. [CD205:7; 24:209]

NOVEMBER 22
11:00 A.M.

Classified ad worker at the *Dallas Morning News* sees Jack Ruby at the elevator; Ruby waves and shouts, "The president is going to be here today!" [25:282]

NOVEMBER 22
11:25 A.M.

Air Force One departs for the short distance from Ft. Worth to Love Field in Dallas. [*The Death of a President*, p. 656]

NOVEMBER 22

Lee Oswald tells Police Captain Fritz on 11-23-63 that he had an apple and a cheese sandwich for lunch which he brought from Mrs. Paine's house. [24:19]

NOVEMBER 22

At lunchtime, Lee Oswald is invited by a co-worker to go with him. Oswald replies, "You go down and send the elevator back, and I'll join you in a few minutes." [CD296:3]

NOVEMBER 22
11:30 A.M.

Lee Oswald eats lunch with fellow employees Piper and Jarman on the first floor. [24:267, 482]

"From their attitude, I believe there is a chance that the program will indicate that there is no CIA connection with Oswald beyond that noted above. This could make a contribution to knocking down the paranoic belief to the contrary. We must, however, insure that Mr. Rather does learn anything which would cause the slightest doubt on the above account before he produces the programs in November."

—W. E. COLBY
CIA Director, concluding his comments on a just-completed interview with CBS correspondent Dan Rather and producer Les Midgley for their 11-75 documentaries on the J. F. K. assassination, September 6, 1975. (Author's note: In the last sentence of Colby's memo, the word "not" would seem appropriate between "does" and "learn"; otherwise, the sentence makes little sense. The above wording is, however, as it appears in Colby's memo.)

NOVEMBER 22
11:45 A.M.
Jarman, TSBD employee, says that all sixth-floor workers leave and are on the streets by noon. [24:213]

NOVEMBER 22
11:40-11:45 A.M.
B. R. Williams sees Lee Oswald on the east side of the sixth floor. Later he says it was the fifth floor. [22:681; CD329:13]

"We do have a dirty rumor [about Oswald being an FBI informant] that is very bad for the Commission . . . and it is very damaging to the agencies that are involved in it, and it must be wiped out insofar as it is possible to do so by this Commission."
—J. LEE RANKIN
Warren Commission chief counsel, during a commission meeting, January 27, 1964

NOVEMBER 22
Between 11:30 and 11:50 A.M., TSBD employee Billy Lovelady says he and four others leave the sixth floor of the building to go see the JFK motorcade. [6:337; 24:214]

NOVEMBER 22
11:50 A.M.
Bill Shelley, a supervisor at the TSBD, sees Lee Oswald on the first floor near a telephone. [7:390; 22:673]

NOVEMBER 22
11:50 A.M.
B. R. Williams eats chicken and drinks a Dr. Pepper, leaving the chicken bones and empty bottle on the sixth floor. He goes to the fifth floor, and at 12:05 says he hears three shots overhead. [CD329:13; CD5:330]

NOVEMBER 22
Shortly before noon Jack Dougherty sees Lee Oswald on the sixth floor. [24:206]

NOVEMBER 22
11:55 A.M.
Presidential motorcade leaves Love Field freight building 28/AA en route to Trade Mart for lunch speech by John Kennedy. The motorcade consists of: (1) motorcycles; (2) pilot car; (3) motorcycle; (4) Police Chief Curry, Sheriff J. E. Bill Decker, and two Secret Service men; (5) John Kennedy, Jacqueline Kennedy, John Connally, Nellie Connally, and two Secret Service men; (6) motorcycles; (7) seven Secret Service men; (8) Lyndon Johnson, Lady Bird Johnson, Senator Ralph Yarborough, and two security men; (9) four Secret Service men; (10) Mayor Earl Cabell, Mrs. Cabell, Congressman Ray Roberts; (11) communications car (wire services and press officer); (12) press pool convertible; (13) newsreel and motion picture car; (14) press pool convertible (local press); (15) four congressmen; (16) and (17) White House press buses; (18) Army Signal Corps; (19) Western Union; (20) and (21) extra vehicles for breakdown. Different sources have different motorcade vehicle orders. [24:351]

"I think this record ought to be destroyed."
—ALLEN DULLES
Warren Commission member and ex-CIA director at the conclusion of a commission meeting dealing with Oswald's alleged intelligence links, January 22, 1964

1963 *(cont.)*

NOVEMBER 22
12:00 NOON
Lee Oswald seen on the first floor by TSBD employee Piper. [6:383]

NOVEMBER 22
12:00 NOON (APPROX.)
Marina Oswald and Ruth Paine watch television reporting of the presidential motorcade. [22:762]

NOVEMBER 22
Employee Jack Dougherty works on the sixth floor until noon, then goes to the first floor lunchroom and eats. Shortly after returning to work on the fifth floor, he hears a shot. [CD5:366; CD206:11]

NOVEMBER 22
12:10 P.M.
Two telephone operators in Oxnard, Calif., on a toll call line serving 12,000 phones report a middle-aged woman's voice at 10:07-10:08 A.M. (P.S.T.) saying "The president is going to die at 10:10," followed by comments about the government and court system.

Then later, "the president is going to die at 12:30" followed by more antigovernment remarks. [CD1107:82, 83]

NOVEMBER 22
12:10 P.M.
TSBD president Jack Cason leaves the building to go home. [22:640]

NOVEMBER 22
12:25 P.M.
Following a noon lunch, three TSBD employees go to the fifth floor and soon hear shots above them. [CD329:12]

NOVEMBER 22
According to Geneva Hine, the only employee in the TSBD second floor office, the power goes off and the phones go dead in the building as the pilot car of the motorcade approaches. (She later changes story in interview with Penn Jones.) [6:395; CD3]

NOVEMBER 22
12:30 P.M.
Going eight to ten miles per hour after the turn onto Elm Street, Police Chief Curry says into police radio channel two, "Approaching triple underpass." [17:456]

NOVEMBER 22
12:30 P.M.
Seventy people are listed as being in the TSBD. [25:851]

NOVEMBER 22
12:30 P.M.
Shots ring out in Dealey Plaza. John Kennedy

"[The CIA's] leadership is now defunct. Allen Dulles is now defunct.

—LEE HARVEY OSWALD

in a radio interview on WDSU, New Orleans, August 21, 1963

is hit. John Connally is hit. A nearby curbstone is hit, sending a chip of cement into the cheek of motorcade observer James Tague. (Time estimates from the Secret Service, FBI, and Dallas Police vary from 12:30 to 12:35 P.M.)

NOVEMBER 22
12:30 P.M.

Jack Ruby, at the *Dallas Morning News* building, looks toward the Texas School Book Depository. [25:189]

NOVEMBER 22
12:30 P.M.

Lee Oswald later tells Dallas Police Captain Fritz that he was eating lunch on the second floor at this time with coworker Jarman and a third party. [4:224, 231]

"The Central Intelligence Agency has inquired if the [Zapruder] film copy in possession of this Bureau can be loaned to that Agency solely for training purposes."

—J. EDGAR HOOVER

in a letter to Warren Commission chief counsel Rankin, December 4, 1964

NOVEMBER 22
12:30 P.M.

Lee Oswald is said to have run from the sixth floor southeast corner to the TSBD front door. This takes one minute, forty-five seconds, according to FBI. [25:859]

NOVEMBER 22
12:30-12:35 P.M.

Dallas Police officer M. L. Baker, riding a motorcycle on the east side of Houston toward

"Life's publisher, the late C. D. Jackson, was so upset by the head-wound sequence [in the Zapruder film] that he proposed the company obtain all rights to the film and withhold it from public viewing at least until emotions had calmed. To this day the film has never been shown publicly."

—RICHARD B. STOLLEY

Life Los Angeles bureau chief who negotiated the film's purchase from Abraham Zapruder November 25, 1963, in *Esquire* magazine, November 1973

Elm from Main hears shots. Baker immediately runs to TSBD main entrance where he and building superintendent Roy Truly go upstairs into the building. Officer Baker, with gun drawn, approaches Lee Oswald on the second floor; Oswald is calm and collected, empty-handed, and wearing a light brown shirt. Truly tells Baker that Oswald is a building employee; they talk to him just inside the

1963 *(cont.)*

west door of the second floor lunchroom. Baker and Truly proceed to roof. [3:227-29, 239, 252, 263; 22:85; 24:199, 307]

NOVEMBER 22
12:30 P.M.

Chief Curry, into police radio channel two: "Get men on top of the underpass! See what happened up there! . . . Move all available men out of my department back into the railroad yards and try to determine what happened!" [17:456]

NOVEMBER 22
12:30-1:15 P.M.

Three shabbily dressed men are picked up by a Dallas policeman in the railroad behind the TSBD. The three are escorted away from the area by the police; no record of the apprehension found in police records. [Rockefeller Commission Report on CIA Domestic Activities, pp. 255-57; *Coup d'Etat in America*]

"It was the [Zapruder] film of the assassination which prompted me to go ahead and support the bill [sponsored by Congressman Henry Gonzalez calling for a new investigation]. When I saw that fatal shot I had that stick-in-the-gut feeling."
—NORMAN MINETA
U.S. Congressman from California, June 1975

NOVEMBER 22
12:30-1:00 P.M.

Pickets across from the Trade Mart, where Kennedy was to speak, are taken into protective custody. Picket signs have anti-Kennedy messages. Five people taken altogether, ages seventeen to thirty-four. [21:577; 25:856]

NOVEMBER 22
12:30-1:00 P.M.

Eugene Hale Brading (aka Jim Braden), an organized crime figure, is questioned coming out of the Dal-Tex building at Dealey Plaza; he says he was on the third floor using the phone. He is taken to the sheriff's office and released after showing his Gulf credit card as I.D. and saying that he had come to Dallas to visit oilman Lamar Hunt. [24:202; CD385:15, 16; see also *Legacy of Doubt*]

NOVEMBER 22

Richard Randolph Carr says he sees four men, including "a Latin," leave the TSBD after the assassination and drive away in a station wagon. [N.O.S.I. 2-19-69]

NOVEMBER 22
12:34 P.M.

Motorcade to Parkland Hospital includes: (1) lead car; (2) president's car; (3) presidential follow-up car (security); (4) vice-president's car; (5) vice-president's follow-up car. [CD677:1]

NOVEMBER 22
12:35 P.M.

FBI agents Shanklin and Clark, in charge of

the Dallas office, are told by a clerk of the assassination. The clerk learned it from watching television. [CD5:16]

NOVEMBER 22
12:35 P.M.
Television newsman Pierce Allman (WFAA) enters TSBD before it is sealed off. [*JFK Assassination File,* p. 55]

NOVEMBER 22
12:35 P.M.
Lee Oswald leaves the TSBD by the main entrance. [6:260, 340; 22:86]

NOVEMBER 22
12:36 P.M.
Presidential car arrives at Parkland Hospital. [*JFK Assassination File,* p. 32]

NOVEMBER 22
12:35-12:38 P.M.
Oswald says he gets on a bus at this time and rides a block or two before getting off in stalled traffic. [24:18, 232; 25:899]

NOVEMBER 22
12:40 P.M.
Lee Oswald gets on the "Marsalis" bus driven

by Cecil J. McWatters, at Elm and Murphy streets, according to McWatters. [2:283; 22:86]

NOVEMBER 22
12:43 P.M.
John Kennedy is wheeled into the emergency room at Parkland Hospital. [CD5:8]

NOVEMBER 22
12:43-12:44 P.M.
Police radio broadcasts a description of the assassin for the first time. [23:916]

NOVEMBER 22
12:40-12:45 P.M.
Captain Will Fritz at the Trade Mart learns of the shooting and rushes to Parkland Hospital. [24:351]

1963 *(cont.)*

NOVEMBER 22
12:45 P.M.
Dr. George Burkely, John Kennedy's physician, arrives at Parkland Hospital. [22:94]

NOVEMBER 22
12:45 P.M.
Jack Ruby calls Carousel Club bartender Andrew Armstrong and tells him "if anything happens we are closing the club," and that he'll be there in thirty minutes. [13:330; CD441:51]

NOVEMBER 22
12:45 P.M.
Police radio dispatch conversation: "Find out from Parkland the situation and see if the president will be able to appear out here [the Trade Mart], got all these people out here; need to know whether to feed them or what to announce. . . . Can you obtain information from [Curry] if the president is going to appear at the Trade Mart." Reply: "Very doubtful."[*JFK Assassination File*, p. 52]

NOVEMBER 22
12:46 P.M.
Lee Oswald gets off the bus, which is stalled in traffic at Elm and Poydras, getting bus transfer first; walks over to a cabstand at Lamar near Jackson. [24:18, 232; 25:899]

NOVEMBER 22
12:47 P.M.
Oswald gets into a cab driven by William Whaley. A lady approaches the cab, Oswald

"*After seeing the Zapruder film, supporting the lone assassin theory is like saying Hiroshima was hit by a firecracker.*"
—PAT SMALL
in the audience at a Zapruder film screening, Milwaukee, Wisconsin, October 1973

offers to give it up. Oswald does not appear to be in a hurry; has the cab take him to the 500 block of N. Beckley. [2:293; 22:86; 24:18, 228]

NOVEMBER 22
12:50 P.M.
Sgt. Gerald L. Hill and Patrolman J. M. Valentine arrive at the TSBD in squad car #207. [23:838, 845]

NOVEMBER 22
12:50 P.M.
Deputy Sheriff Roger Craig sees Lee Oswald jump into a station wagon driven by a dark-complected man. [D.M.N. 2-15-69]

"*I would not like to see vast investigations undertaken that might prove divisive rather than conclusive. . . . I have studied the material and seen the [Zapruder] film, but I don't believe a case has been made.*"
—JOHN TUNNEY
U.S. Senator from California, June 1975

NOVEMBER 22
12:50 P.M.

Plane carrying U.S. cabinet members en route to Japan turns around. [*The Death of a President,* p. 656]

NOVEMBER 22
12:54 P.M.

Dispatch to patrolman J. D. Tippit: "You are in the Oak Cliff area, are you not?" Tippit: "At Lancaster and Eighth." Dispatch: "You will be at large for any emergency that comes in." [21:393]

"I was forced to present a James Bond novel type conspiracy in a trial bound by the old rules. . . ."

—JIM GARRISON

True magazine, April 1975

NOVEMBER 22
12:55 P.M.

Radio dispatch: [Officer #100] has about six men shaking down the railroad yard back toward that direction." 21:393]

NOVEMBER 22
1:00 P.M.

John Kennedy's death is revealed to the Secret Service and Lyndon Johnson. [CD677:3]

NOVEMBER 22
1:00 P.M. (APPROX.)

Lee Oswald comes in the house at 1026 N.

Beckley where he has a room; housekeeper Mrs. Roberts has just heard on television that the president had been shot. Oswald stays no longer than four or five minutes. [CD5:353, 355; 22:86; 24:18]

NOVEMBER 22
1:00 P.M. (APPROX.)

Mrs. Earlene Roberts, housekeeper at Oswald's rooming house, sees a police car stop, honk several times, drive slowly by the house, all while Oswald is in his room. There are two uniformed policemen in the car, which is identified as probably #207. [6:443; 25:170, 909; 26:165]

NOVEMBER 22
AFTER 1:00 P.M.

Jack Ruby calls his sister Eva Grant to tell her about the shooting. [14:467]

NOVEMBER 22
1:10 P.M.

Deputy Sheriff Luke Mooney goes to the southeast corner of the sixth floor of the TSBD and sees a crease on a box propped in

---

"The Attorney General and the President would be glad to get any new information into the killing [from the Garrison conspiracy investigation] so it can be properly analyzed by proper authorities."

—GERALD FORD

in *The New York Times,* February 20, 1967

1963 *(cont.)*

"If they ever reopen the Kennedy assassination, the lid's going to fly right off this country."
—RON DELLUMS
U.S. Congressman from California; quoted in *The San Francisco Bay Guardian*, July 12, 1975

"If the conspiracy is as big and powerful as some Commission critics believe, Schweiker hasn't a prayer of reopening anything."
—WILLIAM RASPBERRY
The Washington Post, September 15, 1975

the window and sees three cartridge cases. Mooney leans out the window to shout this discovery to Sheriff Decker and Captain Fritz below. [3:284]

NOVEMBER 22
1:13 P.M.
Lyndon Johnson decides to leave the hospital before the public announcement of Kennedy's death is made. [CD677:4]

NOVEMBER 22
1:15 P.M.
A pedestrian, walking westward, is stopped by officer J. D. Tippit. [24:253]

NOVEMBER 22
1:15 P.M.
Officer Tippit is shot with a .38 pistol, according to witnesses. One shot enters the head, one the stomach, and one the chest. [1:18; 24:253]

NOVEMBER 22
1:15-1:18 P.M.
Various people see the Tippit murder and give conflicting reports of what they have seen. [*Esquire* 8-67]

NOVEMBER 22
1:16 P.M.

An unidentified citizen using a police radio cuts in on the frequency to inform the police of the killing of an officer (J. D. Tippit) on 10th Street between Marsalis and Beckley. [21:394]

NOVEMBER 22
1:19 P.M.

Lee Oswald runs to the Texas Theater. [17:471; 23:925; 24:253]

NOVEMBER 22
1:20 P.M.

Secret Service puts the bubble and canvas cover on the presidential car and takes it to Love Field to be put on the plane for Washington. [CD3]

NOVEMBER 22
1:23 P.M.

Police dispatch: "Wanted for investigation of assault to murder of a police officer: a white male, approximately 30, 5'8", slender build, black hair, white jacket, white shirt, and dark

---

"There is no hint that somebody else pulled the trigger or that Oswald had an accomplice. Thus there is no reason for reopening the hearing or even disturbing the public. The whole issue fails the test of relevancy."
—JOSEPH KRAFT
syndicated columnist, September 28, 1975

---

trousers. Last seen running west on Jefferson." [21:395]

NOVEMBER 22
1:28 P.M.

Scripps-Howard reporter Seth Kantor at Parkland Hospital feels a tug on his coat—it is Jack Ruby, an acquaintance, who asks Kantor if he should close down his club for three days. Ruby later denies going to Parkland Hospital; the Warren Commission chooses to believe Ruby over Kantor. [5:217; 14:563; 20:50; 24:121]

NOVEMBER 22
1:28 P.M.

Dispatch conversation regarding the Tippit shooting: "Is there any indication that it has any connection with this other [Kennedy's] shooting?" Dispatcher: "Well, the description on the suspects are similar, and it is possible." [This and all dispatcher conversations are from the Warren Commission transcript of the dispatch tapes.]

NOVEMBER 22
1:30 P.M.

Jefferson Avenue shoestore employees see Lee Oswald in the foyer of their store—he is suspicious looking to them. They follow him to the Texas Theater, which is showing Van Heflin in "War Is Hell," and ask ticket taker to call the police. [CD735:267-68]

NOVEMBER 22
1:30 P.M.

Malcom Kilduff, White House press officer,

1963 *(cont.)*

announces that John Kennedy is dead, adding that the fatal shot hit the president in the "right temple." [20:433; see also *Accessories After the Fact*]

NOVEMBER 22
1:31 P.M.
Jack Ruby calls his sister Eva Grant with news of Kennedy's death. [14:431; 15:324]

NOVEMBER 22
1:32 P.M.
Police officer J. D. Tippit pronounced dead on arrival at Methodist Hospital. It is never conclusively ascertained that the bullets in Tippit's body came from Lee Oswald's pistol. [*JFK Assassination File,* p. 67; CD774]

NOVEMBER 22
1:35 P.M.
Jack Ruby arrives at the Carousel Club; tells bartender Armstrong to notify employees that the club would be closed the entire weekend. [25:199]

NOVEMBER 22
1:37-1:54 P.M.
Lyndon Johnson and his party arrive at Love Field from Parkland Hospital. [17:424, 473; 23:924]

NOVEMBER 22
1:40 P.M.
Dallas Secret Service office asks its New Orleans counterpart to check on a Jack W. Martin in Goldonna, La.; twenty-six minutes

"I would favor reopening the investigation by a congressional committee, at least to satisfy those people who keep raising the questions about the original report."
—SAM ERVIN
former U.S. senator from North Carolina; quoted in *Skeptic* magazine, September 1975

later Dallas SS reports that Martin may be an assassin. [CD87:SS450-51]

NOVEMBER 22
1:45 P.M.
Police dispatcher reports that the suspect is in the Texas Theater. [17:424]

NOVEMBER 22
1:44 P.M.
Mrs. Julia Postal, Texas Theater cashier, listens to the announcement of John Kennedy's death on the radio, and sees a man, later identified as Lee Oswald, enter the lobby. Johnny Brewer (shoestore employee from down the street) asks if a man had run into the theater. Brewer and usher/concession attendant Burroughs search unsuccessfully; Julia Postal calls Dallas Police. After hearing the description of the suspect, she tells police that the man in the theater is the suspect. Shortly after, the Dallas police "mobbed the place"—24 patrolmen in the theater. Oswald is in the center section downstairs. The lights go on at the Texas Theater and uniformed police with shotguns walk up each aisle. Offi-

cers "shake down" various customers; one officer comes forward toward the lobby and approaches a lone white male in the center. The officer hollers "Here he is!" Officers contain Oswald after a brief scuffle. Sgt. Gerald Hill ejects six shells from Oswald's pistol. Hill then radios that Oswald is in a green unmarked Ford DPD Special Service Bureau car en route to City Hall. [7:57; 17:424; 21:397; CD735:265, 266; TAG1:75; CD206:68, 69; *Investigation of a Homicide*, p. 107]

NOVEMBER 22
1:45 P.M.
FBI agent R. M. Barret observes the arrest of Lee Oswald. [CD5:841]

NOVEMBER 22
1:58 P.M.
The hearse with Kennedy's body in it leaves Parkland Hospital, arriving at Love Field fifteen minutes later. [CD677; 23:882, 884, 930]

"I am totally opposed to this whole procedure. I will do anything I can to kill it [the bill to reopen the assassination investigation]. . . . I don't know what we have got to gain, even if we proved that Oswald did not even shoot him. I still don't know what difference that is going to make at this stage."

—JAMES SISK

U.S. Congressman from California, opposing the bill to reopen the investigation in the House Rules Committee, March 31, 1976

NOVEMBER 22
2:00 P.M. (APPROX.)
Parkland Hospital employee Tomlinson finds a slug at the hospital, referred to as Commission Exhibit #399 in the Warren Report. The slug had rolled from under a mattress on possibly the president's or Connally's or a third stretcher when Tomlinson was straightening out the stretchers, it is alleged. It is never ascertained how the slug got there in the first place. The slug is in virtually pristine condition, flattened slightly at the base. It is given to Secret Service agent Richard Johnson. [18:800; 24:249, 412; *The Day Kennedy Was Shot*, p. 294]

NOVEMBER 22
2:10 P.M.
Lee Oswald is taken into the homicide office of the Dallas Police Department—on the third floor of City Hall. [7:180; 24:320]

NOVEMBER 22
2:10-2:30 P.M.
Officer M. L. Baker, who stopped Lee Oswald on the second floor of the TSBD immediately after the assassination, identifies Oswald at City Hall. [24:307]

NOVEMBER 22
2:15 P.M.
FBI agent James P. Hosty, Jr., who had previously investigated Lee Oswald, arrives at City Hall the same time as Lt. Revill of the Special Services Bureau (Intelligence), DPD, does. On the way to the third floor, Revill says Hosty makes the statement that the FBI real-

1963 *(cont.)*

ized that Oswald was capable of the assassination. [24:22]

NOVEMBER 22
2:30-4:00 P.M.
Captain Fritz and others interrogate Lee Oswald in the homicide office. No transcript—written or taped—is made of the interview. [7:160; 24:320]

NOVEMBER 22
David Ferrie spends part of the day in federal court in New Orleans as his current employer, mobster Carlos Marcello, is cleared of charges leading to his temporary deportation by the Justice Department 4-4-61. [*They've Killed the President!*, p. 106]

NOVEMBER 22
In custody, Oswald's wallet is catalogued. It contains a Selective Service Registration certificate; Social Security card; U.S. Forces, Japan card; card from a Japanese hotel; snapshot of himself in a Marine uniform; a Department of Defense I.D. card; USMC certificate of service; Selective Service classification; photo of Marina; snapshot of a small baby in a white cap; slip of paper with the address of the Soviet Embassy in Washington, with counselor's name; a slip of paper with the address of *The Worker;* Dallas Public Library card; Fair Play for Cuba Committee membership card, signed A. J. Hidell; another Fair Play for Cuba Committee membership card, signed V. T. Lee; a Selective Service classification card for Alek James Hidell, signed Alek J. Hidell—with a photo of Lee Oswald; USMC certificate of service for Alek James Hidell. [*JFK Assassination File*]

"I now fully realize that only the powers of the presidency will reveal the secrets of my brother's death."
—ROBERT F. KENNEDY
to several students at San Fernando Valley State College, June 3, 1968

NOVEMBER 22
Lee Oswald during interrogation gives Dallas Police detective Sims his ring to hold. [7:180; 22:178; 24:288, 320]

NOVEMBER 22
2:38 P.M.
Dallas police radio conversation: "One of the Secret Service men on the field, Elm and Houston, said that it came over his teletype that one of the Secret Service men had been killed." Dispatcher: "Well, 10-4, I don't have that information." [17:481]

NOVEMBER 22
2:38 P.M.
Lyndon Johnson is sworn in as thirty-sixth U.S. President by Federal District Court Judge Sarah T. Hughes aboard Air Force One. [17:478; 23:934]

NOVEMBER 22
2:40 P.M.

Dr. Malcom Perry at Parkland Hospital, who viewed the president's body, tells NBC News that Kennedy was struck "in front as he faced the assailant." Oswald's position was to the rear. [*Seventy Hours and Thirty Minutes*]

NOVEMBER 22
2:45 P.M. (APPROX.)

Scripps-Howard White House correspondent Seth Kantor calls his office in Washington from Dallas to report on events thus far, and is told to call Scripps-Howard reporter Hal Hendrix in Miami, who already has the accused assassin's full name before anyone else, and identifies him as a Castroite. Hendrix, later identified by ex-intelligence operatives as a reporter the CIA could count on as early as 1962, becomes a top executive for International Telephone and Telegraph in Latin America in 1967. In congressional testimony later he is identified as a CIA operative during the successful military coup against Salvador Allende in 1973. Seth Kantor's telephone records for that day become classified by the FBI, and released to him following a Freedom of Information action in 1975. Notation of only one call was deleted—the call to Hendrix. [*Detroit News* 12-14-75; *The CIA and the Cult of Intelligence,* by Marks and Marchetti; *The Ruby Detail.*]

NOVEMBER 22
2:47 P.M.

Air Force One, with Lyndon Johnson, Jacqueline Kennedy, the casket, and others aboard, takes off from Love Field for Andrews Air Force Base outside Washington, D.C. [*The Death of a President,* p. 657]

NOVEMBER 22
2:50 P.M.

Ruth Paine says she and Marina Oswald are sitting on the couch watching television when deputy sheriffs knock; it is the first she knows that Lee is a suspect. [CD634:3]

NOVEMBER 22
2:55 P.M.

First photo of Lee Oswald, taken forty-five minutes earlier, transmitted over AP wire. [CD897:2; CD723]

NOVEMBER 22

FBI agent Hosty tells Secret Service agents that Lee Oswald had contacts with two known foreign subversive agents. Also, that he cannot tell Captain Fritz about Oswald's previous activities known to the FBI. [CD349:SS974; 24:22]

NOVEMBER 22

In his report of the questioning of Lee Os-

"I think with further investigation we might shed some more light on the Kennedy matter, Martin Luther King's matter, and the matter involving myself."

—GEORGE WALLACE
on KNBC-TV, Los Angeles, August 18, 1975

1963 *(cont.)*

wald, homicide captain Will Fritz says Oswald admits having been in Russia but denies a trip to Mexico; that he does not own a rifle; that he usually works on the second floor of the TSBD; that he was on the first floor eating lunch when the assassination occurred; that he went to his room and changed trousers, got his pistol, and went to the movie. [24:264]

NOVEMBER 22
AFTERNOON

Larry Crafard, who lives in Jack Ruby's office at the Carousel Club, says that Carousel Club bartender Andrew Armstrong tells him Lee Oswald has been to the club. [14:46]

NOVEMBER 22
AFTER 3:20 P.M.

David Ferrie and two others—Alvin Beauboeuf and Melvin Coffey—leave New Orleans and drive to Houston and Galveston, Tex.; the trip is called a celebration for New Orleans organized crime figure Carlos Marcello. Ferrie had worked as a private investigator for Marcello's victorious lawyer Wray Gill. In Houston they go to the Winterland Skating Rink. Ferrie never puts on skates, but instead stands by the pay phone making and receiving calls. He keeps saying, "I'm David Ferrie." [*Heritage of Stone*, p. 116; D.M.N. 2-19-67]

NOVEMBER 22
3:00 P.M.

Three Dallas police detectives go to Mrs.

REPORTER: *Do you think that the Warren Commission should reopen in view of the things that have been revealed in Dallas in the last few weeks?*

GERALD FORD: *I haven't seen any new evidence that would justify a reopening.*

—**exchange at a press conference**
September 13, 1975

Paine's Irving, Tex., home; wait for deputy sheriffs to arrive before beginning a search of the home. [9:448]

NOVEMBER 22
3:15-8:00 P.M. (APPROX.)

Various reporters from WFAA see Jack Ruby at the City Hall police station. [15:350; 21:309]

NOVEMBER 22
3:30 P.M.

Jack Ruby goes to the Ritz Deli to buy food; expresses concern to acquaintances about the effect of the assassination on Dallas convention business. [25:185, 230]

NOVEMBER 22

Sheriff's deputy Walthers gets five or six metal boxes of Lee Oswald's files and correspondence from the Paine residence. [7:548, 549]

NOVEMBER 22
4:00 P.M.

Two detectives take Lee Oswald to the City Hall basement for a lineup; he is searched first. They find: five .38 shells; a bus transfer; $13.87; a bracelet which says "Lee"; a post office box key; other odds and ends. [7:180; 22:178; 24:287, 320]

NOVEMBER 22
4:05-4:20 P.M.
Lee Oswald is in his first lineup with three others. [24:304, 347; see also *Accessories After the Fact*]

NOVEMBER 22
4:00-5:00 P.M. (APPROX.)
According to bartender Andrew Armstrong, Jack Ruby briefly returns to the Carousel Club. [13:336; 19:357]

NOVEMBER 22
4:00-5:00 P.M. (APPROX.)
Jack Ruby calls his synagogue to determine the time of memorial services for Kennedy. [25:142]

NOVEMBER 22
EARLY AFTERNOON
Jack Ruby places CLOSED signs on the Carousel and Vegas clubs. [CD86:498]

NOVEMBER 22
4:00-4:30 P.M.
AP photographer Ferdinand Kaufman of

"I say what's wrong with the old *evidence?"*
—MARK LANE
in numerous speeches, 1965 to the present

Dallas meets Jack Ruby on the third floor of City Hall. Ruby boasts that his ad in the next morning's *News* will be the only one showing a nightclub closed for three days. [25:180]

NOVEMBER 22
4:58 P.M.
Air Force One touches down at Andrews Air Force Base. [CD677:5]

NOVEMBER 22
In Mexico City Mrs. Silvia Duran, a Mexican citizen employed at the Cuban consulate when Lee Oswald visited 9-27-63, is arrested; later she is released. [24:590; D.M.N. 11-29-64]

NOVEMBER 22
5:18 P.M.
Deputy sheriff Roger Craig identifies Lee Oswald as the man who got into a white Rambler station wagon at the TSBD twenty minutes after the assassination. When Craig identifies Oswald in Captain Fritz's office, the suspect stands and says, "That station wagon belongs to Mrs. Paine; leave her out of it. Now everyone will know who I am." [23:817; from the Garrison investigation 11-11-67]

NOVEMBER 22
Washington officials assure the nation that the assassination was the work of one person alone. White House aide Cliff Carter, expressing concern of a possible conspiracy indictment in the assassination, telephones Dallas D.A. Henry Wade to make sure no

1963 *(cont.)*

such indictment will occur. [*They've Killed the President!*, p. 248; also see *Schweiker Report*]

NOVEMBER 22
5:45 P.M.

Marina Oswald and Ruth Paine are brought to the City Hall police station. [24:291]

NOVEMBER 22
6:00 P.M.

Dallas policeman Henry Moore and assistant D. A. Bill Alexander go to Lee Oswald's Beckley Street rooming house. [7:213, 222]

NOVEMBER 22
6:00 P.M.

Through a police interpreter Marina Oswald says that husband Lee probably brought the guns over from Russia and that she had never seen the gun shown her. [9:114, 116]

NOVEMBER 22
6:00-8:00 P.M.

Jack Ruby is seen outside the third floor homicide office interrogation room; he identifies various officers for newspeople, and detectives talk with him. [24:477]

NOVEMBER 22
6:20-6:35 P.M.

Lee Oswald's second interrogation ends, and he is taken to another lineup. [24:347]

NOVEMBER 22
6:37 P.M.

Oswald is questioned by reporters in the hall on his way back to the third floor, according to Scripps-Howard reporter Seth Kantor. [15:78; 20:339, 436]

NOVEMBER 22
6:37-6:40 P.M.

Lee Oswald undergoes his third interrogation of the day; expresses surprise that Governor Connally was shot. [7:315]

NOVEMBER 22

Dallas police announce that Lee Oswald has been arraigned in Captain Fritz's office for the murder of officer Tippit. [7:159]

NOVEMBER 22

While Lee Oswald is being questioned by the FBI, Captain Fritz interrogates Marina Oswald and Ruth Paine in the forgery bureau offices. [24:291; CD5:92-95]

NOVEMBER 22
7:40-7:55 P.M.

Lee Oswald is taken to the basement for his third lineup. [24:347]

NOVEMBER 22
7:55 P.M.

Lee Oswald, speaking to reporters, says, "I'm just a patsy." [15:78; 20:339, 436]

NOVEMBER 22
8:00 P.M.

The plane with motorcade cars arrives at Washington; cars are driven to the White House garage. [*The Death of a President*, p. 656]

NOVEMBER 22
8:35 P.M.

Lee Oswald is fingerprinted. [7:174; 24:287, 321]

NOVEMBER 22
9:00 P.M.

Jack Ruby is seen handing out Carousel Club free admittance cards next to the third floor elevator at City Hall. [24:467]

NOVEMBER 22
AFTER 9:00 P.M.

Assistant District Attorney Bill Alexander tells the press of a "Communist conspiracy." Fifteen minutes later Lyndon Johnson aide Clifford Carter calls Texas Attorney General Waggoner Carr asking him to call Alexander requesting no more allegations of foreign conspiracy. [*Jack Ruby*, p. 70; 5:259]

NOVEMBER 22
9:50-10:00 P.M.

Jack Ruby attends memorial services for Kennedy at Congregation Shearith Israel. Ruby asks people what the rabbi was talking about when he arrives. "I heard the end of it,"

"After the assassination Fidel Castro aptly pointed out that only fools could rejoice at such a tragedy, for systems, not men, are the enemy."

—PHIL OCHS

in the liner notes to his album "I Ain't Marching Any More," 1964

"Through two emissaries—one being Ambassador Attwood, the other a French journalist by the name of Daniel—the young president had implemented secret negotiations with the Castro regime to reestablish relations between the U.S. and Cuba. These negotiations were due to bear fruit on the very day Kennedy died."

—ROBERT D. MORROW

former CIA contract agent, to Congressman Thomas Downing, August 2, 1976

---

he says later. "But my mind was so foggy I didn't know what he was talking about." [5:187; 24:295; TAG5:D28]

NOVEMBER 22
10:00 P.M.

Paraffin casts are made of Lee Oswald's arms and cheeks. Result: some traces of nitrate on hands, none on cheeks. The Warren Commission dismisses the finding as inconclusive. [7:174; 26:699; *Accessories After the Fact*, p. 171]

NOVEMBER 22
10:30 P.M.

Jack Ruby goes straight from *shul* to Phil's Deli and buys sandwiches for Dallas police. (Eight corned beef sandwiches—potato salad and pickle with each; eight black cherry sodas; 2 celery tonics; three cups of butter; half loaf of bread; extra pickles. Total: $9.50.) [CD86:501; 25:146, 176, 201, 202]

1963 *(cont.)*

NOVEMBER 22
11:35 P.M.
The plane carrying six Cabinet members arrives at Washington, D.C., after a midday refueling stop in Hawaii. [*The Death of a President,* p. 657]

NOVEMBER 22
12:10 A.M.
Lee Oswald is brought before reporters for

Dallas strip-joint, May 1974.

© 1974 Jon Whitsell

five to ten minutes; Jack Ruby is present. [7:174; 15:505; 24:321; 25:153]

NOVEMBER 23
Shortly after midnight Dallas policeman Harry Olsen, Carousel Club stripper Kathy Kay Coleman, Jack Ruby, and a parking lot attendant converse at the Simons Parking Garage. [14:630, 642, 646; 25:279, 280, 521]

NOVEMBER 23
12:23 A.M.
Lee Oswald is taken back upstairs to the jail, and District Attorney Henry Wade holds an impromptu press conference which lasts until 1:00-1:30 A.M. When Wade says Oswald is a member of the "Free Cuba Committee, an anti-Castro group," he is corrected by Jack Ruby: "No, Henry, that's Fair Play for Cuba Committee." [5:189; 7:174; 15:458; 25:480]

NOVEMBER 23
2:00-2:30 A.M.
Jack Ruby visits KLIF-radio near City Hall. Shortly after this he calls Larry Crafard at the Carousel Club, tells him to get a polaroid camera and flashbulbs and meet him on Commerce Street. Later, Ruby, Crafard and Ruby's roommate George Senator photograph an "Impeach Earl Warren" billboard and go to the post office to determine the holder of the box number given in the Weissman anti-Kennedy ad in the 11-22-63 *Morning News.* [13:463; 14:87, 324; 15:254; 23:460]

NOVEMBER 23

Jack Lawrence terminates his employment at Downtown Lincoln-Mercury in Dallas because of his arrest the previous day by Dallas Police for suspicious behavior. The dealership is not far from Dealey Plaza. Lawrence had worked there approximately five weeks. [CD85:376]

NOVEMBER 23

School Book Depository records, which show Lee Oswald listed as "Leslie" Oswald, says that Oswald worked a full eight hours every day including 11-22-63. [23:751]

NOVEMBER 23

Lyndon Johnson calls Dallas Police homicide chief Will Fritz asking him to halt the police probe, saying "You've got your man." [*Cover-Up,* p. 186; also *Forgive My Grief III* (rev. ed.)]

NOVEMBER 23

District Attorney Henry Wade says he thinks Oswald had the assassination well-planned, even to what he'd say if caught. He thinks Oswald is of above-average intelligence. [24:844]

NOVEMBER 23
10:25 A.M.

Lee Oswald is taken to the third floor homicide office for further interrogation, which lasts until 11:33 A.M. Oswald says the following: denies he is a member of the Communist party; belongs to the American Civil Liberties Union; picked up the name "Hidell" while in the Fair Play for Cuba Committee; the photo of him holding the rifle is a fake; denies owning a rifle; describes the street fight in New Orleans when he was passing out FPCC leaflets; bought a pistol in Ft. Worth seven months previous; his belongings are in Mrs. Paine's garage; denies carrying a package to the TSBD; brought a sandwich and fruit to work the previous day for lunch; had nothing personal against John Kennedy; did not watch the motorcade; ate lunch with fellow employee Junior Jarman; denies shooting John Kennedy; does not know how John Connally was shot; left the TSBD by bus; changed clothes in his room; wants New York lawyer John Abt for his attorney. Like Oswald's other interrogation sessions, neither tape nor stenographer records the questioning. [24:272]

NOVEMBER 23

Jack Ruby is on the third floor of City Hall between noon and 1:00 P.M. when Lee Oswald is brought to that floor for his fifth interrogation. Oswald is returned to his jail cell at 1:10 P.M. Shortly after this, wife Marina and mother Marguerite visit him for twenty minutes. Oswald tries to call New York lawyer John Abt, and at 2:15 he is taken to another lineup. [7:199; 24:228, 249, 268, 471; 25:154, 286]

NOVEMBER 23
3:00-4:00 P.M.

Jack Ruby visits Dealey Plaza and talks with Dallas police officer James Chaney. [20:42]

1963 *(cont.)*

NOVEMBER 23
4:00 P.M.

Lee Oswald telephones Ruth Paine from the jail twice and asks her to contact New York attorney John Abt. [3:86]

NOVEMBER 23
4:00 P.M.

New Orleans attorney Dean Andrews calls his secretary from his hospital bed to say that he will be representing Lee Oswald. He says he is asked to take the case by a man named Clay Bertrand. [26:357; Garrison investigation]

NOVEMBER 23
4:00-5:00 P.M.

Jack Ruby is seen again on the third floor of City Hall. [15:598]

NOVEMBER 23
5:55 P.M.

Police Chief Jesse Curry announces that Lee Oswald will be transferred to the county jail the following morning. [15:588]

NOVEMBER 23
6:00 P.M.

Lee Oswald is again interrogated and tells homicide captain Fritz that the photos of him with the rifle and the leftist newspapers are fake. He is returned to his jail cell after an hour and fifteen minutes. [24:269, 272, 289, 321, 481]

NOVEMBER 23
7:30 P.M.

Lee Oswald phones Ruth Paine. [3:86]

"The revolution can categorically confirm that it never had the least participation in the death of President John F. Kennedy. Kennedy's death is still a mystery, because the role which the CIA and FBI played has not been cleared up."

—FIDEL CASTRO

on Radio Havana; quoted by United Press, June 7, 1976

NOVEMBER 23

Late in the evening, the Secret Service locates Kerry Thornley, Lee Oswald's old Marine buddy, at a restaurant job in New Orleans. Thornley denies having seen Oswald since 1959. [CD87]

NOVEMBER 23
9:00 P.M.

Dallas police officer Harry Olsen and girl friend/Carousel Club stripper Kathy Kay Coleman talk with Jack Ruby outside the closed Carousel Club about having Lee Oswald "lynched." [14:649; *Playboy* 1-67]

NOVEMBER 23
9:00 P.M.

David Ferrie and friends Alvin Beaubouef and Melvin Coffey leave a Houston restaurant and decide to drive to Galveston. [CD75:289, 290]

NOVEMBER 23
10:45 P.M.

Mrs. A. A. Troon, switchboard operator at

City Hall, says Lee Oswald places a call to a John Hurt in Raleigh, N.C. [Affidavit secured by Bernard Fensterwald 5-29-69]

NOVEMBER 23
11:00 P.M.

David Ferrie and two traveling companions check into the Driftwood Motel in Galveston, leaving at 10:00 A.M. the next morning. [*Kennedy Conspiracy,* p. 28]

NOVEMBER 24

Lyndon Johnson tells Dallas police chief Curry not to say anything regarding a conspiracy. [24:504]

NOVEMBER 24
12:30 A.M.

Captain Fritz thinks that at this time Jack Ruby calls the sheriff's office, threatening harm to Lee Oswald. [4:233; 12:48; 24:353]

NOVEMBER 24
2:15 A.M.

FBI Dallas office receives anonymous phone call warning that Lee Oswald would be shot during the upcoming transfer to the Dallas County Jail from the city lockup. The city police and sheriff's office receive anonymous threats as well. [D.T.H. 11-25-63; 24:429; CD5:402; CD1084b:2]

NOVEMBER 24
6:30 A.M.

A Dallas Police squad car goes to Chief Curry's home; asks him to call the office. His phone is off the hook. [CD1196]

NOVEMBER 24

David Ferrie and his two companions go goosehunting in Galveston. Jim Garrison determines that no one has taken along any shotguns on this goosehunting trip. [*Ramparts* 1-68, p. 46]

NOVEMBER 24
8:00 A.M.

WBAP-TV engineer Rickey sees Jack Ruby outside the station truck parked next to City Hall. Fifteen minutes later another WBAP-TV employee sees Ruby nearby. [D.T.H. 3-11-64; 13:256, 278; 21:300, 530]

NOVEMBER 24
9:00 A.M.

Police begin setting up security for transfer of Lee Oswald through the basement. [24:48]

NOVEMBER 24
9:30 A.M.

Plano, Tex., radio evangelist Ray Rushing goes to City Hall after checking with Sheriff Decker; rides to third floor in elevator with Jack Ruby, with whom he discusses the weather. [12:75, 295]

NOVEMBER 24
10:00 A.M.

WBAP-TV personnel see Jack Ruby again outside City Hall; Ruby asks one of them twice if Lee Oswald has come down yet. [13:256, 278; 24:184]

NOVEMBER 24

Commander J.J. Humes, Chief Autopsy Sur-

1963 *(cont.)*

geon at Bethesda Naval Hospital, burns the first draft of his Kennedy autopsy report at his home. [2:373]

NOVEMBER 24
9:30-10:30 A.M.

Conflicting stories about Jack Ruby's activities; he is evidently on his way to the Western Union office near City Hall to wire money ($25) to a Carousel Club employee Karen Bennett Carlin (aka Little Lynn). Ruby takes his dog with him. [TAG5:B11; CD86:507; 13:211; 14:237; 19:306; 21:436]

NOVEMBER 24
AFTER 10:00 A.M.

Officer Roy E. Vaughn guards the Main Street ramp into the City Hall basement from which Lee Oswald is to be moved. He says Jack Ruby does not pass him. Later, Chief Curry says that Vaughn is responsible for letting Ruby into the basement. Various other stories about how Ruby gains access to the basement include that he has a press pass or comes in through the elevator from above with a high-ranking officer. [12:42, 80, 261, 315, 336; 24:110, 454; CD85:373, 374]

NOVEMBER 24
10:45-11:00 A.M.

Jack Ruby parks his car at the parking lot on the northwest corner of Main and Pearl, leaving his wallet in the glove compartment along with the trunk keys (the trunk contained over $800 in cash). [13:274; 24:330, 495]

NOVEMBER 24
11:00 A.M.

Armored cars arrive at City Hall for the Oswald transfer. [24:29, 48]

NOVEMBER 24
11:10 A.M.

Final interrogation of Lee Oswald ends at the homicide office. Present are two Secret Service men, one FBI agent, one postal inspector, Captain Fritz, and seven detectives. Soon thereafter Oswald is escorted out of the room. [24:91, 169, 272, 289]

NOVEMBER 24
11:16 A.M.

Jack Ruby is at the Western Union office sending a $25 money order to an employee. A pistol is in his right trousers pocket. [22:498; 24:40, 435; 25:523; CD1252:4]

"As soon as Life *magazine published its cover photos with the caption 'Lee Oswald With the Weapons He Used . . . ,' we noticed an inconsistency. While the shadow under Oswald's nose falls directly down, the shadow under his body falls sharply to the right and rear. Now unless the head was superimposed on the photo as Oswald claimed, there is only one other possibility, and that's that the picture was taken in a society that enjoys a dual solar system."*

—MARK LANE

in his lecture, 1965 to the present

NOVEMBER 24
11:19 A.M.

Jack Ruby says he enters the Main Street ramp by walking past the car of Lt. Rio Pierce who was talking with officer Vaughn. [5:199; 14:540]

NOVEMBER 24
11:19 A.M.

Captain Fritz, Detective J.R. Leavelle, and three others surround Lee Oswald upon leaving the jail office; Leavelle is handcuffed to Oswald's right hand. At this time a WBAP-TV employee sees Jack Ruby on the ramp leading into the basement. [13:140; 24:48; TAG1:226]

NOVEMBER 24
11:19 A.M.

Detective Charles Brown drives an unmarked police car up behind the armored car. This car is to be driven to the County Jail. Another detective drives another unmarked police car behind Brown's car; this one is to carry Lee Oswald to the County Jail. [24:48, 289]

NOVEMBER 24
11:20 A.M.

Jack Ruby lunges between detective Blackie Harrison and KRLD reporter R.S. Huffaker, Jr., as a policeman says "Jack, you sonvabich." Ruby shoots Lee Oswald with a .38 Colt Cobra. Ruby shouts, "You all know me. I'm Jack Ruby!" [24:48, 436, 437; 26:499; *Jack Ruby*, pp. 59, 73]

NOVEMBER 24
11:20 A.M.

Marina Oswald is at the home of the Irving, Tex., Police Chief. [CD5:293]

NOVEMBER 24
11:21 A.M.

Lee Oswald is dragged back to the jail office where a medical student massages his chest. [*Coup D'Etat: Three Murders . . .*, p. 40, 41]

NOVEMBER 24
11:21 A.M.

Jack Ruby is arrested in the City Hall basement by detectives L.C. Graves and Harrison. [TAG1:75]

NOVEMBER 24
11:21 A.M.

Funeral home logs call for ambulance for Lee Oswald. [24:48]

NOVEMBER 24
11:00 A.M.-NOON

When arrested, Ruby is carrying: a .38 caliber revolver; five live rounds; one cartridge case; a .38 slug; $2,117.33 in cash and traveler's checks. [25:517, 520; CD101b:4; CD87: SS639:1]

NOVEMBER 24
11:32 A.M.

Lee Oswald is in the Parkland Hospital emergency room. [24:438]

NOVEMBER 24
11:45 A.M.

Secret Service Agent Sorrells says that Jack Ruby refuses to answer some of Captain

1963 *(cont.)*

Fritz's questions at his first interrogation. He does say, however, that he is a Democrat, but

---

"Well, I don't know the facts, see, so I don't know really—I read a lot of things, I hear a lot of things about—and, you know, you see cartoons and so forth. But you can't necessarily get factual information from the cartoons."
—NELSON ROCKEFELLER
Vice-President of the United States, commenting on the drive to reopen the assassination investigation on *CBS Face the Nation*, May 30, 1976

---

votes for the man not the party; he owes the IRS a lot of money; he bought the revolver two or three years ago; he never saw Lee Oswald before 11-22-63; he heard a eulogy for John Kennedy at a synagogue; he came down the Main Street ramp. [24:511]

NOVEMBER 24
1:07 P.M.
Lee Oswald dies at Parkland Hospital. [24:48, 290]

NOVEMBER 24
National Security Action Memorandum #273 shifts U.S. policy in Vietnam from phased withdrawal to "central objective" of "winning"; also calls for authorized planning for specific covert operations, graduated in intensity, against the D.R.V. (North Vietnam). Memorandum approved two days later. [*The Assassinations: Dallas and Beyond*, pp. 406-443]

NOVEMBER 24
3:05 P.M.
Jack Ruby is arraigned before Judge Pierce McBride. [D.M.N. 11-25-63]

NOVEMBER 24
AFTERNOON
David Ferrie tries unsuccessfully to call G. Wray Gill (attorney for Carlos Marcello) from Alexandria, La. He then calls home, learns of allegations against him in connection with the assassination, and drives to New Orleans. [CD75:228]

NOVEMBER 24

In the evening Dallas attorney C. A. Droby arranges a meeting at the apartment of Jack Ruby between Ruby roommate George Senator, lawyers Tom Howard and Jim Martin, and reporters Jim Koethe (*Dallas Times Herald*) and Bill Hunter (*Long Beach Press Telegram,* Calif.). Meeting participants report nothing substantial discussed. [*Forgive My Grief I,* p. 5]

NOVEMBER 25

Texas Attorney General Waggoner Carr announces a state "court of inquiry" to hold public hearings to "develop fully and disclose openly" information about the assassination. Special Counsels are to be Robert Storey and Leon Jaworski. [*Inquest,* pp. 5-6; N.Y.T. 11-26-63]

NOVEMBER 25

David Ferrie and Alvin Beauboeuf are both arrested in New Orleans on their return from Texas; Layton Mortens is arrested at Ferrie's apartment at the same time. All arrests are in connection with the Kennedy assassination. They are questioned by the Secret Service, the FBI, and Jim Garrison. [*Oswald in New Orleans,* p. 21; CD75:285; CD87:SS620:3, 4]

NOVEMBER 25

Assistant District Attorney in New Orleans says that Ferrie was arrested when he denied knowing Lee Oswald; a New Orleans police officer asserted that he was in the Civil Air Pa-

"Our high school is such a drag. The day Kennedy got shot, all the other schools let out after fourth period, but we had to stay till seventh."

—LILY TOMLIN
as a 1960s teenager in her comedy routine

trol with both Ferrie and Oswald, and that Ferrie knew Oswald. [CD75:301]

NOVEMBER 25

Clay Shaw leaves San Francisco for Portland, Ore. [N.O.S.I. 2-27-69]

NOVEMBER 25

Clay Shaw arrives in Portland, Ore., from San Francisco, where he has been for the previous four days. Shaw is later implicated in the assassination by New Orleans District Attorney Jim Garrison. [N.O.S.I. 2-27-69]

NOVEMBER 25

FBI agent James P. Hosty, Jr., tells Secret Service agents Warner and Patterson that Lee Oswald had contacted two known foreign subversive agents within the previous fifteen days, although on whose behalf is unclear. [23:390; CD349:SS774]

NOVEMBER 25

FBI agent Horton contacts Irving Sports Shop where a rifle sight had been mounted with a receipt for mounting marked "Oswald" the previous month. [TAG1:253]

1963 *(cont.)*

NOVEMBER 25
Funeral services for John Kennedy attended by top officials and diplomats from abroad as well as many U.S. officials; casket buried at Arlington National Cemetery. Eternal Flame is lit. [*The Death of a President,* p. 658]

NOVEMBER 25
The CIA reports that Anastas Mikoyan's representation at the Kennedy funeral indicates Russia's peaceful intent; Mikoyan is close to Khrushchev. [CD100:1]

NOVEMBER 25
Jim Braden (Eugene Hale Brading) checks in with the U.S. Probation Office in Houston in the afternoon. [D.M.N. 11-22-73]

NOVEMBER 25
FBI questions anti-Castro activist Frank Bartes, private detective Guy Bannister, and others in New Orleans regarding activity at 544 Camp Street, address given for Lee Oswald's one-man Fair Play for Cuba Committee. Secret Service also investigates the Camp Street address. [CD75:680, 681; CD1495; CE1414; CE3119]

NOVEMBER 25
Marina Oswald tells Secret Service agent Patterson she does not know Jack Ruby. Agent Patterson thinks Marina is a communist. [23:390]

NOVEMBER 25
4:00 P.M.
Lee Oswald buried at Rose Hill Cemetery in Ft. Worth; reporters act as pallbearers. [CD5:412; *Life* special issue]

NOVEMBER 26
Deputy Attorney General Nicholas Katzenbach writes presidential assistant Bill Moyers about the assassination, stating that "the facts should be made public in such a way as to satisfy the people of the U.S. and abroad, that the facts have been told and a statement to this effect be made now." The public should be satisfied that Oswald was the assassin, Katzenbach added, and speculation about his motive ought to be cut off. [*Schweiker Report,* appendix C]

NOVEMBER 26
Illinois Senator Everett Dirksen introduces a motion to have the Senate Judiciary Committee conduct an investigation of the Kennedy assassination. [*Cong. Rec.* 11-26-63]

NOVEMBER 26
The Worker calls for an investigation of the assassination headed by Earl Warren. [*The Worker,* vol. xxviii, no. 198]

NOVEMBER 27
New York Congressman Charles Goodell proposes that a joint committee of fourteen —half from each house of Congress— investigate the assassination. [*Cong. Rec.* 11-27-63]

NOVEMBER 27

David Ferrie calls Roy McCoy at Chalmette, La., to see if McCoy had any pictures of the Civil Air Patrol to which they both belonged in the 1950s, and to which it is alleged Lee Oswald also belonged at the same time. (McCoy does not recall Oswald.) [CD75:212]

NOVEMBER 28

Dallas police officer J. D. Tippit is recommended for the Police Cross Award posthumously. [TAG9]

NOVEMBER 29

Lyndon Johnson sends a letter to J. Edgar Hoover seeking consultation in order to halt the "rash of investigations" into the assassination. Although he wants to get by on just the FBI report, Johnson says, the only way appears to be a high-level committee. [*Schweiker Report*]

NOVEMBER 29

Lyndon Johnson appoints what is called a "blue-ribbon" panel to investigate the assassination of John Kennedy. Earl Warren is the reluctant chairman. Other members include Gerald Ford, Richard Russell, Hale Boggs, John McCloy, John Sherman Cooper, and Allen Dulles. The move preempts congressional inquiries.

DECEMBER 2

Clay Shaw returns to New Orleans from Chicago. [N.O.T.P. 2-28-69]

DECEMBER 2

TSBD employee, Frankie Kaiser, out sick 11-22-63, finds Lee Oswald's clipboard on the sixth floor of the building. Investigators apparently overlooked it. [CE1966, 1980]

DECEMBER 3

Merchants State Bank repossesses Jack Ruby's 1960 Oldsmobile; sells it eight weeks later to Ruby's brother Sam. [CD1500e]

DECEMBER 3

A "straight line" is installed from the home of James H. Martin to White House Communications office in Washington, D.C. Martin was at the time manager of "Six Flags Over Texas" where Marina Oswald had moved to. [TAG5:M3]

DECEMBER 4

An FBI memo from William Sullivan, a Bureau Supervisor, indicates there is no evi-

---

"When I was in high school . . . I witnessed the first military coup against the people . . . accomplished by assassinating the then President John Kennedy. . . . I asked my teachers to tell me the meaning of it. . . . The replies to all my questions then was either silence or a reply filled with confusion and lies."

—NANCY LING PERRY
SLA soldier; quoted in *The Strange Case of Patty Hearst*

1963 *(cont.)*

dence that Oswald was inspired or directed by pro-Castro organizations or by any foreign country. [*Schweiker Report*, appendix C]

DECEMBER 4
Five top aides to Teamsters Union president Jimmy Hoffa resign because of a dispute over the death of John Kennedy. Reportedly, Hoffa had opposed a move by the five to issue a press release extending condolences to the Kennedy family; Hoffa also reportedly opposed a decision to close the Teamsters' Washington, D.C., headquarters on the day of the Kennedy funeral (11-25-63). [*Wall Street Journal* 12-9-63]

DECEMBER 5
The Secret Service conducts tests in Dealey Plaza to determine how the president could have been shot in the front from behind. [N.Y.T. 12-6-63]

DECEMBER 5
The Warren Commission meets for the first time: two hours forty-five minutes. They discuss news leaks and a few areas of research. [*The New Republic* 9-27-75]

"You know, ever since John Kennedy was assassinated, this country has fallen apart."
—PHIL OCHS
in an anti-hard drug radio spot, circa 1973

DECEMBER 6
National Life and Accident pays off Lee Oswald's life insurance policy after deducting a loan. [CD126:63]

DECEMBER 6
The Warren Commission meets again. [*The New Republic* 9-27-75]

DECEMBER 9
U.S. Deputy Attorney General Nicholas Katzenbach writes the Warren Commission recommending that it immediately state the FBI report clearly shows that Oswald was a "loner." [*Schweiker Report*, appendix C]

DECEMBER 9
The FBI completes its five-volume report on the assassination. [*Schweiker Report*, appendix C]

DECEMBER 10
After receiving a report on the investigative "deficiencies" in the handling of the preassassination Oswald file, J. Edgar Hoover brings disciplinary action against seventeen agents. [*Schweiker Report*, appendix C]

DECEMBER 10
Jack Ruby's attorney, Tom Howard, is given $1,500 by brother Earl Ruby. [TAG5:P5]

DECEMBER 13
A Joint Resolution of Congress authorizes the Warren Commission to subpoena wit-

nesses and take other judicial authority. [*Cong. Rec.* 12-13-63]

DECEMBER 14
Dallas deputy sheriff Allen Sweatt tells *Houston Post* reporter Alonzo H. Hudkins that Lee Oswald was FBI informant #S172, and was paid $200 monthly. [CD320:SS767:1]

DECEMBER 16
Warren Commission meets for the third time between 2:00 and 4:30 P.M. [*The New Republic* 9-27-75]

DECEMBER 16
Almost four weeks after the assassination, Lee Oswald's blue jacket is found lying on a window sill in the first floor lunchroom of the TSBD. [CD205:209]

DECEMBER 17
Lyndon Johnson orders a review of U.S. policy towards Cuba, seeking new ways to combat Castro. [*Wash. Daily News* 12-18-63]

DECEMBER 19
The *National Guardian* runs the first article questioning Oswald's lone guilt: "Oswald Innocent? A Lawyer's Brief," by Mark Lane.

DECEMBER 28
Warren Commission staff attorney Howard Willens, liason to the Justice Department, proposes the structural format of the Commission's inquiry. There is no category for "Who killed the president?" Most categories revolve around Oswald. [*Inquest,* p. 12]

DECEMBER 28
Citing adverse publicity, the national office of the Fair Play for Cuba Committee in New York closes down. [CD365:50]

DECEMBER 31
The Fair Play for Cuba Committee national office officially disbands. [10:87]

1964
JANUARY 14
Mrs. Harry A. Fredrickson forfeits twenty-five-dollar bond for hitting Adlai Stevenson with a placard during his 10-63 visit to Dallas. [D.M.N. 1-15-64]

JANUARY 21
The Warren Commission meets and discusses procedural questions and decides to hold its sessions closed rather than open. [*Inquest,* p. 14]

JANUARY 22
The Warren Commission meets and discusses the links between the intelligence community, particularly the FBI, and Lee Oswald. At the end of this discussion, Commissioner Allen Dulles suggests that "this record ought to be destroyed." [*Presumed Guilty,* p. 15]

JANUARY 27
Warren Commission staff, along with representatives from the FBI and Secret Service,

1964 *(cont.)*

views the Zapruder film. It is a copy of the original, not the original itself. [*Inquest*, pp. 16, 93]

JANUARY 27

Warren Commission meets; discusses the possibility that Lee Oswald was an FBI informant, and how to go about asking J. Edgar Hoover. The transcript was classified until obtained in 1974 by Harold Weisberg. Chief Counsel Rankin calls the Oswald-FBI link a "dirty rumor" that "must be wiped out." [See *Whitewash IV*]

JANUARY 28

Dallas County Judge Sterrett refuses to renew the beer and wine license for the Carousel Club. A new application under another name two weeks later is also denied. [D. T. H. 1-28-64; D. M. N. 2-12-64]

JANUARY 28

Warren Commission counsel J. Lee Rankin meets privately with J. Edgar Hoover to discuss allegations that Oswald was an FBI informant. Three days later Hoover indicates in a memo that he does not appreciate a statement by Earl Warren that the bureau's summary of assassination was a "skeleton report." [*Schweiker Report*, appendix C]

FEBRUARY 5

Marina Oswald is questioned by the Warren Commission in their search for John Kennedy's assassin(s). Asked commission counsel Rankin: "Do you have any idea of the motive which induced your husband to kill the president?" [1:76]

FEBRUARY 6

J. Edgar Hoover writes the Warren Commission telling them that Lee Oswald was never an informant for the FBI. He repeats this in person 5-14-64. [*Inquest*, p. 34]

FEBRUARY 18

Questioning of jurors in the Jack Ruby murder trial begins before Judge Joe Brown; ends two weeks later. All but one of the jurors selected had seen Jack Ruby shoot Lee Oswald on television.

FEBRUARY 21

Lee Oswald is on the cover of *Life* magazine shown holding a rifle, wearing a pistol, and carrying copies of the Socialist Workers party newspaper *The Militant* and the Communist party newspaper *The Worker*, with the caption "Armed for Murder." Neither *Life* nor the Warren Commission noted that a person who adheres to the Communist party line would not likely support the Socialist Workers party as well (or vice-versa). Physical discrepancies in the photo—the shadow, chin line, and proportions—lead to suspicion that it is a composite photo. [*They've Killed the President!*, pp. 78-80; 2:34; 7:410-18]

"I understand that the height of the wiretaps was when Robert Kennedy was attorney general in 1963. I don't criticize it however. . . . But if he had had ten more and, as a result of wiretaps, had been able to discover 'the Oswald plan,' it would have been worth it."

—RICHARD NIXON

in response to a press conference question from *St. Louis Post-Dispatch* reporter James Deakin, August 22, 1973

FEBRUARY 22

Robert Oswald, in his testimony before the Warren Commission, says that he is of the opinion that Ruth and Michael Paine were involved with brother Lee in killing John Kennedy, and that Lee knew Jack Ruby. [1:348, 404]

FEBRUARY 22

The Warren Commission meets. [*The New Republic* 9-27-75]

FEBRUARY 25

The Warren Commission asks American Bar Association president Walter Craig to advise whether their "proceedings conformed to the basic principles of American Justice." Craig subsequently attends two Warren Commission sessions in six months of hearing. [*Inquest*, p. 18]

FEBRUARY 25

The Warren Commission receives from *Life* magazine the original copy of the Zapruder film. [*Inquest*, p. 93]

MARCH 4

Jack Ruby's trial begins. [D. T. H. 3-4-64]

MARCH 4

Attorney Mark Lane testifies before the commission; at his request the session was open. [*Inquest*, pp. 19, 20]

MARCH 14

Last day of the Jack Ruby trial. The defend-

1964 *(cont.)*

ent is found guilty of murdering Lee Oswald. The conviction is for "murder with malice." The jury, which deliberates two hours and nineteen minutes, directs punishment by death. [D. M. N. 3-15-64]

MARCH 16

The Warren Commission meets.

MARCH 16 AND 17

FBI and Army test the "Oswald rifle" at the Warren Commission's request. None of the experts could duplicate the accomplishments attributed to Oswald using the rifle. The one expert whose time was better than that attributed to Oswald was using a stationary target and could pick his own starting time. In addition, the rifle sight had been slightly altered for the test. [*Inquest*, pp. 114-16]

MARCH 17

Hank Killam, a housepainter whose wife worked at the Carousel Club for two years, is found dead, with a cut throat, on the streets of Pensacola, Fla., having jumped, fallen, or been pushed off a building. Wife Wanda Joyce Killam says Hank had been hounded by inquisitive federal agents from job to job because of his association with Ruby and acquaintanceship with a boarder at the Oswald rooming house on Beckley Street. [*Forgive My Grief I*, pp. 7-8]

MARCH 18

Three Warren Commission staff attorneys go to Dallas to lay the groundwork for their field investigation. Two days later staff attorneys David Belin and Joseph Ball conduct an off-the-record reconstruction of Oswald's assumed movements. Eyewitnesses who would appear later before the commission participate. [*Inquest*, p. 19]

MARCH 24

The Warren Commission asks the USSR for its file on Lee Oswald 1959-1962. [CD704]

MARCH 26

The Warren Commission requests the FBI to respond to fifty-two questions in writing. Eight days later an FBI supervisor tells bureau official William Sullivan that the commission was cross-examining the FBI regarding its assassination investigation. [*Schweiker Report*, appendix C]

MARCH 26

Warren Commission counsel J. Lee Rankin requests the FBI furnish the commission with information on certain pro- and anti-Castro organizations. [*Schweiker Report*, appendix C]

APRIL 19

Warren Commission meets in executive session. [*The New Republic* 9-27-75]

APRIL 21

Dr. Robert Shaw, a physician who examined Governor Connally five months earlier at Parkland Hospital and said that the governor's wounds came from one bullet, sees the Zapruder film and tells the Warren Commission that he now thinks that it is possible that Connally was hit by separate bullets— possibly three different bullets. If this is true, then a second gun must have been used in the assassination. [4:109]

APRIL 23

Bill Hunter, *Long Beach* (Calif.) *Press Telegram* reporter who attended a meeting at Jack Ruby's apartment on the night of 11-24-63 with Ruby's roommate George Senator, lawyers Jim Martin and Tom Howard, and *Dallas Times Herald* reporter Jim Koethe, is shot to death from three feet in the press room of the Long Beach police station by a policeman. The death occurs literally hours after George Senator testifies to the Warren Commission "not recalling" the 11-24-63 meeting. [*Forgive My Grief I*, pp. 5-6; *In the Shadows of Dallas*, p. 11]

APRIL 23

An executive session meeting of the Warren Commission is held.

APRIL 27

Under the direction of Warren Commission attorney Arlen Specter, Army ballistics experts conduct tests on the alleged murder weapon and the penetration force of the bullets. [*Inquest*, p. 97]

APRIL 30

The Warren Commission holds an executive session meeting. [*The New Republic* 9-27-75]

MAY 14

CIA official Richard Helms and FBI director J. Edgar Hoover testify to the Warren Commission that the assassination case will always be open. [*Schweiker Report*, appendix C]

MAY 24

The Warren Commission stages a reenactment of the assassination at Dealey Plaza, complete with limousine and stand-ins for Kennedy and Connally. [*Inquest*, p. 22]

JUNE 1

This is the first self-imposed deadline the Warren Commission has. It is not met. [*Inquest*, p. 60]

JUNE 4

Executive session meeting of the Warren Commission.

JUNE 5

The Warren Commission visits the home of Jacqueline Kennedy to receive her testimony. [*Inquest*, p. 23]

JUNE 7

Earl Warren and Gerald Ford interview Jack Ruby in the Dallas County Jail. They refuse Ruby's pleas to be taken to Washington where he could talk more freely. Earl Warren: "Jack, if you fear for your safety, perhaps it's better you don't tell us." [*Inquest*, p. 23; Warren Commission testimony transcript]

1964 *(cont.)*

JULY 1

New Orleans private detective Guy Bannister dies of a heart attack. Bannister had an office at 544 Camp Street, the same address listed as headquarters for Oswald's one-man Fair Play for Cuba Committee on leaflets. Bannister, a former FBI agent, had extensive right-wing connections with anti-Castro activists and others. [*Plot or Politics*, p. 111; *Garrison Case*, p. 77]

JULY 18

Jack Ruby undergoes a polygraph test in the Dallas County Jail for the Warren Commission. [*Jack Ruby*, p. 182]

SEPTEMBER 4

Galley proofs of the final draft of the Warren Commission report circulate among staff for comments; attorney Wesley Liebler has substantial criticisms, few of which are acted upon. [*Inquest*, pp. 24, 111-20]

SEPTEMBER 7

Marina Oswald is requestioned by the Warren Commission in Dallas; substantial parts of her earlier testimony are contradicted. [*Inquest*, p. 24]

SEPTEMBER 9

Fifteen days before the Warren Commission report is completed and turned over to Lyndon Johnson, the FBI informs the White House that "the commission's report is se-riously inaccurate insofar as its treatment of the FBI is concerned." [*Schweiker Report*, appendix C]

SEPTEMBER 21

Jim Koethe, *Dallas Times Herald* reporter who attended a meeting at Jack Ruby's apartment 11-24-63 P.M. with Ruby's roommate George Senator, lawyers Jim Martin and Tom Howard, and *Long Beach* (Calif.) *Press Telegram* reporter Bill Hunter, receives a karate chop to the throat as he emerges from the shower in his home. He dies; Jim Martin successfully represents the accused. Koethe was working on a book about the assassination at the time. [*Forgive My Grief I*, pp. 5-6; *Vol. II*, p. 8; *In the Shadow of Dallas*, p. 9]

SEPTEMBER 24

The entire Warren Commission visits the White House to present its final report to Lyndon Johnson.

SEPTEMBER 27

The Warren Commission report is released to the public at 6:30 P.M. E.S.T.; within ten days over a million copies are sold by the government and various private publishers.

SEPTEMBER 30

Federal Bureau of Investigation disciplines certain Special Agents following issuance of the Warren Commission report the preceding week. [*Schweiker Report*, appendix C]

OCTOBER 5
FBI Agent James P. Hosty, Jr., is suspended for thirty days without pay and transferred to Kansas City, Mo., after ten years in the Dallas office. [D. T. H. 10-13-64]

OCTOBER 16
Soviet Premier Nikita Khrushchev is overthrown.

NOVEMBER 20
The government announces that the Warren Commission's twenty-six volumes of evidence and documents and testimony will be made available to the public; sets go on sale for seventy-six dollars each.

1965
MARCH 27
Forty-eight-year-old Tom Howard, another participant in the 11-24-63 meeting at Jack Ruby's apartment, dies; cause unknown. [*In the Shadow of Dallas*, pp. 11-13]

APRIL 6
Burglars break into the Texas School Book Depository, take $25. [D. T. H. 4-6-65]

"I shouted out 'who killed the Kennedys?' when after all, it was you and me."
—MICK JAGGER
from the song "Sympathy for the Devil"

Clay Shaw goes to Europe to get permission to translate a play called "The Trees Die Standing," by Spanish playwright Alejandro Casona. [*Plot or Politics*, p. 61]

SEPTEMBER
Clay Shaw resigns as Director of the International Trade Mart at age fifty-two. [*Garrison Probe*, p. 64]

1966
Midlothian (Texas) *Mirror* publisher Penn Jones, Jr., releases the first of his four-volume *Forgive My Grief* series.

1966
Several works critical of the Warren Commission appear: *Rush to Judgment* by Mark Lane, *Whitewash* by Harold Weisberg, *The Oswald Affair* by Leo Sauvage, *Inquest* by Edward Jay Epstein, and *The Second Oswald* by Richard Popkin.

1966
New Orleans District Attorney Jim Garrison charges that Clay Shaw this year asks the post office to forward mail to another New Orleans address where mail for Clem Bertrand is delivered as well. [N. O. S. I. 2-6-69]

1966 *(cont.)*

JANUARY 31

Autograph merchant Charles Hamilton auctions off two letters allegedly smuggled out of the Dallas County Jail by Jack Ruby. The sale is at the Waldorf-Astoria Hotel in New York. One letter is purchased for $950.00 by Penn Jones, Jr., editor of the *Midlothian* (Tex.) *Mirror*. In it, Ruby alleges a neo-Nazi conspiracy killed Kennedy. [*Forgive My Grief I*, pp. 64-66; *Ramparts* 2-67]

JUNE 13

Jack Ruby is ruled sane by a Texas state court; the issue of his sanity arose regarding his competency to hire and fire attorneys. [D. T. H. 6-14-66]

AUGUST 13

Authorities in the Soviet Union halt distribution of the Warren Report. [N. Y. T. 9-1-66]

SEPTEMBER 28

New York Congressman Theodore Kupferman asks Congress to review the Warren Commission's findings. [*Cong. Rec.* 9-28-66]

OCTOBER 5

Jack Ruby's conviction for murdering Lee Oswald is reversed. Reasons given are that Judge Brown should have granted a change of venue, and that Jack's statements to police should have been ruled inadmissible. [*Jack Ruby*, p. 181]

NOVEMBER

Jim Garrison officially begins his probe into the Kennedy assassination. [*Playboy* 10-67; *Heritage of Stone*]

NOVEMBER 25

FBI director J. Edgar Hoover in a public statement says that, "all available evidence and facts point to one conclusion—that Oswald acted alone in his crime."

NOVEMBER 27

Warren Commission member and U. S. Congressman Hale Boggs says that "if it would please anyone" the classified autopsy X-ray results of John Kennedy should be looked at to resolve any questions in the Kennedy assassination. [D. T. H. 11-28-66]

DECEMBER 9

Jack Ruby is admitted to Parkland Hospital for pneumonia. [D. T. H. 1-3-67]

DECEMBER 10

Doctors at Parkland Hospital discover cancer in Jack Ruby. [D. T. H. 1-3-67]

1967
JANUARY

Ramparts magazine publishes a special report on "The Case for Three Assassins" by David Lifton and David Walsh.

JANUARY 3

Jack Ruby dies of cancer at Parkland Hospital. [N. Y. T. 1-4-67]

JANUARY 30
Murder charges against Jack Ruby are post-humously dropped in Wichita Falls, Texas (where the retrial was to be held). [D. T. H. 1-30-67]

FEBRUARY
Playboy magazine publishes lengthy interview with Mark Lane; follows up eight months later with a lengthy interview with Jim Garrison.

FEBRUARY 17
New Orleans Parish District Attorney Jim Garrison's investigation becomes public for the first time in an article published by the *New Orleans States-Item*. David Ferrie, a strange man with innumerable ties to the political right wing and intelligence communities, is named as the key figure in the conspiracy to assassinate John Kennedy.

FEBRUARY 22
David Ferrie dies of "natural causes." Elidio del Valle, a friend of Ferrie's and fellow militant anti-Castroite, dies of a bullet wound in the heart, with his head axed open. [N. O. S. I. 2-23-67; *The Kennedy Conspiracy*, p. 19]

MARCH 1
Prominent New Orleans businessman Clay Shaw is arrested and charged with "conspiring with Ferrie, Oswald, and others" to assassinate John Kennedy. Shaw had official CIA connections at the time. [N. O. S. I. 3-2-67; Zodiac News Service 12-21-73]

MARCH 2
Attorney General Ramsey Clark says that Clay Shaw has already been checked out by the FBI and was not involved in the Kennedy assassination. (Later Clark backed down from this statement.) [W. P. 3-3-67]

MARCH 17
Lyndon Johnson presses the FBI to probe allegations that the Kennedy assassination was retaliation by Castro, but the FBI is reluctant to enter controversy while Garrison probe is on. [*Schweiker Report*]

APRIL 1
A CIA memo to overseas offices concerning the Kennedy assassination controversy urges "book reviews and feature articles" to "refute the attacks of the critics." The memo's goal is "to provide material for countering and discrediting the claims of the conspiracy theorists, so as to inhibit the circulation of such claims in other countries." The action is taken, the memo says, because "efforts to impugn [the] rectitude and wisdom [of Warren Commission members and staff] tend to cast doubt on the whole leadership of American society." [CIA memorandum #1035-960]

APRIL 4
Following charges that Cubans were involved in the John Kennedy assassination, Marvin Watson, an aide to Lyndon Johnson, calls FBI official Cartha Deloach advising him that Johnson is convinced of a plot in the Kennedy assassination. Garrison's probe had

1967 *(cont.)*

"An autographed book co-authored by President Ford when he was a Congressman, was sold at auction in New York last month for $300. The book was Portrait of the Assassin, *written with John R. Stiles in 1965. In the inscription in the book, which dealt with Lee Harvey Oswald, Ford made a spelling error. It read: 'Warmest personel regards.' "*

—*Crawdaddy* magazine

April 1975

---

been front-page news for weeks. [*Schweiker Report*, appendix C]

APRIL 5

Clay Shaw is arraigned on charges of conspiring to kill John Kennedy. [*The Kennedy Conspiracy*, p. 213]

APRIL 21

Luis Castillo, a Puerto Rican national, seeks political asylum in the Philippines. Castillo, twenty-four, says he was part of a fifteen-member plot in Dallas 11-22-63 to kill John Kennedy. Acting in Dallas as an agent under deep hypnosis for an undetermined intelligence agency, Castillo says he was handed a gun and instructed to shoot "a man in an open car," and to run to the building's fourth floor if things got too rough. Someone called "Joe" was able to hit the "man in the open

car" first, and Castillo was hustled off to Chicago. The Philippine National Bureau of Investigation questions Castillo intensely, using hypnosis, truth serum, and polygraph techniques. Castillo's story does not change. Press reports indicate "Castillo's mind must have been conditioned to remember only what it has been 'taught' to remember." The U.S. Embassy in Manila expresses keen interest in the case; the FBI in Washington has "no comment." [*The Manila Times* 4-22, 23, 24, 25-67; *Operation Mind Control*]

JUNE 26-29

CBS-TV presents a four-part series on its nine-month assassination investigation; concludes through manipulated evidence that the Warren Commission findings were essentially accurate. [*Citizens Dissent*, pp. 75-120]

JUNE 27

A New Orleans Parish grand jury begins two days of hearings into allegations of improprieties made on NBC-TV eight days earlier against Jim Garrison and the conduct of his probe. Later, one of those who accuses Garrison on NBC-TV is found in contempt of court for refusing to comment on his previous allegations. [*The Kennedy Conspiracy*]

JULY 5

New Orleans District Attorney Jim Garrison files a motion for an early trial date for Clay Shaw, citing slanted pretrial publicity in national publications and broadcast media. [N.O.S.I. 7-6-67]

DECEMBER 20
Edgar Eugene Bradley of North Hollywood, Calif., an employee of fundamentalist conservative Dr. Carl McIntyre is charged by New Orleans District Attorney Jim Garrison with conspiracy to assassinate John Kennedy. Possible case of mistaken identity by Garrison's office. [See *Legacy of Doubt.*]

1968
FEBRUARY 16
Former CIA director and Warren Commissioner Allen Dulles, whose CIA career was terminated in September 1961 by JFK, is subpoenaed to appear at the Clay Shaw trial in New Orleans. He refuses to appear. [N.O.T.P. 2-17-68]

FEBRUARY 27
Lyndon Johnson visits Dallas for the first time since 11-22-63, in an unannounced trip, riding in an unmarked car. [D.T.H. 2-29-68]

MARCH
Jim Garrison, assembling evidence to present in the Clay Shaw trial, subpoenas the original print of the Zapruder film from Time, Inc. Time, Inc., supplies the film. [*The Kennedy Conspiracy,* p. 242]

MARCH 31
Lyndon Johnson announces he will not run for reelection.

APRIL 4
Martin Luther King is killed in Memphis, Tennessee.

JUNE 5
Robert Kennedy is killed in Los Angeles, California.

AUTUMN
European release of the controversial *Farewell America* by "James Hepburn," about the John Kennedy assassination. This book is alleged to be the work of a French intelligence organization. [Garrison investigation]

NOVEMBER 8
Edgar Eugene Bradley, a suspect in Garrison's New Orleans probe, stays in California where Governor Ronald Reagan refuses to extradite him to Louisiana. (See *Legacy of Doubt.*) [N.O.T.P. 11-9-68]

LATE 1968-1969
Formation of the Committee to Investigate Assassinations, headed by Washington, D.C., lawyer Bernard Fensterwald.

1969
JANUARY 17
A panel of four medical experts appointed by Attorney General Ramsey Clark examines secret autopsy photos and X-rays from the Kennedy probe. The group confirms the Warren Commission's conclusions. The effort appears to be directed at heading off Jim Garrison's attempt to get the autopsy mate-

1969 *(cont.)*

rial for the upcoming Clay Shaw trial. [N. Y. T. 1-18-69]

JANUARY 21
Formal beginning of the Clay Shaw trial in New Orleans; D. A. Jim Garrison charges that Shaw with David Ferrie, Lee Oswald, and others plotted in New Orleans to assassinate John Kennedy. Garrison also states that the evidence will conclusively demonstrate that Kennedy was killed in a crossfire. [N. O. T. P. 1-22-69]

MARCH 1
New Orleans businessman Clay Shaw acquitted on conspiracy charges. Some jury members admit that evidence pointed to conspiracy, but not that Shaw was a participant. [N. O. T. P. 3-2, 3-69]

MARCH 2
Garrison announces he will charge Clay Shaw with perjury. [N. O. T. P. 3-3-69]

AUTUMN
Lyndon Johnson, out of office, tells CBS-TV interviewer Walter Cronkite that he is not sure Oswald acted alone. That portion of the interview is deleted on grounds of "national security" and finally aired in April 1975.

1970
Computers and Automation begins its lengthy series of articles on political assassination with Richard E. Sprague's "The Assassination of President Kennedy: The Application of Computers to the Photographic Evidence."

FEBRUARY 27
Clay Shaw sues Jim Garrison and others for $5 million in damages. [N. O. S. I. 2-28-70]

AUGUST 30
Abraham Zapruder, Dallas businessman and one-time amateur photographer, dies at age sixty-five. [D. T. H. 8-31-70]

1972
APRIL 29
At the Athens Transfer & Storage Co., Athens, Tex., fixtures from the Carousel Club are auctioned off. Seventy-five people show, including Aubrey Mayhew, temporary owner of the Texas School Book Depository in Dallas, who buys items for a museum he hopes to put in the building. Jack Ruby's kitchen sink sells for $22.50, and a rusty can opener is purchased for one dollar. Two nights before the auction, a locked Carousel Club safe, considered the prime item on the block, was stolen from the warehouse. [*SunDance Magazine* #2, p. 17]

MAY 15
George Wallace, a strong contender for the Democratic presidential nomination, is shot while campaigning in Laurel, Md., putting him out of the race. Incumbent president

Richard Nixon's reelection chances are significantly increased as a result.

JUNE 17

Five men picked up bugging and burglarizing Democratic National Committee headquarters in Washington, D.C., all with connections to CIA and anti-Castro exile community. A later addition to the group is E. Howard Hunt, head of political operations for the Bay of Pigs invasion.

NOVEMBER 7

Richard Nixon and Spiro Agnew are reelected to their second four- year term as president and vice-president. Neither victor serves a full term.

NOVEMBER 20

U.S. Supreme Court refuses to consider setting aside the court order which barred Jim Garrison from prosecuting Clay Shaw for perjury. [N.Y.T. 11-20-72]

DECEMBER

On public television, Earl Warren says Lyndon Johnson feared an outbreak of nuclear war after the assassination, and that he (Warren) was persuaded to take the commission job because of this.

1973

In the first part of the year, a small fire breaks out in the Texas School Book Depository; charged with arson and placed on probation

"If we had learned on November 22, 1963, that the premier of Russia had been shot by a lonely capitalist sympathizer, we immediately would have pierced the government lie and recognized that new hands had taken over in the Soviet Union.

"Government investigators could be expected to produce truckloads of incendiary capitalist literature found hidden in the assassin's apartment. A photograph would be produced of the lone assassin proudly holding aloft in one hand the murder weapon and the other a copy of the Wall Street Journal. *Positive evidence would be exhibited proving that he had lived for a period of time in Chicago.*

"The assassination of President Kennedy demonstrated that many Americans will believe the most unlikely inventions rather than confront the fact that their government is lying to them."

—JIM GARRISON
in *A Heritage of Stone*

is Win Anderson, an employee of building owner Aubrey Mayhew, who defaulted on the building purchase shortly thereafter. Anderson goes on to promote rock music festivals in the Dallas area in the following years. [*Texas Sun* 9-17-76]

MARCH

Dallas newspapers run following ad: "For

1973 *(cont.)*

Sale or Lease: Famous Historic Dallas Landmark. It was from a window in this building, according to the Warren Commission Report, that a sniper fired the shots that killed President John F. Kennedy and wounded Governor John Connally, on November 22, 1963." The ad also says that the building has 80,000 square feet of office space, a sprinkler system, elevators, and "excellent rail and freeway access." The ad runs again in September 1975.

MAY 22-23
WWL-TV in New Orleans broadcasts an interview with Pershing Gervais, a former investigator for Jim Garrison who admits a role in a Justice Department-Internal Revenue Service frame-up of Garrison.

AUGUST 22
Garrison trial on charges of accepting bribes from pinball dealers begins in federal court in New Orleans. [N.O.T.P. 8-23-73]

SEPTEMBER 27
Jim Garrison found not guilty on bribery charges brought by Mitchell Justice Department. Federal District Court Judge Herbert Christenberry presided over the trial. [N.O.S.I. 9-28-73]

OCTOBER 10
Congressman Gerald Ford, a former member of the Warren Commission, is nominated to be Vice-President of the U.S. by Richard Nixon after Spiro Agnew resigns that position.

NOVEMBER
Another alumnus of the Kennedy assassination investigation, Leon Jaworski, reappears in the news as the Watergate Special Prosecutor. In late 1963 and 1964 he represented the State of Texas in its dealings with the Warren Commission as Special Counsel to the Texas Court of Inquiry.

NOVEMBER 23-24
"Decade of Assassinations" conference held at Georgetown University under sponsorship of the Committee to Investigate Assassinations, first of the latter-day researcher gatherings.

1974
JANUARY 25
Dallas policeman Roy Vaughn, who was present when Ruby shot Oswald, files a $3 million libel suit against the producers of the movie "Executive Action." Vaughn claims the movie depicts him as allowing Ruby into the police station basement. The suit is later dropped.

"History is the trick the living play on the dead."

—GEORGE BERNARD SHAW

AUGUST 9

Richard Nixon resigns U.S. presidency; Gerald Ford assumes office.

AUGUST 15

Clay Shaw dies of cancer. [N.O.S.I. 8-16-74]

SEPTEMBER

The Assassination Information Bureau formally begins operation as the first national organization to propagandize facts on the Kennedy assassination in an overall political context.

OCTOBER

Penn Jones, Jr., editor-publisher of the *Midlothian* (Tex.) *Mirror,* retires, turning the weekly over to its employees.

1975
JANUARY

David Belin, a former counsel to the Warren Commission, is appointed Staff Director of the Rockefeller Commission investigation of CIA domestic activities.

JANUARY 31-FEBRUARY 2

"The Politics of Conspiracy" conference, sponsored by the Assassination Information Bureau, is held at Boston University. Many significant researchers attend, as well as a large turnout from the general public. The conference plays a catalyzing role in building interest in the subject around the country in the following years.

FEBRUARY 19

Congressman Henry Gonzalez introduces a resolution calling for a congressional reinvestigation of the assassinations of John Kennedy, Robert Kennedy, Martin Luther King, and the attempt on George Wallace. (Gonzalez was in the Kennedy motorcade in Dallas.)

MARCH

The "Citizens' Commission of Inquiry" is established in Washington, D.C., by Mark Lane with the goal of agitating Congress with facts and petitions to reopen the assassination investigation. (Lane had used the same name for a group in 1964 to rally support for an independent investigation.)

APRIL 8

A resolution is introduced in the California State Legislature calling on Congress to carry out an independent investigation of the John Kennedy assassination. The resolution passes the Assembly, fails in the Senate.

APRIL

Congressman Thomas Downing introduces a resolution to reopen the John Kennedy assassination investigation.

APRIL 9

Time, Inc., announces it is releasing the original of the Zapruder film and all commercial rights to it to the heirs of Abraham Zapruder for the sum of one dollar. [N.Y.T. 4-10-75]

1975 *(cont.)*

APRIL 18

New Times magazine publishes Robert Sam Anson's "JFK: The Truth Is Still At Large," first national magazine to start with critics' point of view, putting Warren Report on the defensive.

MAY 15

Roger Craig, former Dallas County sheriff's deputy, dies of self-inflicted wounds. Craig had witnessed evidence of conspiracy on 11-22-63. [D. T. H. 5-15-75]

MAY 16-18

The "Campaign for Democratic Freedoms" puts on a well-received conspiracy conference in Los Angeles. National conferences on conspiracy and the Kennedy assassination are also held in the spring in Wisconsin, Connecticut, and Michigan.

AUGUST 20

Joachim Joesten dies in Germany; was responsible for popularizing conspiracy theories about Kennedy death throughout Europe.

SEPTEMBER

Senators Richard Schweiker and Gary Hart are asked by Senator Frank Church to conduct an investigation into the role of intelligence agencies in the Kennedy assassination investigation.

NOVEMBER 17-22

The "November 22nd Coalition" coordinated by the Assassination Information Bureau holds a week of teach-ins, rallies, and media appearances around the country to generate interest in the Kennedy assassination investigation. Boston, Los Angeles, Milwaukee, Madison, and Washington, D. C., are among the cities where "Coalition" activities take place.

NOVEMBER 22

David W. Belin, a Warren Commission and staff director of the Rockefeller Commission investigation of CIA domestic activities, calls for a new inquiry into the Kennedy assassination. [N. Y. T. 11-23-75]

NOVEMBER 25-26

CBS-TV reinvestigates the Kennedy assassination; accepts the likelihood of Warren Commission conclusions but calls for a reinvestigation, particularly of intelligence community connection to Oswald and others.

NOVEMBER 26

The Massachusetts State House passes a resolution asking Congress to investigate the assassination of John Kennedy.

1976
JUNE 23

The *Schweiker Report* is released; prepared by a subcommittee of the Senate select Committee on Intelligence, it concludes that there was substantial interference by intelligence operatives and agencies and Johnson administration officials in the assassination investigation.

AUGUST 2

Johnny Roselli, a CIA contact in organized crime who was active in U.S. sponsored attempts on Fidel Castro's life, is missing from his Florida home; a few days later he is found dead, murdered gangland style. The previous April 23 he had testified in secret before the Schweiker Committee probe of the government's Kennedy assassination investigation.

SEPTEMBER 17

U.S. House of Representatives passes a resolution creating a select committee to investigate the assassinations of John Kennedy and Martin Luther King. Richard A. Sprague, a Philadelphia lawyer, is named chief counsel of the twelve-member committee.

NOVEMBER 2

President Gerald Ford, a former Warren Commission member, is defeated in his first presidential candidacy by former Georgia governor Jimmy Carter. It is the first presidential election since 1960 which is not determined by a bullet.

1977
MARCH 2

Congressman Henry Gonzalez, chairman of the House committee investigating the John Kennedy and Martin Luther King assassinations, resigns, sharply criticizing committee

counsel Richard A. Sprague. A few days later (March 7), Ohio Congressman Louis Stokes is named committee chairman.

MARCH 8

Twenty-five-year-old Larry Reaume, on the campus of St. Clair Community College at Port Huron, Mich., where he was not a student, shot off a gun in the College Center building while yelling, "Who killed John F. Kennedy? Who killed Martin Luther King?" When bystanders tried to restrain him, Reaume, still yelling about the two assassinations, set himself on fire. A few seconds later he dived into a nearby fountain from which he was pulled, alive.

MARCH 29

George De Mohrenschildt dies of a gun shot to the head in Palm Beach, Florida. De Mohrenschildt, a Russian-born Dallasite with many connections to the intelligence and petroleum industries, had befriended Lee Oswald after the latter's return from Russia until his death. De Mohrenschildt's death came shortly after he learned that the House assassinations committee wanted to interview him; it was ruled "an apparent suicide." [*Crime and Cover-Up*, pp. 34-36; Associated Press 3-31-77]

MARCH 30

Richard A. Sprague, chief counsel to the House Select Committee on Assassinations, resigns. [Cong. Rec. 3-30-77]

1977 *(cont.)*

MARCH 30

The House of Representatives extends the life of the Select Committee on Assassinations through December 1978. [Cong. Rec. 3-30-77]

2039

This is the year originally scheduled as the time when certain classified documents used by the Warren Commission would be released to the public unless declassified earlier by the agency of origin (CIA, Justice Department, etc.). All documents are expected to be declassified in the course of the House of Representatives Select Committee investigation of the John Kennedy assassination.

Elegy for John F. Kennedy
by Ed Sanders

I grieve for the day it happened for the sallow light of the
        Dallas morn, framed on the TV screen, a day which always
        seemed, in the tear-cleansed circuits of memory, to carry
        a haze of greenish yellow

I grieve for the interceding years—how each new revelation bristles
        like a flag of pain upon the map of our lives—and each new
        fact subsumes itself beneath a pyramidal battlement of
        criminality, which we must bear upon our collective shoulders
        until that time—o joyous day—'when we may collectively
        dash it into the sea

I grieve for the legacy of Abraham Zapruder, his mere 8mm film
        blown up full color and shown by necessity in the audit-
        oriums of America—I grieve for the innocent eyes that
        see the head twist back and the scattering skull rise up
        upon the Dealey Plaza day

I grieve upon the carcinogenic winds I grieve at the mountains of
        detritus I grieve for the children fed insects by hungry
        parents I grieve for the causes, instant and searing, which
        have long lain desolate in desuetude because of the Presi-
        dent's death—and he has been the president, and the only
        president, for 15 years—and we have been held in a writhing
        national stasis by the trauma of his execution

I grieve for the children of the murderers who will live to know
        what sort of mutant twerps rode berserk in the war of money
        and power and rifle teams and racist payoff—o how our
        democracy lies besmirched if Kennedy were slain by men who
        never ended WW II but took that war's most evil worst and
        brought it back all bloody smears upon the pages of the
        Dallas Morning News

I grieve for the era of behavior modification—o how the specter of
        robo-wash engulfs us—and why! o America do we allow these

intelligence agency turkeys to practice turning mammals
into robots—Worse than the worst dope dealer selling
heroin to children is the agency that makes some hypnotized
mod manchurian malefactor rise up to kill for the cause of
a secret persuasion

I grieve that when the last dour plotter is caught and the last rifle
is x'd in on the last permanent map of Dealey Plaza and the
last dollar bill is traced to the last secret courier and
the last secret cash cache, I grieve that John F. Kennedy
won't have helped this country as it hurtles toward that
signpost year in the 1980's

Raise a hand of knowledge o America
that holds a tape recorder

and another hand holding
a telescope—& let us focus our
symbols of awareness
upon those
                    assassinatious tracks
whose bloody marks
                    we see to grow
each day of our recent lives.

For this is the age of investigation
and every citizen must investigate.

And we will see the names embossed in beauty,
of those who placed, I believe,
their lives on the line—all across the
country the investigators arose to
face a chorus of spittle and boos
and sabotage—to dare to declare
that evil can not place
a veil of garbage
upon the history of our country

That this country is not Rome
and the Kennedys
were not the Gracchi
whose murders by
the Roman oligarchy were
veiled in silence

for the pallid tracks of guilt and death—slight
as they are—suffuse upon the retentive electromagnetic
data-retrieval systems of our era.

And let th' investigators
not back away one micro-unit
from their endeavors,

for only a tide of love-zap zeal,
love-zap mixed with a crosscountry
investigative ceaselessness, a seething relentless pressure
of ink and airwaves and videotape: a seething relentless
pressure upon the official investigative agencies
who carry in their wounded computers the bloody tracks
of this assassination
                    only by this will we
                    drag these murderers
                    from their jive-jargon'd lairs
                    of murder & wire-up & poisons
                    &
o how serious it is!

            I stand here
        in Boston, Massachusetts—
    in the state where John Kennedy lived—
                        in a country
            caught in a struggle for democratic freedom
            that tries to write something new in the gore-writ
                    pages of history.

The truth will
not blow our country apart
"The truth," to quote
the verse from WE SHALL OVERCOME,
"The truth shall set us free"

But the times are perilous
and I can feel the Spirit
of America walk weeping
around and around the
burning circular henge of stone
past Kennedy's grave

and up to the
hill base where his
brother lies slain—

and we must join the circling spirit
of our country
to stop the anvil of evil
before it falls too far
into the pit
of Tartarus

And let us take this vow, o Americans:

Get those people
who killed John Kennedy
Get them, haul them
away from wherever they are
away from their ambassadorships,
from their commodities markets
or beet cartels,
or wherever they are
and yank their hematoidal cover stories
and groans of national security
into the harshest and purest light

o women o men
of America
let them see
the searing light

get them get them get them!

4 READ ALL ABOUT IT!

"Freedom of the press is guaranteed only to those who own one," wrote critic and essayist A. J. Liebling. And so it is usually difficult for topical literature critical of the conventional wisdom to gain wide circulation. J. Edgar Hoover sent an emissary to Holt, Rinehart & Winston when it considered publishing Mark Lane's *Rush to Judgment*. The publishing house was advised that Mr. Hoover would prefer that the book not gain a U.S. publisher (it was already out in England). Knowledge of this pressure helped explain why for a year every previously contacted publisher in the United States sheepishly turned Lane's book down after first tentatively accepting it. (Hoover's advice was ignored.)

Lane's 1966 book has been by far the most commercially successful volume critical of the government's contention that Oswald was a lone-nut assassin, but it was not the only one to encounter interference. Among the most highly respected books in the field is Josiah Thompson's *Six Seconds in Dallas,* a detailed analysis of what happened in Dealey Plaza based on information gleaned from the Zapruder film, other photographs, and witness testimony. It is at once scientific and quite readable, and its conclusions contradict the Warren Report. In the course of preparing the manuscript, Thompson was retained by *Life* magazine to help in its ongoing investigation of the Kennedy assassination, thus giving him access to that most valuable of resources, the original Zapruder film. Frames from the Z-film, as it is called, had been published elsewhere, and when Thompson requested permission to likewise print crucial and illustrative frames in his book, he fully expected it to be granted. Instead, *Life* refused.

Thompson and his publisher (Bernard Geis) tried to persuade the magazine to relent. Finally Geis offered *Life* the entire profits from the book in exchange for permission. The magazine still refused. Chagrined at *Life* for withholding valuable historical documentation, Thompson and Geis had accurate charcoal renditions of the pertinent Z-frames sketched for use in the book. The sketches appeared throughout *Six Seconds in Dallas* and served their purpose well. Then, in December 1967, *Life* sued Thompson for using the charcoal sketches, claiming it was essentially the same as using the originals.

In September 1968 Federal District Court Judge Inzer D. Wyatt ruled that while Thompson had, in fact, infringed on a copyright held by Time, Inc., the historical value of the material superseded Time's copyright restrictions. Through this application of what is called the "fair use doctrine," Thompson won the case. (In October 1976 the book had a paperback publication which substituted the original Z-frames for the charcoal drawings.)

Books that support the Warren Commission are fewer in number, and are, as a group, defensive. They include Gerald Ford's only literary output, *Portrait of the Assassin* (coauthored with John Stiles), summaries of the official line of events by on-the-scene reporters, and a rather shallow attack on the Warren Commission critics themselves (*Scavengers,* by Lewis and Schiller). The most ambitious of the Warren Commission defenses was the work of one of its staff lawyers, David Belin (*November 22, 1963: You Are The Jury*).

Some writers have ignored the entire publishing circus and printed their own books. Best known of the self-publishing authors are Harold Weisberg and Penn Jones, Jr. After receiving numerous turndowns on his original *Whitewash* manuscript, Weisberg decided to publish it himself in August 1965. A few months later, Dell, which had earlier refused Weisberg's work, contracted to publish the book following Weisberg's private edition. The same chain of events followed between Weisberg and Dell with *Whitewash II.* In the twelve years since his first of many self-published books on the Warren Commission's malfeasance, Weisberg estimated that he has sold in excess of 50,000 copies of his own books out of his Maryland home.

Penn Jones, Jr., started with a printing press, which made publishing easier. As editor of the weekly *Midlothian* (Texas) *Mirror,* Jones wrote regular essays based on research and speculation about the Kennedy assassination, law enforcement investigation of it, and the rapidly decreasing list of living witnesses. Over 35,000 copies of his books (*Forgive My Grief,* vols. I-IV) are in circulation, including 10,000 he gave away at a 1969 rock music festival outside Dallas. At one point Jones was approached by a New York paperback house with the idea of condensing his first two books—which included a list of material witnesses who had died under suspect circumstances—into one. According to Jones, the publishing house added some dead witness names to the list for their edition, names Jones had never heard of. "So they'd publish the book," Jones recalls, "and some of these people would call and say, 'Hey! You sumvabitch! I'm not dead!' I didn't let them print it, and I haven't gone to any publisher since."

At least one lawsuit has emerged from recent assassination books. In July 1976 convicted Watergate burglar and former CIA official E. Howard Hunt sued the authors of *Coup d'Etat in America* for, among other things, suggesting that he was in Dealey Plaza November 22, 1963. The authors expressed delight at the opportunity to question Hunt for the record.

If books are *de facto* interesting because of their scarcity, then the literature of the assassination is filled with fascinating volumes. It is not just the obscure entries such as *Is John F. Kennedy Alive . . . and Well?* and *Everything You Wanted to Know . . .* (consult bibliographic entry for full title) which generate curiosity, but the unpublished manuscripts as well. These labors of frustration and diligence are unencumbered by the constraints of published works, and circulate from hand to hand and Xerox machine to Xerox machine on the sleuth underground.

By far the most respected manuscript of this type is Peter Dale Scott's *The Dallas Conspiracy*, used as a basic reference for others in the field. Like the Russian *Samizdat*, a new manuscript in the field is pounced upon, digested, copied, and passed along the network.

The mystery of Dallas has enough loose ends to be a fertile territory for fiction, drawing from basic facts and suppositions. *Winter Kills* by Richard Condon is among the best, as is *The Parallax View* by Loren Singer. Ex-lieutenant William Calley was reported in July 1976 to be working on a presidential assassination novel called *Zulu 3*. Bostonian Luke Salisbury has written a novel about grave-diggers who plan to exhume the president's body and sell the photographs to a European magazine. He has never found a publisher for it.

The following bibliography includes English-language books which deal either substantially or altogether with the John Kennedy assassination. Self-published and

'Let's see . . . Warren Commission . . . ;
contribution by C.I.A. and F.B.I. . . . '

unpublished works are also included. Ceremonial books—those which simply chronologize the official line of events that weekend—are not listed, but magazines and pamphlets are included if they concern themselves directly with the assassination. As much bibliographic data as could be collected is presented; in some cases year of publication or publisher was not available. Descriptive comments are intended as a guide where there is knowledge of the book or its writer.

Most secondhand book stores carry some Kennedy assassination books, while the more scarce volumes are valued at high prices among rare book dealers. In the following list self-published books contain the author's address, and hard-to-find entries are marked "HTF."

This is a strange breed of book. It will, in all probability, get stranger before the mystery is solved.

BOOKS

Accessories After the Fact; The Warren Commission, the Authorities, and the Report, by Sylvia Meagher. New York: Bobbs-Merrill, 1967; Vintage, 1976.
If you have time for just one book on the deficiencies of the Warren Commission and its report, this is it. Bookstores and libraries.

According to Zapruder, by Chris Scally. London: Unpublished manuscript.

An Irish computer programmer now living in England, Scally is an authority on the Zapruder film.

After the Assassination; A Positive Appraisal of the Warren Report, by John Sparrow. New York: Chilmark Press, 1967.
Professor Sparrow ignores much obvious documentary evidence in this 77-page volume. Some libraries.

Aftermath of an Execution—The Burial and Final Rights of Lee Harvey Oswald as Told by His Mother, by Marguerite Oswald. Dallas: Self-published, 1964.
Brief, HTF [Hard To Find].

An Almanac of Jim Garrison's Investigation; The Crime of Silence. Austin, Texas: Research Publications, 1968.
229 pages, 13 photos, one document. HTF.

American Grotesque: An Account of the Clay Shaw-Jim Garrison Affair in New Orleans, by James Kirkwood. New York: Simon & Schuster, 1970.
Emotional attack on Garrison which strays from the evidence. In some libraries.

American Political Assassinations: A Bibliography of Works Published 1963-1970 Related to the Assassination of John F. Kennedy, Martin Luther King, and Robert F. Kennedy, compiled and published by the Committee to Investigate Assassinations. Washington, D.C.: 1973.
Contains magazine articles as well as books; also some non-English language entries. Breaks down JFK subject matter into catego-

ries (Garrison, Ruby, world opinion, conspiracy, etc.).

Appointment in Dallas: The Final Solution to the Assassination of JFK, by Hugh C. McDonald as told to Geoffrey Bocca. New York: Zebra Books, 1975.
An undocumented adventure story; sold extremely well. Bookstores and newsstands.

The Assassin, by Evelyn Anthony. New York: Coward McCann, 1970; Dell paperback, 1971. HTF.

Assassin: The Lee Harvey Oswald Biography, by Gene Ringgold and Roger La Manna. Hollywood: Associated Professional Services, 1964.
66 pages, illustrated. An instant biography. HTF.

Assassination; A Special Kind of Murder, by W. A. Heaps. New York: Meredith, 1969. HTF.

The Assassination Chain, by Sybil Leek and Bert R. Sugar. New York: Corwin Books, 1976.
A clearly written primer for newcomers to the assassination field, this book summarizes known facts pointing to conspiracy conclusions involving the CIA, FBI right-wing Americanism, the Mafia, Communism, and the military-industrial complex. The book also includes an "Assassination's Who's Who," giving capsule descriptions of many actors in America's assassination drama. Jack Anderson's foreword is awful. Bookstores.

Assassination by Consensus; The Story Behind the Kennedy Assassination, by William E. Smith. Washington, D.C.: L'Avant Garde Books, 1966.
Speculative, behavior-modification theory. HTF.

The Assassination Conspiracy; The Judas Movement, by Libra (pseud.). Los Angeles: unpublished manuscript, 1976.
The author relates an account of a former employer who was tormented because he knew too much about the Kennedy assassination. Also includes resource material.

Assassination: The Death of President John F. Kennedy, by Relman Morin. New York: New American Library-Signet, 1968.
A review of the facts as put forth by government and investigative agencies, by an Associated Press reporter who was at the assassination scene. A chapter is devoted to ridiculing investigation critics. Some used bookstores.

Assassination of a President, by the *New York Times* Editors. New York: Viking Press, 1964. Reprints from the *Times* from November 23 to November 28, 1963. HTF.

Assassination! The World Stood Still, by John Cottrell. London: New English Library, 1964.
128 pages, HTF.

The Assassination of John Fitzgerald Kennedy; An Annotated Bibliography, by David R. Wrone. Madison, Wis.: Wisconsin Magazine of History, Autumn, 1972.
Scholarly. Fifteen pages of basic sources, arti-

cles and books. Perceptive comments; with an introduction. (Available from the State Historical Society of Wisconsin, 816 State St., Madison, Wis. 53706.)

The Assassination of John F. Kennedy; A New Review, by Ian MacFarlane. Melbourne, Australia: Book Distributors, 1974.
Analysis by Australia's foremost JFK assassination researcher.

The Assassination of John F. Kennedy; The Reasons Why, by Albert H. Newman. New York: Potter, 1970.

This staunch Warren Commission defense ignores the body of evidence and dwells on Oswald's mental state as perceived by the author. Refers to Mark Lane's "little pink fingers in the cookie jar of truth." Excellent chronology, however. HTF.

The Assassination of President Kennedy, compiled and designed by Michael Rand, Howard Loxton, and Len Deighton. London: Cape, 1967.
A jackdaw kit, containing documents and cutout model of Dealey Plaza. HTF.

The Assassination of President Kennedy; A Study of the Press Coverage, by Dean C. Baker. Ann Arbor, Mich.: University of Michigan Department of Journalism, 1965.
A 100-page academic survey of U.S. print media and how the assassination weekend was handled in terms of space, subject, advertising, headlines, photos, readership, circulation, etc. Interesting section on headline writers who had already tried and convicted Oswald. Try journalism school libraries.

The Assassination Story: Newspaper Clippings from the Two Dallas Dailies. Dallas: American Eagle Publishing Co., 1964.
Sixty pages of valuable clippings between November 22 and December 11, 1963. Originally published by an associate of Major General Edwin Walker, ret., later reduced to booklet size. (Available from Penn Jones, see *Forgive My Grief, Vol. I* for address.)

The Assassination Tapes; An Electronic Probe Into the Murder of John F. Kennedy and the Dallas Cover-Up, by George O'Toole. New York: Penthouse Press, 1975.
Relies on the new Psychological Stress Evaluator device said to reflect on a speaker's veracity based on the level of vocal stress. The author, a former chief of problem analysis for the CIA, asserts Oswald was innocent. Few libraries and bookstores.

The Assassinations: Dallas and Beyond—A Guide to Cover-Ups and Investigations, edited by Peter Dale Scott, Paul L. Hoch and Russell Stetler. New York: Random House/ Vintage Press, 1976.
Contains evidentiary studies on the major assassinations. *The* text in its field. Many bookstores, some libraries.

The Assassins, by A. V. Syme. Sydney, Australia: Horwitz Publications, 1967.
A sentimental documentary-style review of the Warren Commission case against Oswald, put in the context of assassinations around the world. The author leaves Warren Commission veracity an open question. Syme also wrote *Vietnam: The Cruel War.* Libraries in Australia.

Assassins From Tomorrow, by Peter Heath. New York: Lancer Books, 1967.
The Kennedy murder is the setting for a science-fiction journey. HTF.

This Awesome Challenge, by Michael Amrine. New York: Putnam, Popular Library paperback, 1964.
HTF.

The Bane in Kennedy's Existence, by Bernard M. Bane. Boston: BMB Publishing Co., 1967.
Conspicuous title, contents less so. HTF.

The Bastard Bullet: A Search for Legitimacy for Commission Exhibit 399, by Raymond Marcus. Los Angeles: Randall Publications, 1966.
A short but piercing study of the Warren Commission's magic bullet theory. HTF.

The Bay of Pigs: The Leaders Story of Brigade 2506, by Haynes Johnson. New York: W. W. Norton; Dell paperback, 1964.
This inside story of the CIA's invasion was written before the Warren Report came out; it could shed light on who killed Kennedy—and why. Some used bookstores.

Betrayal: A Reconstruction of Certain Clandestine Events From the Bay of Pigs to the Assassination of John F. Kennedy, by Robert D. Morrow. Chicago: Henry Regnery Co., 1976.
Seems to depend heavily on the Garrison investigation. Reconstructed events are between alleged conspirators now anonymous, dead, or missing. The author, a former CIA contract agent, presents a tidy package of not-

Cover-up Lowdown BY JAY KINNEY & PAUL MAVRIDES

"NO. 399 WITH A BULLET!"

© 1976 by Kinney & Mavrides

(A) ACCORDING TO THE WARREN COMMISSION, **BULLET** "A" (NO. 399) SHATTERED **2** BONES & CAUSED **7** WOUNDS!

(B) YET **BULLET** "B", FIRED THRU EQUIVALENT OBSTACLES SHOWS UNIQUELY DIFFERENT "WEAR & TEAR"!

quite credible events. Some of the confusion caused by this book is cleared up in the author's statement issued by Congressman Thomas Downing in August 1976. Bookstores.

A Bibliography of Books, Newspaper and Magazine Articles, Published in English Outside the United States of America, Related to the Assassination of John F. Kennedy, by T. H. Irwin and Hazel Hale. Belfast, Ireland: Self-published, 1975.

A valuable addition to the field; lists television programs as well. Goes chronologically, even includes six entries from the Soviet Union. (Available from T. H. Irwin, 32 Ravensdene Crescent, Ravenhill, Belfast BT6 0DB, Ireland, for $3.00 U.S.)

A Bibliography of Literature Relating to the Assassination of President John F. Kennedy, compiled by W. C. Thompson. San Antonio: Carleton Printing Co., 1968; revised with supplement, Jiffy Press, 1971.
A most comprehensive listing of books, records, and movies on the subject. Relied upon by many researchers.

The Biggest Lie Ever Told; The Kennedy Fraud and How I Helped Expose It, by Joachim Joesten. Munich: Self-published, 1968.
Four volumes published in mimeo form. HTF.

Bulletin From Dallas; The President Is Dead, by John B. Mayo. New York: Exposition Press, 1967.
Contains radio and TV coverage of the assassination. HTF.

The Case Against the Kennedy Clan in the Assassination of President John F. Kennedy, by Joachim Joesten. Munich: Self-published, 1968.
Mimeo supplement to *Oswald—The Truth.* Twenty thousand words, very speculative. HTF.

The Case Against Lyndon B. Johnson in the Assassination of President Kennedy; The Detailed Story of the First Coup d'Etat in American History, by Joachim Joesten. Munich: Self-published, 1967.
Two-volume mimeo supplement to *Oswald—The Truth.* Speculative. HTF.

Citizen's Arrest: The Dissent of Penn Jones, Jr., in the Assassination of JFK, by Harry C. Nash. Austin, Texas: Latitudes Press, 1977.
The first book about a researcher—covers the exploits of the still active Midlothian, Tex., conspiracist. The author, a Morehead, N.C., teacher, includes an appendix listing "Forty-five Basic Objections to the 'Single-Assassin' Findings of the Warren Report."

A Citizen's Dissent, by Mark Lane. New York: Holt, Rinehart & Winston, 1968.
Subtitle: "Mark Lane replies to the defenders of the Warren Report, to the press and communications industry, to the Establishment intellectuals and commentators, and tells the often grim story of how his dissent was almost silenced." Informative book. Available in many libraries and used bookstores.

Children and the Death of a President, by Martha Wolfenstein and Gilbert Kliman. Garden City, N.Y.: Doubleday Anchor, 1966.
Academic papers analyze the effect of the assassination on children; originally presented at a conference on the subject. Few libraries.

Closing In: The Search for JFK's Assassins, by Dick Russell, with photographs by Richard E. Sprague. New York: Dial Press, 1977 (scheduled).
This free-lance journalist has hustled around the country interviewing subjects other researchers merely exchange footnotes about, including CIA hit men, the alleged "second Oswald," and others. Bookstores.

College Students Reactions to the Assassination, by Fred I. Greenstein. Stanford, Cal.: Stanford Univerity Press.
Draws on the author's 1965 article in the *American Journal of Psychiatry.* HTF, try Stanford University library.

Coincidence—or Conspiracy? by Bernard Fensterwald, Jr., and the Committee to Investigate Assassinations, compiled by Michael Ewing. New York: Zebra Books, 1977 (scheduled).
Describes possible involvement in the Kennedy assassination of over two hundred people, many well known. This lengthy book (700 pages) draws no conclusions, but rather presents gathered facts. Also includes the Senate report on assassinations and a sizable bibliography. Newsstands.

The Complete Kennedy Saga, four volumes compiled and published by Associated Professional Services. Hollywood: 1967.
A review of the official line of events. HTF.

Computers & People Magazine (formerly *Computers and Automation*) edited and published by Edmund Berkeley. Newtonville, Mass.: Berkeley Enterprises, Inc.
Every issue from May 1970 to April 1975 contained an article on assassination or conspiracy. A gold mine, check local science libraries. (Series continued in *People in the Pursuit of Truth,* effective May 1975.)

Conspiracy Interpretations of the Assassination of President Kennedy, by Alfred Goldberg. Los Angeles: University of California Security Studies Project, 1968.
An Air Force historian and Warren Commission staffer writes an undocumented attack on critics he labels "demonologists." Security studies?? A few libraries.

A Conspiracy Murdered President Kennedy, by Ross Ralston. East Grand Forks, Minn.: Unpublished manuscript.
27 pages, mainly visual evidence. HTF.

The Conspirators: (The Garrison Case), by Sandy Hockberg and James T. Valliere. New York: Special Edition of *Win Magazine,* February 1, 1969.
This 45-page resource guide to the Garrison inquiry is both fair and informed. Published by a magazine of gentle integrity.

Controlled Brinkmanship, by Bernard M. Bane. Boston: BMB Publishing Co., 1968.
Eight-page pamphlet; theoretical, incomprehensible (by the author of *Is John F. Kennedy Alive . . . And Well?*). HTF.

Counterplot, by Edward J. Epstein. New York: Viking Press, 1969.
An attack on Jim Garrison with the wrong facts for the wrong reasons. In libraries.

Coup d'Etat in America: The CIA and the Assassination of John F. Kennedy, by Michael Canfield and Alan J. Weberman. New York: Third Press, 1975.
Well-researched chronicle of CIA anti-Castro cabal; includes revealing interview with CIA/Watergate operative Frank Sturgis. Marred by

apocryphal theory that E. Howard Hunt and Frank Sturgis were in Dealey Plaza, and other assumptions. Few bookstores and libraries.

Coup d'Etat! Three Murders That Changed the Course of History; President Kennedy, Reverend King, and Senator Robert F. Kennedy, by Stanley J. Marks. Los Angeles: Bureau of International Affairs, 1970.
Theories posing as history, redeemed by appendix of documents and photos. Few libraries.

Cover-Up; The Governmental Conspiracy to Conceal the Facts About the Public Execution of John Kennedy, by Larry R. Harris with J. Gary Shaw. Cleburne, Tex.: published by Shaw, 1976.
Primer on JFK assassination for newcomers to the field. Well-documented with many photos never published before. Easy to read and absorb. (Available from the authors: P.O. Box 722, Cleburne, Texas 76031.)

Crackpot or Crack Shot, by Kenneth Goff. Englewood, Colo. Self-published, 1965.
Blames Communism. HTF.

Crime and Cover-Up; The CIA, The Mafia, and the Dallas-Watergate Connection, by Peter Dale Scott. Berkeley, Calif.: Westworks (P.O. Box 2071, Station A, Berkeley, Cal. 94702), 1977.
Scott's web of interconnections between organized criminals in and out of government is so thick that it's virtually opaque. Generously footnoted, with a foreword by Sylvia Meagher. Eighty pages. Available from the publisher.

Critical Reactions to the Warren Report, compiled by the editors of Marzani and Munsell. New York: Marzani and Munsell, 1965.
A 65-page collection of articles by Kempton, Lane, Buchanan, Sauvage, and others. HTF.

Crossfire: Evidence of Conspiracy, by R.B. Cutler. Beverly, Mass.: Omni-Print, 1972.
Charts and theories of bullet flightpaths in Dealey Plaza. (Available from the author: P.O. Box 1465, Manchester, Mass. 01944.)

Dallas Conspiracy, by David Nord, Jr. Hollis, New Hampshire: 1968.
The Commies did it. HTF.

The Dallas Conspiracy, by Peter Dale Scott. Berkeley, Cal.: Unpublished manuscript.
Cited heavily in *They've Killed the President!* by Anson; widely circulated and respected by researchers. An underground gem, focusing on organized crime, anti-Castroites, and U.S. intelligence operations. Scott is so thorough that even the footnotes have footnotes.

Dallas Justice: The Real Story on Jack Ruby and His Trial, by Melvin Belli with Maurice C. Carroll. New York: David McKay, 1964.
A Ruby lawyer, the author accepts that his client acted impulsively and on his own. In some libraries.

Dallas, Public and Private; Aspects of an American City, by Warren Leslie. New York: Grossman Publishers, 1964.
The author was an executive of Nieman-Marcus; a behind-the-scenes look at the Dallas power structure. HTF.

"YES, WE STOCK ALL THE NEW JFK ASSASSINATION BOOKS AND THE WASHINGTON SEX SCANDALS... BUT WE RAN OUT OF ROOM FOR CUSTOMERS!"

Stayskal—Chicago Tribune

The Dark Side of Lyndon Baines Johnson, by Joachim Joesten. London: Peter Dawnay, 1968.
Background material on LBJ leads to speculation. HTF.

The Day Kennedy Died, by Dan Wise and Marietta Maxfield. San Antonio: Naylor, 1964.
One of the very first full-length books on the assassination. The authors were S. M. U. law students at the time. HTF.

The Day Kennedy Was Shot, by Jim Bishop.

New York: Funk & Wagnalls, 1968; Bantam paperback, 1969.
Saturated with innumerable factual errors. Available in many used bookstores and libraries.

"The Death of a President," by M. S. Arnoni. Passaic, New Jersey: *Minority of One,* 1964.
Published by one of the first magazines to critically scrutinize the Dallas events. HTF.

The Death of a President: November 20-25, 1963, by William Manchester. New York:

Harper & Row, 1967; Popular Library paperback, 1968.

Drama and research in abundance; answers scarce. Not worth all the controversy it provoked. Good chronology. Available in many used bookstores and most libraries.

The Death of the President: The Warren Report on Trial in New Orleans! by John B. West. Covina, Cal.: 1967.

One-hundred-page quickie exploitation book on Garrison with Warren Report highlights. HTF.

Destiny in Dallas: On the Scene Story in Pictures, by R. B. Denson. Dallas: Denco Corp., 1964.

The author was a private investigator hired by Ruby's relatives. HTF.

The Destruction of the Temple, by Barry N. Malzberg. New York: Pocket Books, 1974.

"The year is 2016," says the blurb on this science-fiction paperback, "and President Kennedy is being murdered again and again and again." HTF.

Diary of a Nightmare, by Ursula Von Kardorff. London: 1965. HTF.

Document Addendum to the Warren Report, by David Lifton. El Segundo, Cal.: Sightext Publications, 1968.

When published, this was an indispensable resource tool. HTF.

Editorials U.S.A.; Editorials Relating to the Assassination of President Kennedy, collected by Ronald Rains. Dallas: Self-published, 1965.

Twenty pages, tabloid. HTF.

Everything You Wanted to Know About Jacqueline Kennedy's Behavior at the Moment of the Assassination of President John F. Kennedy in Dallas on Nov. 22, 1963, Including the Way the News Media Described It at the Time and the Way Mrs. Kennedy Described It Three Years Later, by Veritas (pseud.). Washington, D.C.: Self-published.

Jackie could have saved Jack if she had her wits about her, says this mysterious 16-page pamphlet. Many photos. HTF.

The Evidence: An Appendix to Executive Action Providing Supportive Documentation, by Steve Jaffe, Mark Lane, and Donald Freed. Unpublished, August 1971.

Correlates to the book *Executive Action,* likewise to the movie; 56 pages.

Executive Action, by Mark Lane and Donald Freed. New York: Dell paperback, 1973.

A novel of fact; reconstructs events based on in-depth research. Better than the movie of the same name. Some bookstores and newsstands.

Executive Action; Facts Behind the Making of This Film, by Stephen Jaffe, with special research by Martin Gates and David Lifton. 1973.

A handout to viewers of the movie, this eight-page fact-filled booklet contains key particles of documented material that lead to a conspiratorial conclusion. HTF.

Farewell America, by James Hepburn (pseud.). Liechtenstein: Frontiers Publishing Co., 1968.

This most mysterious book, published where libel laws do not apply, appeared at the time of Garrison. Its grandiose right-wing conspiracy is led by oil interests. Fact or fiction, it is believed to be based on foreign intelligence files. An underground enigma. Distributed mainly in Canada. HTF.

Fifty-One Witnesses: The Grassy Knoll, by Harold Feldman. San Francisco: Idlewild Publishers, 1965.

Fifty-five pages reprinted from *Minority of One,* March 1965. An important early contributor. The author also wrote on Oswald in *The Nation.* HTF.

Files of Evidence Connected With the Investigation of the Assassination of President John F. Kennedy, by Leon Jaworski. 21 volumes, 2 reels microfilm. Washington, D.C.: Microcard Editions, 1967.

Little-known facts from the Texas Attorney General's inquiry. Jaworski gets around. HTF.

The Flight of CE-399; Evidence of Conspiracy, by Robert B. Cutler. Beverly, Mass.: Omni-Print, 1969; Cutler Designs, 1970.

Excellent critique of the Warren Commission's single-bullet theory. Material also appears in the author's book, *Two Flightpaths.* HTF.

Forgive My Grief, Volume I: A Critical Review of the Warren Commission Report, by Penn Jones, Jr. Midlothian, Texas: *Midlothian Mirror* (newspaper), 1966.

Critique of the Warren Report based almost exclusively on testimony before the commission. Published by a courageous small-town editor. Includes first of the mysterious deaths of witnesses. (Available from the author: Box 1140, Midlothian, Texas 76065.)

Forgive My Grief, Volume II: A Further Critical Review of the Warren Commission Report, by Penn Jones, Jr. Midlothian: *Midlothian Mirror,* 1967.

The count is up to twenty-four "strange" deaths of witnesses. The author includes further evidence of conspiracy with insight into the Texas power structure. (Available from the author, see *Forgive My Grief, Vol. I.*)

Forgive My Grief, Volume III: Now the People Know Who Killed Their President and They Are Totally Afraid, by Penn Jones, Jr. Midlothian: *Midlothian Mirror,* 1969 (reissued with photo-illustrated appendix, 1976).

The count is at sixty-eight victims—the hits just keep on comin'. Also includes pro-Garrison coverage of the D.A.'s inquiry. 1976 edition includes new information. (Available from the author, see *Forgive My Grief, Vol. I.*)

Forgive My Grief, Volume IV: A Further Critical Review of the Warren Commission Report on the Assassination of President John F. Kennedy, by Penn Jones, Jr. Midlothian: *Midlothian Mirror,* 1974.

Years of research leads to wide speculation.

(Available from the author, see *Forgive My Grief, Vol. I.*)

Four Dark Days in History; November 22, 23, 24 and 25, 1963, by Jim Matthews. Los Angeles: Special Publications, 1963.
A 64-page quickie, with photos. HTF.

The Gaps in the Warren Report, by Joachim Joesten. New York: Marzani and Munsell, 1965.
A 47-page addition to the original edition of the author's *Oswald; Assassin or Fall Guy?* HTF.

The Garrison Case, by Milton E. Brenner. New York: Potter, 1969.
Somewhat emotional harangue against Garrison. Some libraries.

The Garrison Enquiry; Truth and Consequences, by Joachim Joesten. London: Peter Dawnay, 1967.
Highly speculative. HTF.

Government by Gunplay; Assassination Conspiracy Theories from Dallas to Today, edited by Sid Blumenthal and Harvey Yazijian of the Assassination Information Bureau. New York: Signet, 1976.
Essays by the best and the brightest; covers major assassinations, Watergate, and clandestinism. Try bookstores and newsstands.

The Gun—A "Biography" of the Gun That Killed John F. Kennedy, by Henry S. Bloomgarden. New York: Grossman, 1975.
The author says that the Mannlicher-Carcano and Oswald could have done it. Also contains comments on gun control. Few bookstores.

Guns of the Regressive Right: Or How to Kill a President, by Morris A. Bealle. Washington, D.C.: Columbia Publishing Co., 1964.
According to the bookjacket, this is "the only reconstruction of the Kennedy assassination that makes sense." HTF.

The Harrassment of Roger Craig; The Case History of an Uncooperative Witness, by Harry Irwin. Belfast: Self-published, 1977.
This nine-page pamphlet outlines the trauma Dallas County Sheriff's Deputy Roger Craig went through in the years between John Kennedy's death and his own.

David Milne

Much of the material is in the form of letters from his widow. Craig had solid unshakable evidence that Oswald had accomplices in the assassination but was ignored by authorities and harrassed by others until his suicide.

He Gave His Life; A Newspaper's Account of the Assassination of a President and the Two Weeks That Followed, compiled by the editors of the *Nashville Tennessean.* Nashville: *Nashville Tennessean,* 1965.
Reprints from the *Tennessean,* whose editor John Siegenthaler was a close Kennedy friend. HTF.

A Heritage of Stone, by Jim Garrison. New York: Putnam, 1970; Berkeley paperback, 1972.
A reasonable political analysis of the assassination motive, by the New Orleans D.A. who led an independent probe of the murder. Used bookstores and libraries.

Highlights of the Warren Report, by Marc Davis and Jim Matthews. Los Angeles: Associated Professional Services, 1964.
A very condensed Warren report. HTF.

History's Verdict, by Ross Ralston. Unpublished manuscript.
Excellent on the shooting of Major General Edwin A. Walker, ret., and policeman J.D. Tippit.

A Hog Story; From the Aftermire of the Kennedy Assassination, by Bill Smith. Washington, D.C.: L'Avant Garde Publications, 1968.
A convoluted theory which has right-wing plotters cashing in on hog-market speculation. Hard to follow, HTF.

How Kennedy Was Killed; The Full Appalling Story, by Joachim Joesten. London: Peter Dawnay, 1968.
The title is overstated. HTF.

Illuminatus, Part I; The Eye in the Pyramid, by Robert Shea and Robert Anton Wilson. New York: Dell, 1975.
Combines Vonnegut and Castaneda; result is a strange visionary perspective of conspiracy. Only a small portion deals with the assassination *per se,* however. Some bookstores and newsstands.

In the Shadow of Dallas: A Primer on the Assassination of President Kennedy, by the editors of *Ramparts.* San Francisco: *Ramparts Magazine,* 1967.
Articles from the only magazine which consistently probed conspiracy through the sixties. HTF.

Incident at Credibility Gap and the Innocent Child; A Fairy Tale of Courage and Grief, by G.Z.A. Barkus. Greenwich, Conn.: Paper Bag Books, 1967.
A 28-page allegory. HTF.

Index of Basic Source Materials in Possession of the Warren Commission, compiled by the National Archives. Washington, D.C.: Government Printing Office, 1967.
Was a tool for those researching at the National Archives. Outdated now, however.

Inquest; The Warren Commission and the

Establishment of Truth, by Edward Jay Epstein. New York: Viking Press, Bantam paperback, 1966. Viking reissue, 1969.
Reveals scope and causes of Warren Commission cover-up through interviews with its staff and members. One of the first major criticisms. Later, the author opposed those who stayed critical. Libraries and used bookstores.

Investigation of the Assassination of President John F. Kennedy; Hearings Before the President's Commission, 26 volumes, by the President's Commission on the Assassination of President John F. Kennedy. Washington, D.C.: Government Printing Office, 1964; Washington, D.C.: Zenger Publishing Co., 1977 (anticipated).
Over 18,000 pages—*the* basic source for researchers. The first 15 volumes are testimony, the balance is exhibits. Many conspiracy leads contained in the 26 volumes were not followed up or else omitted from the final report. In most major libraries. Few sets elsewhere, unfortunately.

The Investigation of the Assassination of President John F. Kennedy: Performance of the Intelligence Agencies, by the Select Committee on Intelligence. Washington, D.C: Government Printing Office, 1976.
This "Schweiker Report" is significant as the first official federal government criticism of the assassination investigation. It asserts the FBI and CIA withheld crucial data from the Warren Commission, but is marred by lending credence to the "Castro's Revenge" theory. Publication was delayed while intelligence agencies reviewed the contents and requested deletions. Available at Government Printing Office bookstores (major cities) and some libraries.

Investigation of a Homicide; The Murder of John F. Kennedy, by Judy Whitson Bonner. Anderson, S.C.: Droke House, 1969.
"Investigation" probes no further than Oswald. Relies heavily on Dallas police tapes. Some libraries.

Invitation to Hairsplitting: A Hypercritical Investigation Into the True Function of the Warren Commission and the True Nature of the Warren Report, by J. Zwart. Paris-Amsterdam: 1970.
HTF.

Is John F. Kennedy Alive . . . And Well? by Bernard M. Bane. Boston: BMB Publishing Co., 1973.
No. HTF.

It Is As If: Curious Aspects Concerning the Matter of President Kennedy's Death, by Thothnu N. Tastmona. New York: Thothmona Book Co., 1966.
Mormons, Christianity, and Middle East monuments are involved. Indigestible. HTF.

Jack Ruby; The Man Who Killed the Man Who Killed Kennedy, by Gary Wills and Ovid Demaris. New York: New American Library, 1967; N.A.L. paperback, 1968.
An orthodox account, nice anecdotes about Ruby, however. Some libraries.

Jack Ruby's Girls, by Diana Hunter and Alice Anderson. Atlanta: Hallux, Inc., 1970.

The authors' dedication says "Our raging boss, our faithful friend, the kindest-hearted sonuvabitch we ever knew." Enlightening. HTF.

Jackdaw Kit; The Assassination of President John F. Kennedy. New York: Grossman, 1967.
Cutout sections form a three-dimensional replica of Dealey Plaza. HTF.

Jackie, Bobby and Manchester; The Story Behind the Headlines, by Arnold Bennett. New York: Bee Line Books, 1967.
About the controversy surrounding Manchester's *The Death of a President.* HTF.

JFK Assassination File: Retired Dallas Police Chief Jesse Curry Reveals His Personal File, by Jesse Curry. Dallas: American Poster and Publishing Co., 1969.
Curry defends his actions that weekend. The book contains valuable photos and documents. Locatable in some Dallas bookstores and newsstands.

JFK: The Case for Conspiracy, by F. Peter Model and Robert J. Groden. New York: Manor Books paperback, 1976.
Photoanalysis of the Zapruder film with a text surveying conspiracy evidence. Groden's photo-enhancement of the Zapruder film is acknowledged as one of *the* major advances in the field. Try bookstores and newsstands.

Joshua Son of None, by Nancy Freedman. New York: Delacorte, 1973; Dell, 1974.
President cloned! A novel. Few libraries.

Kennedy and Big Business, by Alvin Gerenson. Beverly Hills, Cal.: Book Company of America, 1964.
Speculation that Big Business killed JFK. (What was Kennedy, small business?) HTF.

The Kennedy Assassination and the American Public; Social Communication in Crisis, by Bradley S. Greenburg and Edwin B. Parker. Stanford, Cal.: Stanford University Press, 1965.
Academic analyses of how the assassination affected various groups. Includes among other studies, one by the National Opinion Research Center on public apathy and public grief. HTF, try Stanford University library.

The Kennedy Conspiracy; An Uncommissioned Report on the Jim Garrison Investigation, by Paris Flammonde. New York: Meredith, 1969.
A favorable report on the specifics of the Garrison investigation, highlighted by a chapter on the media hysteria it provoked. Some libraries.

The Kennedy Curse: An Astrologer's View of the Destiny of America's First Family of Politics, by Arthur Gatti. Chicago: Henry Regnery Co., 1976.
"John Kennedy was born with the Sun in Gemini, the Moon in Virgo, his Ascendant in Libra." Well! No *wonder* organized crime, petroleum interests, and elements of the cryptocracy had him assassinated. Few libraries, generally HTF.

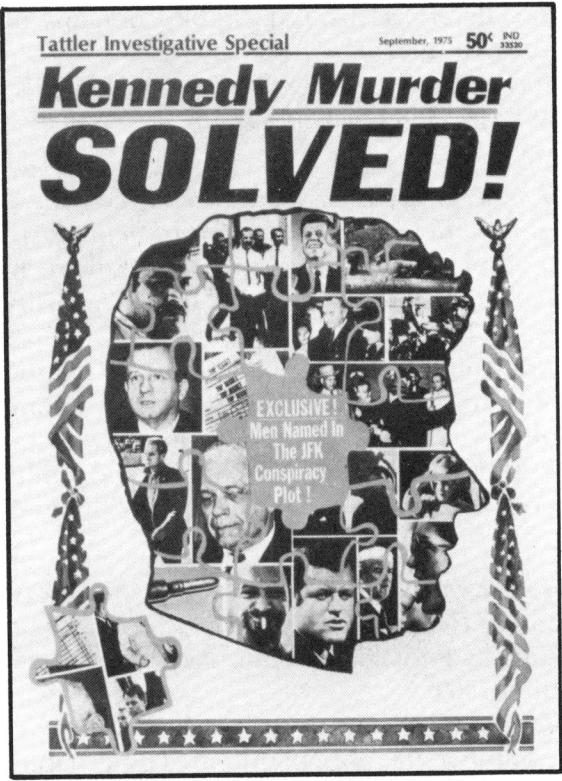

Tattler Investigative Special   September, 1975   50¢ IND 33530

Kennedy Murder

SOLVED!

EXCLUSIVE!
Men Named In
The JFK
Conspiracy
Plot!

Lee Harvey Oswald, Allen W. Dulles, Ronald Lee Augustinovich, J. Lee Rankin, Eugene Hale Brading, Elaido del Valle, Lawrence Howard Jr., Thomas Kane, Luis Angel Castillo, Earl Warren, Gerald Ford, Richard Russell, John McCloy, Gary Patrick Hemming, Hale Boggs, Bill Turner, David Belin, Mark Lane, Dean Fallon, Loran Hall, Jim Garrison, Peter Dale Scott, Harold Weisberg, Al Chapman, John Cooper, Mrs. Sylvia Odio, David Ferrie, Albert E. Jenner, William Wood, Arlen Specter, Richard Sprague, Donald Freed, Richard Popkin, Jack Ruby, Clay Shaw, Carlos Marcello, Dean Andrews, Lee Odom, Andy Anderson, The National Tattler.

The Kennedy Literature, by James Tracy Crown. New York: New York University Press, 1968.
A detailed annotated review of books on John Kennedy, divided into subjects including the assassination. The author shows some respect and great doubt of books by the critics, and is warm towards the Conventional Wisdom. Some libraries.

Kennedy Murder Solved! by the editors of the *National Tattler.* Chicago: Publishers Promotion Agency, Inc., 1975.
A supermarket tabloid overstates the case.

Khrushchev Killed Kennedy, by Michael H. B. Eddowes. Dallas: Self-published, 1975. Using a telescopic sight, of course. HTF.

Last Man at Arlington, by Joseph Dimona. New York: Arthur Fields Books, 1973.
Novel by former *Washington Post* reporter tells of CIA murders which surround the JFK assassination. HTF.

Lee Harvey Oswald, by Michael Hastings. Baltimore: Penguin Books, 1966.
A play, eventually performed in Atlanta and elsewhere, which draws out the psychological pressures on the "loner assassin." Involves Marina and Marguerite as well. HTF.

Lee Harvey Oswald and the American Dream, by Paul Sites. New York: Pageant Press, 1967.
Intriguing title. HTF.

Lee; A Portrait of Lee Harvey Oswald, by Robert L. Oswald, with Myrick and Barbara Land. New York: Coward-McCann, 1967.
Interesting background on Lee's upbringing, by his brother. Some libraries and used bookstores.

Legacy of an Assassination, by Norbert Murray. New York: Pro-People Press, 1964.
"Exposes red treachery," says the bookjacket. Also, "The book that powerful people in Washington don't want you to read." The powerful people had their way. HTF.

Legacy of Doubt, by Peter Noyes. New York: Pinnacle Books paperback, 1973.
Half of this book documents that a Mafia operative was in Dealey Plaza; the other half attacks Garrison's motives, suggesting organized crime ties. The author is at least half right. Try bookstores and newsstands.

Life-Itek Kennedy Assassination Film Analysis, by the Itek Corporation. Lexington, Mass.: Itek Corporation, 1967.
Be wary—Itek is very technical but is supported by CIA contracts and contacts to some extent. HTF.

The Lingering Shadow, by Bernard Gauzer and Sid Moody. Dallas: 1967.
A reprint from the *Dallas Times-Herald* of Sunday, June 25, 1967. Two Associated Press writers in a scholarly report, discuss the Warren Commission critics. It is not supportive of the critics. HTF.

MacBird! by Barbara Garson. Berkeley, Cal.: The Grassy Knoll Press, 1966; Grove/Evergreen Black Cat, 1967.
An appropriately vicious and successful morality play about LBJ's usurpation of power. Done in Shakespearean fashion. A classic in its time. Used bookstores.

The Making of the President, 1964, by Theodore White. New York: Atheneum Publishers, 1965.
The author propagates conventional wisdom. Most libraries, also used bookstores.

The Man Who Knew Kennedy, by Vance Bourjaily. New York: Dial Press, 1967.
Uses the JFK assassination as a reference point for a look at his generation. A novel. Some libraries.

The Manchester Affair, by John Corry. New York: Putnam, 1967.
More about the book, *The Death of a Presi-*

dent, and the problems encountered by its author. HTF.

Marina Oswald, by Joachim Joesten. London: Peter Dawnay, 1967.
Heavily speculative about Lee's querulous wife. HTF.

The Men Behind the Guns, by W. R. Morris. Loretto, Tenn.: Angel Lea Books, 1975.
Asserts that retired Major General Edwin Walker and former California Congressman Rousselot conspired with Birchers. Thirty pages, tabloid style, by the author of the novel on which the movie "Walking Tall" was based. HTF, try major newsstands.

Moment of Madness: The People vs. Jack Ruby, by Elmer Gertz. Chicago: Follett Publishing Co., 1968.
The author, an attorney, writes an accurate account of the trial and argues that the murder was not premeditated. Some libraries.

Motorcade—November 22, 1963, by Tom Dunshee and Richard Duncan. Trenton, N. J.: Self-published, 1975.
(Available from the authors: Box 4547, Trenton, N. J. 08611.)

A Mother in History; Mrs. Marguerite Oswald, by Jean Stafford. New York: Farrar, Straus, and Giroux; Bantam paperback, 1966.
An elongated version of an interview originally in the October 1965 *McCall's* magazine. About the mother who stuck by her son. Few libraries.

Murder From Within, by Fred Newcomb. Van Nuys, Cal.: Unpublished manuscript.

This manuscript, privately circulated among a select group of researchers, indicates that the Secret Service was involved in the assassination.

Murder Most Foul! The Conspiracy That Murdered President Kennedy, by Stanley J. Marks. Los Angeles: Bureau of International Affairs, 1967.
Subtitle: "975 Questions and Answers." Whew! HTF.

The Murder of Police Officer J. D. Tippit, by Gary Murr. Canada: Unpublished manuscript, 1971.
The author does a microstudy of the Tippit murder.

The Mysterious and Unpublicized Facts Behind the Assassination of John F. Kennedy, by Gerald L. K. Smith. Los Angeles: Christian Nationalist Crusade, 1965.
The author delights in calling Oswald's assassin "Rubenstein." Fifteen pages of heavy anti-Communism. HTF.

A Nation Grieved; The Kennedy Assassination in Editorial Cartoons, compiled by Raymond B. Rajski. Rutland, Vt.: Charles E. Tuttle, 1967.
HTF.

National Archives Lawsuit, by Sherman H. Skolnick and the Citizen's Committee to Clean Up the Courts. Chicago: Self-published, 1970.
Text of this lawsuit, with documents, details a plot to kill JFK in Chicago, November 2,

1963. (Available from the plaintiff: 9800 S. Oglesby Avenue, Chicago 60617.)

Neither the Fanatics nor the Faint-Hearted, by John H. Jenkins, Austin, Texas: Pemberton Press, 1963.
Subtitle: "The Tour Leading to the President's Death and the Two Speeches He Could Not Give." HTF.

Nomenclature of an Assassination Cabal, by William Torbitt (pseud.). Unpublished manuscript, 1970.
Parallels Garrison evidence, suggests a right-wing clique from U.S. intelligence and organized crime. Participants range from J. Edgar Hoover to Roy Cohen to Joe Bonannos. One of most mysterious and best circulated manuscripts on the sleuth underground. The author is believed to be a prominent attorney in Waco, Texas.

Now It Can Be Told! Festival of the Fiends, by Allan Witwer. Unpublished manuscript.
The author points a finger at J. Edgar Hoover.

November 22, How They Killed Kennedy, by Michael Eddowes. London: Neville Spearman Ltd., 1976.
First book originating in England on the subject since 1968. Hard to find in U.S., try ordering through bookstores. Basically the same book as *Khrushchev Killed Kennedy.*

November 22, 1963: You Are the Jury, by David W. Belin. New York: Quadrangle Books, 1973.
The author, a Warren Commission attorney,

became one of the most fanatical defenders of the Party Line. Later, staff director of the Rockefeller Commission peek at the CIA. This book retells the Warren Report. Few bookstores, some libraries.

Of Poetry and Power; Poems Occasioned by the Presidency and Death of John Kennedy. New York: Basic Books, 1964.
Has one Allen Ginsberg poem. HTF.

One and One Make Two Sometimes: The Kennedy Assassination, by Bruce Gordon. 1968.
HTF.

One Day; This Being the Day in November the Word from Dallas Was Heard in Escondido, by Wright Morris. New York: Atheneum, 1965.
A novel which juxtaposes an abandoned infant with the death of the President. HTF.

1:33 In Memoriam: John F. Kennedy, by Bruce Henderson and Sam Summerlin. New York: Cowles Education Corp., 1968.
A global look at the assassination's effect. HTF.

Operation Mind Control, by Walter Bowart. New York: Delacorte, 1977 (scheduled).
The first book to document substantial U.S. government activity in the field of mind control; posits that the Kennedy assassination was planned and carried out by the ruling "cryptocracy." The author, a founder of the *East Village Other* in 1965, presents data on mind control techniques used in the Kennedy murder and other assassinations.

Oswald, by Kerry Thornley. Chicago: New Classics House, 1965.
The author wrote a novel based on Oswald in 1960 after serving in the Marines with him. This book includes Thornley's testimony before the Warren Commission and, it advertises, "what he did not tell the commission." HTF.

The Oswald Affair; An Examination of the Contradictions and Omissions of the Warren Report, by Leo Sauvage. Cleveland: World Publishing Co., 1966.
An early critique of the commission's findings by a French journalist. Some libraries.

Oswald: Assassin or Fall Guy? by Joachim Joesten. New York: Marzani and Munsell, 1964. Reprinted with a critique of the Warren Report, 1965.
This remarkable book was the first book (June 1964) to take a critical view of the official lone assassin theory. A few libraries.

Oswald in New Orleans; Case for Conspiracy With the CIA, by Harold Weisberg. New York: Canyon Books, 1967.
The author makes an impressive and well-documented case in not unreadable style. Foreword by Jim Garrison. Few libraries.

Oswald: The Truth, by Joachim Joesten. London: Peter Dawnay, 1967.
Oswald rumors collected. HTF.

Panel Review, by Joachim Joesten. Munich: Self-published, 1968.
A description of the report on the JFK autop-

Quinan—Washington Star

sy made by a government-selected panel to Attorney General Ramsey Clark in April 1968. HTF.

The Parallax View, by Loren Singer. New York: Doubleday, 1970.
A novel based on assassination of a politician; the hero is an investigative reporter who

sees witnesses turn up dead left and right. Later a movie. Some used bookstores.

A Physicist Examines the Kennedy Assassination Film, by Luis W. Alvarez. Unpublished manuscript.
Prepared under a government contract. Says one lone assassin could do it.

Photographic Whitewash; Suppressed Kennedy Assassination Pictures, by Harold Weisberg. Hyattstown, Md.: Self-published, 1967.
The author demonstrates that shoddy and biased photoanalysis was used to support the lone assassin case. (Available from the author: Route 12, Old Receiver Rd., Frederick, Md. 21701.)

The Plot to Kill JFK, by David M. Warren. Chicago: Novel Books, 1965.
Subhead: "Explosive Documentary Novel of Three Men and Their Diabolical Plot to Assassinate John Fitzgerald Kennedy." HTF.

Plot or Politics? The Garrison Case and Its Cast, by Rosemary James and Jack Wardlaw. New Orleans: Pelican Publishing House, 1967.
The authors attempt to present both prosecution and defense sides of the controversy. Good background. HTF.

Portrait of the Assassin, by Gerald R. Ford and John R. Stiles. New York: Simon and Schuster, 1965; Ballentine paperback, 1966.
The authors, who crib heavily from Warren Commission hearings, publish material from a classified "top secret" document for chapter one (and unlike Daniel Ellsberg, were not prosecuted for it). Follows the Oswald-as-deranged-loner line. Author Ford, a Warren Commission member, later became Vice-President and President of the United States. Some libraries.

Post Mortem, by A. Edwards. New York: Coward-McCann, 1971.
HTF.

Post Mortem: JFK Assassination Cover-Up Smashed, by Harold Weisberg. Frederick, Md.: Self- published, 1975.
A probing look at the physical evidence leads to conclusion of conspiracy. (Available from the author: See *Photographic Whitewash* for address.)

The Press Corps and the Kennedy Assassination, (Journalism Monograph #15-1970), by Darwin Payne. Lexington, Kentucky: Association of Education for Journalism, 1969.
A reporter who covered the assassination events for the *Dallas Times Herald* (later a teacher at S. M. U.) writes an academic analysis of the problems the press coverage created. He now teaches at S. M. U. HTF.

Presumed Guilty: How and Why the Warren Commission Framed Lee Harvey Oswald, by Howard Roffman. Cranbury, N. J. Fairleigh Dickinson Press, 1975; London: Thomas Yoselaff, 1976; New York: A. S. Barnes & Co., 1976.
A law student probes the physical evidence and rejects the presumption of Oswald's guilt; a clear presentation of how the Warren

Commission functioned is also included. One of the best such books in print. Some bookstores, few libraries.

Proof of Conspiracy in the Assassination of President Kennedy, by Ian MacFarlane. Victoria, Australia: Book Distributors, 1975.
A summary of the best evidence for conspiracy; also includes essays from other writer-researchers on the case. (This resource guide is available from the author: c/o Book Distributors, 59 Talbot Crescent, Kooyong 3144, Victoria, Australia; or the Assassination Information Bureau, 63 Inman Street, Cambridge, Mass. 02139.)

The Quest for Truth; A Quizzical Look at the Warren Report—Or How President Kennedy Really Was Assassinated, by George C. Thomson. Glendale, Cal.: G. C. Thomson Engineering Co., 1964.
An early critique of the Warren Report interpretation of the physical evidence. Political preconception detracts greatly from this fifty-page effort. HTF.

Red Roses From Texas, by Nerin E. Gun. London: Frederick Muller, 1964.
One of the first full-length books published on the assassination; attacked by J. Edgar Hoover. Never published in the U. S. HTF.

Red Friday: November 22, 1963, by Carlos Bringuier. Chicago: C. Hallberg, 1969.
The Commies did it. Undocumented tripe from a Cuban exile who knew Oswald in New Orleans. HTF.

Report to the President by the Commission on CIA Activities Within the United States (The Rockefeller Commission Report). New York: Manor Books, 1975.
Chapter 19 says that convicted Watergaters E. Howard Hunt and Frank Sturgis did not participate in the assassination, that no bullet struck Kennedy from anywhere but the rear right, and that the CIA was not involved in the assassination. Staff director David W. Belin was an attorney for the Warren Commission. Some bookstores and libraries.

Report of the President's Commission on the Assassination of President John F. Kennedy ("The Warren Report"), by the President's Commission (Earl Warren, Chairman, Richard B. Russell, John Sherman Cooper, Hale Boggs, Gerald R. Ford, Allen W. Dulles, and John J. McCloy). Washington, D. C.: Government Printing Office, 1964. (Also published by Doubleday, McGraw Hill, Bantam, Popular Library, and the Associated Press, 1964.)
Speculates that Oswald alone killed JFK and that Ruby likewise acted with no conspirators in killing Oswald. Authors started with conclusion and worked backwards. Every library and most used bookstores.

The Ruby Detail (tentative title) by Seth Kantor. New York: Zebra Books, 1977.
Details of Ruby's connections with organized crime and pre-Castro Cuba. Also includes previously unpublished Warren Commission "problems" with Jack Ruby. The author is a reporter for the *Detroit News.* Bookstores and newsstands.

Rush to Judgment; A Critique of the Warren Commission's Inquiry Into the Murders of President John F. Kennedy, Officer J. D. Tippit, and Lee Harvey Oswald, by Mark Lane. New York: Holt, Rinehart & Winston, 1966; Fawcett Crest paperback, 1967; Dell paperback, 1975.

This international best-seller picks apart the Warren Report, using the commission's own evidence plus personal interviews with witnesses by the author. Most libraries and used bookstores.

Scavengers and Critics of the Warren Report, by Richard W. Lewis based on the investigation of Lawrence Schiller. New York: Delacourte Press, Dell paperback, 1967.

Inaccurate, emotional, baseless attempt to prop up the Warren Report by attacking the critics. Refers to women researchers as "housewives underground," etc. Some libraries.

The Schweiker Report—see *The Investigation of the Assassination of President John F. Kennedy: Performance of the Intelligence Agencies.*

Scop, by Barry N. Malzberg. New York: Pyramid, 1976.

A twenty-first-century museum employee, Scop returns to the scene of the sites of the two Kennedy, King, and Malcolm X assassinations in a vain attempt to thwart them. Newsstands.

A Search for Justice, by John Siegenthaler. Nashville: Aurora Publishers, circa 1970.

The author, a friend of the Kennedy family and editor of the *Nashville Tennessean,* examines the James Earl Ray, Sirhan Sirhan, and Clay Shaw trials. Raises conspiracy likelihood in the Ray case; is very anti-Garrison.

The Search for a Master Assassin. Shreveport, La.: Councillor Newspaper, 1972.

A right-wing newspaper (White Citizen's Council) thinks former New York Governor Herbert Lehman, a liberal mistaken for a communist, might have been responsible for the assassination. HTF.

The Second Oswald, by Richard H. Popkin. New York: Avon Books, 1966.

The author, a philosopher on the history of skepticism, documents the existence of a phony Oswald used to set up the actual Lee. Few libraries, HTF.

Seventy Hours and Thirty Minutes: The Weekend No One Will Ever Forget, by NBC News. New York: Scarecrow Press, 1966.

See *There Was a President.* Try used bookstores.

The Shooting of John F. Kennedy; One Assassin, Three Shots, Three Hits—No Misses, by William H. Hanson. San Antonio: Naylor Co., 1969.

You *can* judge a book by its cover. The author is a retired Air Force colonel. HTF.

Should We Now Believe the Warren Report? by Stephen White. New York: Macmillan, 1968.

No, notwithstanding Walter Cronkite's two-page preface. (Also contains the text of the CBS-TV 1967 documentary on the JFK death.) Few libraries.

David Milne

Six Seconds in Dallas: A Microstudy of the Kennedy Assassination, by Josiah Thomp-

son. New York; Bernard Geis Associates, 1967; revised, Berkley House paperback, 1976.
Originally a *Life* consultant on the Zapruder film, the author's scholarly and definitive study of witnesses and physical evidence led him to conclude that three gunmen fired shots at the motorcade. Includes valuable "Dealey Plaza Chart; Location of Witnesses" with information on 268 witnesses. A must for researchers. Some libraries.

Sixteen Questions on the Assassination, by Bertrand Russell. Passaic, N. J.: *Minority of One,* 1964.
British philosopher Russell was among the very early questioning the lone assassin line, and spoke out about it in England. This article contains errors of facts, however. HTF.

Stifle the Legend, by Lyle H. Munson. New York: Bookmailer, 1964.
An ex-CIA man implicates Fidel. HTF.

Subject Index to the Warren Report and Hearings and Exhibits, by Sylvia Meagher. New York: Scarecrow Press, 1966; Ann Arbor, Mich.: University Microfilms (enlarged reprint), 1971.
A most indispensable research tool, indexing all 26 volumes of evidence. Many libraries.

The Star Spangled Contract, by Jim Garrison. New York: McGraw Hill, 1976.
Like the author, this novel of conspiracy is always exciting and sometimes outrageous. Some bookstores and libraries.

The Taking of America 1-2-3, by Richard E. Sprague. Hartsdale, N.Y.: Self-published, 1976.

Speculation about the invisible government, called "the power control group," manipulating high-level government affairs over the past fifteen years. [This is not the same Richard Sprague who was appointed Chief Counsel to the House of Representative committee investigating the assassination.] (Available from the author: 193 Pinewood Rd., Hartsdale, N.Y. 10530.)

The Tears of Autumn, by Charles McCarry. New York: Saturday Review Press/Dutton, 1974.

A novel of international conspiracy in which an intelligence officer searches for the real killer. Few libraries.

A Texan Looks at Lyndon; A Study in Illegitimate Power, by J. Evetts Haley. Canyon, Tex.: Palo Duro Press, 1964.

Good dirt on LBJ, flawed by heavy right bias. Few libraries, some used bookstores.

Texas Supplemental Report on the Assassination of President John Kennedy and the Serious Wounding of Governor John B. Connally November 22, 1963, by Texas Attorney General Waggoner Carr. Austin, Tex.: State of Texas, 1964.

Formal correspondence between state officials and the Warren Commission.

There Was a President, by NBC News. New York: Ridge Press, 1966.

Summary of that Dallas weekend; contains the earlier book *Seventy Hours and Thirty Minutes* with some 200 additional photos. The title is one of NBC's more accurate statements on the assassination. Some used bookstores.

"They've Killed the President!" The Search for the Murderers of John F. Kennedy, by Robert Sam Anson. New York: Bantam paperback, 1975.

Best pop version of conspiracy evidence to date. Easy reading. Some bookstores and newsstands.

This Captive Land, by Pat Matteo. Yonkers, N.Y.: Self-published, 1968.

HTF.

Through the Looking Glass, by John Joerg. New Orleans: Unpublished manuscript, 1969.

Novel has CIA plan to eliminate D.A. Garrison halted at zero hour by the first front-page story on the new probe. The author aided the Garrison investigation.

The Torch Is Passed; The Associated Press Story of the Death of a President, by the Associated Press. New York: Associated Press, 1963; Parallax paperback, 1967.

Wire service copy. Some used bookstores.

Trauma, vol. 6, no. 4 (Dec. 1964) of *Medico-Legal Journal*. Albany, N.Y., San Francisco, New York: Matthew Bender and Co., Inc., 1964.

Details medical aspects of Jack Ruby. A forensic pathologist's delight. Try medical libraries.

The Trial of Jack Ruby: A Classic Study of Courtroom Strategies, by John Kaplan and Jon R. Waltz. New York: Macmillan, 1965.
Good analysis. Some libraries and used bookstores.

Trilogy of Murder; A Novel Analysis and Interpretation of the John F. Kennedy, Robert F. Kennedy, and Dr. Martin Luther King Assassinations, Viewed as a Whole (12 volumes, 2 supplements) by Joachim Joesten. West Germany: Self-published, 1971.
Nine of the twelve mimeographed volumes concern the Kennedy assassination, including "Highlights of the Shaw Trial," "The Case Against LBJ," ditto the Kennedy clan, ditto Hoover, "The Biggest Lie Ever Told," and "Cuba, Vietnam, and Oil: Three Reasons Kennedy Had to Die." Joesten, Europe's leading Warren Report critic for many years before his death in August, 1975, put all his eggs in this basket. Some are boiled, some are scrambled, some won't cook at all. HTF.

Trumpets of November, by Wesley S. Thurston. New York: Bernard Geis Associates, 1966; Signet paperback, 1967.
Satanic plot indicts a group called "The Militants." Intriguing novel. Some used bookstores.

The Truth About the Assassination, by Charles Roberts. New York: Grosset & Dunlap, 1967.
Self-righteous liberal attack by an ex-*Newsweek* correspondent on the critics and their motives. Often strays from available documentation; title is a misnomer. Few libraries.

The Two Assassins, by Renatus Hertogs and Lucy Freeman. New York: Thomas Crowell, 1965; Zebra Books, 1976.
A psychological approach to solving the Kennedy and Oswald murders; authors succeed with neither. Newsstands and some libraries.

Two Days of Infamy; Relating to the Murder of President Kennedy, by Stanley J. Marks. Los Angeles: Bureau of International Affairs, 1969.
A diatribe against the Warren Commission. HTF.

Two Flightpaths: Evidence of Conspiracy, by Robert B. Cutler. Manchester, Mass.: Cutler Designs, 1971.
The author concentrates on bullet flightpaths using precise drawings; book is successful at demonstrating more than one murderer. (Available from the author; see *Crossfire: Evidence of Conspiracy* for address.)

The Umbrella Man: Evidence of Conspiracy, by Robert B. Cutler. Manchester, Mass.: Self-published, 1975.
The author reaches the novel and questionable conclusion that the fatal shot was fired by a man on the sidewalk using a black umbrella. Reviews the gunshot theories of six other researchers as well. (Available from the author, see *Crossfire: Evidence of Conspiracy* for address.)

The Unanswered Questions About President Kennedy's Assassination, by Sylvan Fox. New York: Award Books, 1965 and 1975.
Original version raised valid questions; reissue revises and distorts by blending Castro into the mix. Some bookstores and newsstands.

Uncertain Mandate, by Ernest W. Lefever. Baltimore: Johns Hopkins Press, 1967-68.
HTF, try Johns Hopkins University library.

The Untold Story: Why the Kennedys Lost the Book Battle, by Lawrence Van Gelder. New York: Award Books, 1967.
About the William Manchester book controversy. HTF.

The Warren Report—see *Report of the President's Commission on the Assassination of President John F. Kennedy.*

Was Oswald Alone? by Gil and Ann Chapman. San Diego: Publishers Export Co., 1967.
An overview of the criticisms. HTF.

The Weight of the Evidence: The Warren Commission and Its Critics, by Jay David (pseud.). New York: Meredith Press, 1968.
Presents both sides. Author is a UFO expert. HTF.

Were We Controlled? The Assassination of President Kennedy, by Lincoln Lawrence (pseud.). New Hyde Park, N.Y.: University Books, 1967.
Speculates that mind control was used in the assassination with stock market windfall the motive. Very strange. The author is a prominent New Yorker. HTF.

What Was Back of Kennedy's Murder? by John R. Rice. Murfreesboro, Tenn.: Sword of the Lord, 1964.
Ponderous, religious. HTF.

What Was Behind Lee Harvey Oswald? by W. S. McBirnie. Self-published. HTF.

What We Do, Not What We Say, by Stanley J. Marks. Los Angeles: Bureau of International Affairs, 1971.
HTF.

When They Kill a President, by Roger Craig. Dallas: Unpublished manuscript.
The author, the decorated Dallas County Sheriff's deputy, writes about the lack of security and strange occurrences in Dallas law enforcement on November 22, 1963. Craig is best known as the officer who witnessed evidence of conspiracy (a getaway car, phony Secret Service credentials) that day at the assassination site. He died of self-inflicted gunshot wounds in mid-1975.

Where Death Delights; Adventures in Courtroom Medicine, by Marshall Houts. New York: Coward-McCann, 1967.
Contains objections of forensic pathologists, including Dr. Milton Halpern, to the Warren Report's medical conclusions. Try medical libraries.

The White House Case, by Col. Victor J. Fox (pseud.). Pleasantville, N. Y.: Fargo Press, 1968.
A novel by the author of *The Pentagon Case,* distributed through American Opinion (John Birch Society) Bookstores, touches on characters in the Kennedy assassination. Subjects are thinly disguised (e. g., Soviet Premier Krushyou). Says Russia responsible.

Whitewash; The Report on the Warren Report, by Harold Weisberg. Hyattstown, Md.: Self-published, 1965; New York: Dell, 1966.
One of the first and most methodical analyses of the Warren Commission. Excellent research overshadows crowded writing. (Available from the author, see *Photographic Whitewash* for address.)

Whitewash II; The FBI-Secret Service Cover-up, by Harold Weisberg. Hyattstown, Md.: Self-published, 1966; New York: Dell, 1967.
The author did the Schweiker-Hart subcommittee's homework ten years early. (Available from the author, see *Photographic Whitewash* for address.)

Whitewash IV; Top Secret JFK Assassination Transcript, With a Legal Analysis by Jim Lesar. Frederick, Md.: Self-published, 1964.
Except for Gerald Ford's edited pirate edition (see *Portrait of the Assassin*) this was the first publication of the January 27, 1964, Warren Commission executive session dealing with Oswald's FBI link. Includes many other documents never before published. Introduction difficult to follow. (Available from the author,

see *Photographic Whitewash* for address.) [N.B. Chronologically, *Photographic Whitewash* was *Whitewash III.*]

Who Killed JFK? Opposing Views on the Question That Keeps Coming Back, prepared by *Skeptic Magazine,* Special Issue #9. Santa Barbara: Forum for Contemporary History, 1975.
Sixty-four excellent and balanced pages on the Kennedy assassination. Some libraries and secondhand magazine stores.

Who Killed Kennedy? by Thomas G. Buchanan. New York: Putnam, 1964; London: Secker & Warburg (slightly different text), 1964; New York: Macfadden, 1965.
Criticizes the Warren Report, speculates widely, settles on oil monopolies as culprits. As one of the earliest published critics, the author, a former *Washington Evening Star* reporter, was often maligned in the press. Jack Ruby recommended this book shortly before his death. Some libraries.

Who Killed Kennedy? Compiled by Marc Davis and Jim Matthews. Hollywood: Associated Professional Services, 1966.
A reprint of *Highlights of the Warren Report* along with biographical material on the Kennedys. HTF.

Who Killed the President? by Dale G. Warner. New York: American Press, 1964.
Wandering essay which touches on the subject less than one would hope. HTF.

Who Shot Kennedy? by David Moses. England: Church of God, 1973.
Everyone's getting into the act. Four pages.

Why Did They Assassinate President Kennedy? by George W. Snyder. Self-published.
Good question. HTF.

Why Did You Kill Your President? by Kyrill Goranoff. West Berlin: 1970.
In the form of a dialogue between a lady symbolizing Public Opinion and a man symbolizing The Man on the Street. HTF.

Why Lee Oswald Would Have Been Acquitted for the Murder of John F. Kennedy, by Joe H. Tonahill. 1967.
The author, an attorney for Jack Ruby, brings forth a provocative thesis. HTF.

Winter Kills, by Richard Condon. New York: Dial Press, 1974.
Novel about a Kennedy-like assassination involving right-wing conspiracy. By the author of *The Manchurian Candidate.* Bookstores.

The Witnesses: The Highlights of Hearings Before the Warren Commission on the Assassination of President John F. Kennedy, selected and edited by the *New York Times.* New York: Bantam paperback 1964; McGraw Hill, 1965.
The *Times* selected only those witnesses whose testimony supported the lone assassin conclusions. Book smacks of profiteering, a charge the *Times* would later level at critics. Some libraries, few used bookstores.

The Wounded Land: Journey Through a Divided America, by Hans Habe, translated from German by Ewan Butler. New York: Coward-McCann, 1964.
Interesting foreign perspective of America in the aftermath. HTF.

The Yankee and Cowboy War; Conspiracies from Dallas to Watergate, by Carl Oglesby. Kansas: Sheed, Andrews & McMeel, 1976.
Well-developed theory that two ruling elites struggle for power, sometimes resulting in coups, countercoups, and assassination. Eastern money versus South and West entrepreneurs. Bookstores and some libraries.

Young Men and the Death of a Young President, by Fred I. Greenstein.
An expansion of the author's January 1965 article in *The American Journal of Psychiatry.* HTF.

The Zionist Conspiracy Behind the President Kennedy Assassination, by Mark Koral. Rochester, N. Y.: Self-published, 1976.
"John Kennedy was killed because his domestic and foreign policy conflicted with the Zionist program," the author claims. Agnew redux?

Movies

A Child's Eyes: November 22, 1963, produced by Group VI Productions. Released by Pathe Contemporary Films, 1968.
8 minutes, in color. 16 mm.

The Eternal Frame, produced by T. R. Uthco

and The Ant Farm. Premiere at the First Unitarian Church, San Francisco, November 22, 1975.

A 24-minute videotape reenactment of the assassination, filmed in Dealey Plaza, August 1975, with actors dressed like participants. Footage contains interviews with real tourists, who alternately laugh and cry; also commentary on media role in shaping opinions of leaders such as JFK. Outrageous and brilliantly conceived. Shown on a few cable-TV stations. Underwritten in part by *The National Lampoon* magazine.

Executive Action, directed by David Miller, screenplay by Dalton Trumbo. Based on a novel by Donald Freed and Mark Lane. Produced by Edward Lewis. Distributed by National General, 1973.

Good cast (Will Geer, Burt Lancaster, Robert Ryan), good idea, poorly executed. Appeared ten years after. Some TV stations refused to run ads for it. Free eight-page handout with factual background to the film available at theaters. Worth seeing for its historical value; involves a right-wing intelligence plot. In color; occasionally on campuses and rerun houses.

The Fateful Trip to Texas; The Assassination of a President, produced by Arthur M. Schlesinger and Fred Israel. New York: Chelsea House Educational Communications, 1969. Super-8 mm.

A 7-minute black and white summary of major events in JFK's last six months—comments on civil rights, test-ban treaty,

A picture is worth. . . .

© 1974 Jon Whitsell

Vietnam. Also includes background on quarrel within Texas Democratic party in which JFK was to be a peacemaker that weekend. Contains Kennedy speeches in Texas prior to assassination; also motorcade.

Four Days in November, produced by David Wolper Productions. Released by United Artists, 1964. 16 and 35 mm.

A documentary in black and white. 122 minutes long.

Greetings, directed by Brian de Palma. Distributed by Sigma III, 1968.
One of three young characters is an obsessed and paranoid assassination buff. The only feature-length political comedy on the subject. Contains references to author Weisberg, the magic bullet theory, and *The Rat,* a now-defunct NYC underground newspaper. A classic, in color; occasionally on campuses and rerun houses. Robert DeNiro is in *Greetings.* 88 minutes long.

The Hughes Film. Filmed by Robert J. E. Hughes. Dallas: 1963.
Shows the presidential motorcade turning onto Elm Street with School Book Depository in the background only seconds before Kennedy's death. Filmed from the corner of Main and Houston Streets.

The Muchmore Film. Filmed by Mary Muchmore. Dallas: 1963.
Motorcade footage.

The Nix Film. Filmed by Orville O. Nix. Dallas: 1963
Captures the deadly head shot from a position opposite Zapruder. Rights purchased by UPI shortly thereafter.

The Parallax View, directed by Anthony Pakula. Paramount Pictures, 1974.
Investigative reporter tries to expose an assassination cover-up, finds his witnesses dead. Feature-length film, in color, stars Warren Beatty and Paula Prentiss. Quite heavy on the violence. (Pakula later directed *All the President's Men.*) Based on the novel. 100 minutes.

The President's Last Hours, produced by WFAA-TV. Dallas: 1964.
30 minutes of 16 mm newsfilm.

Rush to Judgment, produced by Emile de Antonio and Mark Lane, directed by de Antonio. Impact Films, 1967.
Over two hours—a good early documentary with on-the-screen interviews. Lane does narration and interviews. Still screened as a fund raiser for resource groups, or in conjunction with a Lane speech. Usually on campuses. 122 minutes.

The Two Kennedys: A View from Europe, directed by Gianna Bisiach. American premiere at the Orson Welles Cinema, Cambridge, Mass., 1976.
Images of America from the KKK to HUAC to Capone to the Kennedy clan to Dallas. Posits an organized crime, anti-Castro Cuban, oil baron plot. According to the *Boston Globe:* "Shrewdly edited, it makes political connections about the possible conspiracy in mind-dizzying speed." 2 hours.

Two Men In Dallas: John Kennedy and Roger Craig. Alpa Productions, 1977.
This sixty-minute videotape is based on a lengthy interview in his last year with Roger Craig, the Dallas deputy sheriff whose unshaken testimony about events 11-22-63 reveals a number of assassination plot partici-

pants. The tape is intercut with supporting material from Warren Commission files and a congressional investigation of document destruction by the FBI. Also included is evidence that Jack Ruby and Lee Oswald met in Houston months before the assassination. Narrated by Mark Lane, this videotape is intended for distribution to television stations.

The Zapruder Film. Producers and directors still at large; filmed by Abraham Zapruder. Dallas: 1963.

Of home-movie quality, this film offers convincing proof of conspiracy by revealing time sequence of shots and backwards direction of Kennedy head explosion. Used by virtually all researchers. Has been shown on national television after years of suppression by Time, Inc. Optical enhancement by Robert Groden sharpens precise analysis. Bootleg copies abound, and are available from many resource centers.

Plays

A Die-Hard for Dallas (tentative title), by J. C. Louis. 1976. As yet unperformed.

Drawn from known facts, this play follows Jack Ruby through gunrunning to Cuba, his extensive police contacts, his Jewishness, and his knowledge of the conspiracy to have Kennedy murdered. An anatomy of Ruby's head, as manipulated and manipulator.

Fact Finders, by Hans Steinkellner. As yet unperformed.

A three-act play situated mainly in the Warren Commission's hearing room; content is taken primarily from the Warren Report and testimony.

Jack Ruby, All American Boy, by John Logan in association with Paul Baker, director. Opened at the Dallas Theater Center, April 23, 1974.

"He was human," said the ad. "He was an American. He had a dream." Chastity Fox played a stripper.

J. F. K. Lives, by Mark McIntyre. Opened at the Montgomery Playhouse, San Francisco, February 1977.

A one-man show, in which actor Mark McIntyre builds up, then dismantles the mythology surrounding J. F. K. The original run closed after eight performances, following which it was reworked and performed again. "In the tradition of *Give 'em Hell, Harry,*" said the advertisements.

Lee Harvey Oswald: A Far Mean Streak of Indepence Brought On By Negleck, by Michael Hastings. U. S. opening at Theatre Atlanta, April 17, 1968. Directed by Jay Broad.

Concentrates on the dynamics in Oswald's life rather than ascertaining involvement in assassination. Uses mother Marguerite's Ft. Worth apartment, Marina's suburban Dallas room, and Lee and Marina's Russian apartment as locales, with commentators roaming the audience. Uses testimony from the Warren Commission hearings. (Yes, the title is spelled that way.)

MacBird! by Barbara Garson. Opened at The Village Gate Theater, New York, January 19,

Assassination figures take to the stage.

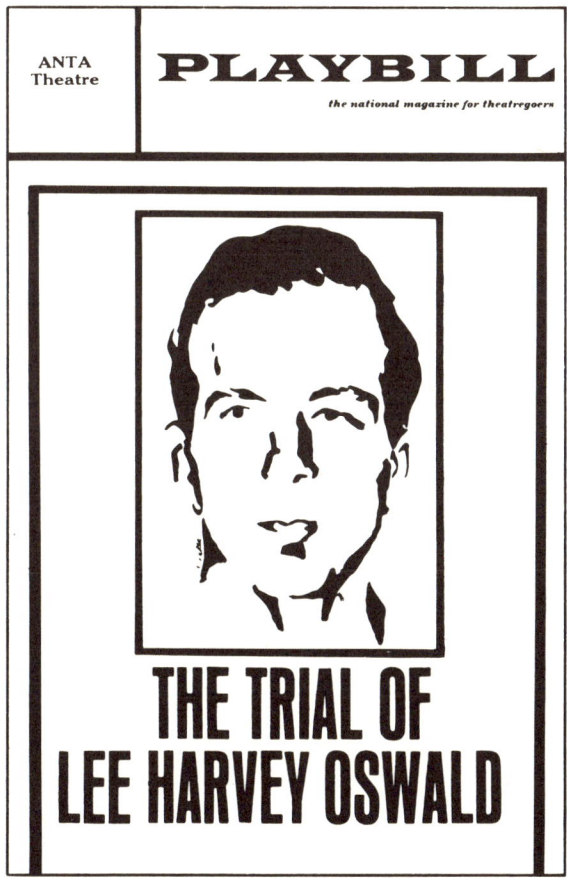

1967. Produced by Julia and David Dretzin.
Directed by Ron Levine.
Started out as political theater for Berkeley activists, blossomed into an immensely successful play with national road troupes, long runs, and controversy. Aggressive art, theatrical politics. Radical theater using traditional mode. See comment on the book.

Sparky and the Truth Detector, by the DNA Collective, developed in a college course in Contemporary Political Assassinations. Opened in San Francisco in the spring of 1975 at the First Unitarian Church.
"Sparky was Ruby's early nickname; almost the entire dialogue is taken from Warren Commission testimony, court hearings, and

other public information on Ruby. Tabloid theater at its best. Employs slides and music (Ray Charles singing "Ruby") as well.

A Time to Die, A Time to Cry, by Stanley J. Marks. Los Angeles: Bureau of International Affairs, 1971.
A three-act play, performance unknown.

The Trial of Lee Harvey Oswald, by Amram Ducovney and Leon Friendman. Opened at the Anta Theater in New York, November 5, 1967.
This play, which used slides and film clips as well as actors, operated on the premise that Ruby's attempt to kill Oswald failed, and that Lee had his day in court. The audience was the jury, as Oswald insisted he was the victim of a conspiracy. Panned by the *New York Times* as "a perversion of democratic processes."

Records

"The Actual Voices and Events of Four Days That Shocked the World." Colpix Records, 1964.
Includes an insert by Merriman Smith, UPI correspondent. HTF.

"Can't Keep From Crying; Topical Blues on the Death of President Kennedy," featuring Otis Spann, Big Joe Williams, and others. Testament Records, 1974.
Eleven songs written out of the despair of the moment. Historical blues. Check rare record lists and major stores.

"The Controversy. The Death of John F. Kennedy; The Warren Report and Controversy." Lawrence Schiller and Richard W. Lewis. Capitol Records, 1966.
What was controversial about this record was the deceit employed for interviews and how it was marketed (see *Citizen's Dissent* by Lane for details). The interviewers were equally shrill against conspiracists in their book *Scavengers,* which was based on this record. HTF.

"The Fateful Hours; A Presentation of KLIF News in Dallas." Capitol Records, 1964.
A valuable recording; coverage of JFK events, Tippit, and Oswald. HTF.

"Four Dark Days in November." A Presentation of WQMR News. Connie B. Gay Broadcasting Corp., 1964.
Representative of radio news coverage over that weekend. HTF.

"Lee Harvey Oswald's Letters to His Mother (with footnotes by Mrs. Oswald)." Broadside, 1964.
HTF.

"Lee Harvey Oswald Speaks: A Personal Interview with Lee Harvey Oswald in New Orleans, August 17, 1963." Truth Records, 1967.
Oswald tells interviewer Bill Stuckey about his political and personal life. The tape and transcript became Warren Commission documents. HTF.

"*Mac Bird!* A Play by Barbara Garson." Songs and Music by John Duffy. Evergreen Records, 1967.
See comment on the book and play. HTF.

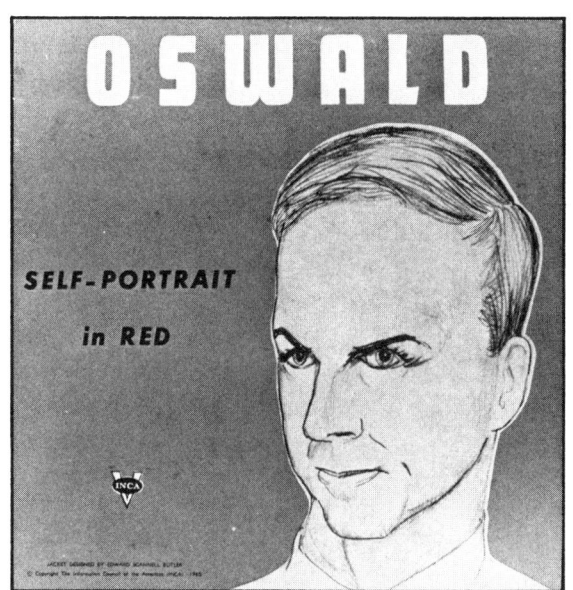

Cover reproduction from Folkways Records—used by permission

"November 22; Dialogue in Dallas. The Assassination of President Kennedy as Reported by Newsmen Malcolm Kilduff, Jerald ter Horst, Robert Donovan, and Sid Davis—Jim Snyder, Moderator." Liner notes by Donald H. McGannon, 1964.
Kilduff, and then ter Horst later, worked in the White House press office. HTF.

"November 22, 1963; An Historical Document in Sound—Radio Reported to the Nation Throughout 80 Hours Following the First Broadcast at 1:36 P.M. On the ABC Radio Network," 1963.
HTF.

"The Oswald Case—Mark Lane's Testimony to the Warren Commission." Includes text. Broadside, 1964.

For visually handicapped Warren Commission critics. HTF.

"Oswald, Self Portrait in Red," Information Council of the Americas (INCA), 1964. (Two record set.)
Oswald's August 21, 1963, radio debate on WDSU in New Orleans, with Carlos Bringuier and Ed Butler of INCA. Contains Oswald's revealing slip about his life in the Soviet Union: " . . . I was under, uh, the protection of the uh—of the uh—that is to say, I was not under the protection of the uh—American government . . . "

"Rush to Judgment; The Living Testimony by the Actual Witnesses on the Original Sound Track of the Emile de Antonio and Mark Lane Film." Vanguard, 1967.

Contains some interviews which only appeared in the film and not in the book. A soundtrack. HTF.

"Rush to Judgment; With New Insights on the Assassination of President John F. Kennedy," by Mark Lane. Happening Records, 1967.
Lane's basic college speech (since updated, of course). Touches on the single bullet theory, the Zapruder film, and FBI activity. HTF.

"A Time to Keep." NBC Reporting by Robert McNeil, Chet Huntley, and Tom Pettit. RCA Victor, 1963.
Pettit is the calm reporter with a microphone on the right in photos of Ruby shooting Oswald. HTF.

Sources for Chapter 4

The American Book Collector (Private Collectors' Directory): "The Assassination Industry; A Tentative Checklist of Publications on the Murder of President John F. Kennedy," by Thomas M. McDade. Chicago, June 1968.

Ibid.: "The Legend of John F. Kennedy," by Earl C. Kubicek. In four installments, beginning September 1971.

American Political Assassinations: A Bibliography of Works Published 1963-1970 Related to the Assassination of John F. Kennedy, Martin Luther King, and Robert F. Kennedy, compiled by the Committee to Investigate Assassinations. Washington, D. C., 1973.

A Bibliography of Books, Newspaper and Magazine Articles, Published in English Outside the United States of America, Related to the Assassination of President John F. Kennedy, by T. H. Irwin and Hazel Hale. Belfast, Ireland, 1975.

A Bibliography of Literature Relating to the Assassination of President John F. Kennedy, by W. C. Thompson. San Antonio, 1968; with 1971 supplement.

Wisconsin Magazine of History: "The Assassination of John Fitzgerald Kennedy: An Annotated Bibliography," by David R. Wrone. Madison, Wis., autumn 1972.

Various researchers' private libraries, as well as the author's personal collection.

PART 2
OTHER
ASSASSINATIONS

5 OFFICEHOLDERS

Assaults on politicians in the United States have been fairly consistent since the first major assassination attempt in 1835 against President Andrew Jackson. From the most innocuous bureaucrat to members of Congress and presidents, officeholders have been the targets of numerous murder attempts.

The assassination attempts in the following list—more than 115 of them—were carried out for many reasons. They include political jealousy, economics, rulings thought unfair, legislation, favoritism, investigations, party rivalry, election results, foreign policy, organized crime vengeance, and morality. In each attempt, the attacker—or the attacker's sponsors—wanted to bring about an immediate shift in political power and policy. In very few instances were those goals met.

The list which follows contains the more significant assassination attempts as well as many obscure ones. The major problem encountered in assembling it was that so little study has been done in the field, and what there is often lacks an understanding of political motive. Chip Berlet, who researched this chapter, found this particularly so with the staff report to the 1969 U.S. government's "National Commission on the Causes and Prevention of Violence in America," *Assassination and Political Violence.* "The biases and attitudes of the individuals responsible for writing the descriptions and analyses in this government report are very transparent,"

Berlet said. "The inability to understand legitimate political motivations, albeit obscure, of anarchists and nationalists is disturbing and offensive. The racism and naivete concerning leftist political motivation is especially clear in the description of the attack by Puerto Rican nationalists on President Truman. By denying rational or emotionally legitimate motivations of a political nature, it becomes simple to ascribe assassination attempts to unstable lone nuts rather than politically motivated individuals."

In reviewing entries from the government report on political assassination in American history, errors of fact were found. Still, the book *Assassination and Political Violence* is the primary source in the field. Like other studies used, each entry required, whenever possible, independent verification.

There were, no doubt, many other assassination attempts against officeholders in American history. The following entries are those that were prominent enough to enter history books or merit news coverage over the years.

1835

President Andrew Jackson, while walking through the Capitol rotunda in January, was shot at twice from thirteen feet by British-born Richard Lawrence, whose two pistols misfired. Thirty-five-year-old Lawrence believed at various times that he was king of England, owner of vast holdings in Europe, and that the U.S. government owed him much money, which Jackson was party to withholding. Lawrence also thought that since Jackson had vetoed rechartering the Bank of the United States that the president's death would help the working class by causing the bank to regain its charter.

Lawrence was found not guilty by reason of insanity, and became the first in a long line of lone-nut potential assassins. Prosecuting for the government was part-time songwriter Francis Scott Key. [1]*

1836

U.S. Congressman Sam Houston attacked fellow Congressman William Stanbury with a cane following the latter's accusation of misconduct. Stanbury retaliated by pulling a gun on Houston. The fight took place on Pennsylvania Avenue in Washington and neither congressman was seriously hurt. [1]

1856

Three days following Massachusetts Senator Charles Sumner's strong antislavery speech, which singled out Senator Andrew Butler of South Carolina, Butler's nephew, Congressman Preston Brooks, severely assaulted Sumner on the Senate floor. Press reports say that a group of Southerners plotted the May attack, which left Sumner unconscious, and intended to kill the senator. [1]

1857

California State Supreme Court Justice

---

*The numbers in brackets refer to sources listed at the end of this chapter which contain supportive information.

David Terry challenged his opponent in a U.S. Senate race, incumbent officeholder David C. Broderick, to a duel following a political feud over the slavery question (Broderick was antislavery). Terry won the duel; Senator Broderick died of a bullet wound in his left lung. Terry was later acquitted in court (see 1889). [1]

1865

Two people who were part of an earlier unsuccessful ambush attempt on Abraham Lincoln joined with actor John Wilkes Booth in April in a plot to kill the president, Vice-President Andrew Johnson, and Secretary of State William Seward.

Lewis Paine (aka Rev. Lewis Wood) was to take medicine to the ailing Seward whose servant stopped him, got slugged, recovered, and alerted neighbors. Paine then severely injured Seward's son and daughter, and stabbed the secretary of state numerous times, failing to kill him.

Vice-President Johnson was to be killed by one George Atzerodt, who at the last minute preferred booze to assassination and never followed through.

Booth attacked Lincoln while the latter was attending a play at Ford's Theatre in Washington in mid-April. With the president's box unguarded (the bodyguard was out drinking with the valet and coachman), Booth approached the president and shot him below the left ear during audience laughter at a line from the play, "Our American Cousin."

Assailant Booth, a Confederate loyalist

seeking revenge, whispered the Virginia state motto *sic semper tyrannis* and leaped to the stage, breaking his fall on the bunting, and escaped out a stage door. He was cornered twelve days later in a nearby Maryland barn, which was set afire, and died of a gunshot wound as it burned. (Revisionist theory postulated in *Rolling Stone* magazine, July 1, 1976.) Lincoln died the morning following the shooting. Booth's fellow conspirators and others were convicted and hanged.

"In a drawer of the huge desk, he [Lincoln] had a file marked 'Assassination' and in another had been the words 'hazarded attempts.' They were neatly labelled in chronological order and numbered eighty-two." [5] One of the plots was foiled during President-elect Lincoln's train ride to Washington when he assumed a disguise and switched trains. [1, 2, 3]

1866

In February Louisville, Kentucky, Justice of the Peace J. G. Smart was killed by "guerillas." [1]

1867

A pro-Union Republican delegate to the Georgia Constitutional Convention during Reconstruction, G. W. Ashburn, was shot and killed by unknown assailants. Implicated were ten prominent citizens. [1]

1867

In January a Tennessee state senator, Almon Case, was killed by Frank Farris, the leader of an anti-Union guerilla band. The daylight attack was made in the town of Troy, Tennessee. The Confederate guerillas had killed and threatened other officeholders and Union sympathizers during and after the Civil War. [1]

1867

In Texas the assistant collector of revenues, H. W. Fowler, was killed by D. B. Bonfoey, his boss. [1]

1867

Following a December resolution backed by New Mexico Territorial Senator William Rynerson which ordered the removal of Territorial Chief Justice John P. Slough, the chief justice made insulting remarks to the senator, who insisted that Slough retract his comments. The chief justice refused to do so, and Rynerson killed him. [1]

1867

In December at Mobile, Alabama, the local D.A. shot a local judge named Busteed in front of the Customs House after a verbal exchange. [6]

1868

A St. Mary's Parish, Louisiana, judge, V. Chase, was murdered for his pro-Union sentiments by a band of rebels. [1]

1868

Two Alabama state senators, Harrington and Pennington, were ambushed and fired upon while canvassing for the Republican party. Their attacker was never apprehended, and the two escaped injury. [1]

1868

A Louisiana justice, Robert Gray, was shot and killed by party(ies) unknown. [1]

1868

An Arkansas congressman, James Hinds, was killed by Monroe County, Arkansas, Democratic party Secretary George M. Clark, who was drunk at the time. [1]

1868

Another unsolved Louisiana murder, this time the victim was Caddo Parish Sheriff B. Saulet. [1]

1868

The former Lt. Governor of Wisconsin, Samuel W. Beall, was murdered in Montana by George M. Pinney. Pinney had written articles that provoked Beall to attack him; Pinney was brought to trial, claimed the killing was self-defense, and was acquitted. [1]

1869

Illinois State Senator M. McConnell was murdered at home. The local press assumed the killing was prompted by McConnell's involvement in property litigation in Chicago. [1]

1870

Ex-New York Congressman William S. Lincoln was caned by an unsuccessful applicant for a seat-at-large in the House, Joseph Segar. The Virginian's attack occurred in the Baltimore railroad station after a local paper ran a story ridiculing Segar's claim for the seat and his conduct. Lincoln lived. [1]

1870

A particularly grisly affair, North Carolina State Senator John W. Stevens was stabbed and hanged by two men named Mitchelle and Wiley. The killing of the Republican legislator was apparently carried out with the knowledge of the local Caswell County Democratic party apparatus. [1]

1870

Frank Williams, a Republican office seeker, killed Gaylord Clark, who got a local District Judgeship in El Paso which Williams had sought. Clark was awarded the position when local party officials figured he could unite extremist factions among Republicans. [1]

1871

A U.S. Customs Inspector, Alden McLaughlin, was killed by illegal importers. [1]

1871

Republican Florida state legislator John P. Mahoney was killed at Lake City in early May. He was the fifth Republican to be killed in Florida in a six-month period. [6]

1871

Reportedly, a Ku Klux Klansman killed Clarendon, South Carolina, school commissioner Benbow in May. [6]

1873

In November New York City Controller Andrew H. Green was the intended recipient of a package with explosives inside. The contents were discovered and disarmed before reaching the destination. There was no return address. [6]

1873

After a rather controversial campaign and election, Louisiana Governor William Pitt

Kellogg was fired upon by Charles R. Rainey and Melvin H. Cohen. The disputed election led to open rebellion in many parts of the state. [1]

1873
It was a double murder in September for Monroe, Louisiana, officials T. S. Crawford and Arthur H. Harris. The assumed murderers were members of the "Tom Wayne gang," one of whose members had escaped prison, having been sentenced by Judge Crawford and prosecuted by D. A. Harris. [1]

1873
In the Dakota Territory P. P. Wintermute, involved in an argument over railroad bonds, tried to settle the dispute by killing Edwin S. McCook, the territorial governor. [1]

1873
The U. S. Attorney for Georgia, H. P. Farrow, was clubbed soon after a strenuous effort to indict five men on serious charges. His assailant(s) was unknown. [1]

1874
Four men, Richard Croker, John Sheridan, and George and Henry Hickey, tried to kill ex-New York State Senator James O'Brien in a New York political feud involving the Tammany group. Charges were never pressed because the four were already under indictment for killing a man who was earlier the intermediary between the four and O'Brien. [1]

1875
E. G. Johnson, a revenuer and Florida state legislator, was killed by unknown assailant(s) while visiting a still. [1]

1875
A former Louisiana parish judge named Belden was killed by the man who later held the job, named Sherburn. [1]

1875
Grant Parish, Louisiana, ex-Sheriff John B. McCoy killed local tax collector G. A. Roderty. [1]

1875
One of the militant Irish immigrants known as the Mollie Maguires fired upon and killed Squire Gwither, a Girardville, Pennsylvania, justice of the peace when he attempted to serve an arrest warrant on several suspected Mollies. [13]

1877
Another Louisiana murder attempt. This one was directed at Governor Stephen B. Packard, whose election was contested by political opponents. W. H. Weldon was charged with the crime, which was apparently motivated by the election challenge. [1]

1880
The former sheriff of Abbeville, South Carolina, Pem Guffin, was killed by a thug employed by local Democrats in October. The Democrats had been offended by something Guffin, a radical Republican, had said. [6]

1881
In July Charles J. Guiteau, a layabout job

seeker, shot President James A. Garfield, who had been in office only four months and was embarking on his first vacation from Washington. The weapon used was a fifteen-dollar .44 caliber British revolver with a white bone handle (a cheaper model was available, but Guiteau wanted a gun which would look nice in a museum). Guiteau had been following Garfield for some time, thus becoming the first of the "stalking assassins." Because he felt that the train station crowd's reaction would be angry, he arranged to have a cab waiting to carry him to jail following the shooting. Guiteau, who had spent much of his adult life in legal and religious hustles, felt he was particularly responsible for Garfield's slim victory (under 10,000 votes) the previous November, and thought he was entitled to a consulship in Paris, if not the Austrian ambassadorship. Garfield died eleven weeks later on September 19 despite periodic improvement in his condition.

During the murder trial, Guiteau claimed that his actions were inspired by God. Public opinion ran quite strongly against him, and there were at least two attempts on his life. January 25, 1882, a jury found him guilty, and on June 30, 1882, he was hanged.

A second gunman theory was advanced by Guiteau's sister, who admitted that while her brother did shoot at and injure the president, the fatal shot was fired by another person in a dark doorway. [1, 9]

1881

Tennessee attorney John Vertress, having accused State Senator Smith of accepting a bribe, shot and wounded him. Following Vertress' direct action, the state legislature promptly voted to conduct an investigation of the accusation. [1]

1889

In August California State Supreme Court Justice David S. Terry, who was involved in an 1857 assassination, ran into a bitter political enemy at the Lathrop, California, train station dining room. The enemy, U.S. Supreme Court Justice Stephen Field, was guarded by David Nagle, a U.S. marshal, sent by the Justice Department to protect Field from attack (presumably by Terry). Terry walked over to the Field table and interrupted their meal by slapping the justice. Nagle then interrupted Terry's meal by pumping a bullet from a Colt six-shooter into his heart.

Nagle was acquitted, and Justice Field served out nine more years of his thirty-six years on the Supreme Court. [1]

1889

John M. Clayton, who narrowly lost an Arkansas congressional race, contested the November 1888 election and was killed two months later by parties unknown before the official victor was declared. [10]

1889

W. S. Clendennin, angered at an unfavorable ruling by Superior Court Judge W. L. Pierce in San Diego, California, shot Pierce and seriously wounded him. [1]

1890

The Washington correspondent for the *Louisville Times* shot and killed ex-congressman William P. Taulbee of Kentucky. After Charles E. Kincaide, the reporter, had published a story linking Taulbee with a Patent Office scandal, the former representative harrassed and attacked the correspondent. A day following the attack, Kincaide shot Taulbee "in self-defense." Public sentiment was on the reporter's side, and he was acquitted of the murder. [1]

1893

In October, Chicago's mayor, Carter H. Harrison, owner of the *Chicago Times* and enemy of the wealthy for his toleration and acceptance of socialist and anarchist elements in the city, was killed by a Patrick E. Prendergast. The assassin claimed he was promised a job as city corporation counsel in exchange for his efforts to get Harrison elected. Prendergast also cited broken campaign promises by Harrison as a motive. [1]

1896

A former New Mexico Territorial state legislator, Col. Albert Jennings Fountain, was ambushed, along with his son, by parties unknown. He was presumed killed. Fountain was the head of one faction in a feud with Democratic party judge Fall over control of cattle rustling. [1]

1898

A black postmaster at Lake City, South Carolina, was killed, along with his family, by a white mob that didn't like the idea of their town having a black postmaster. The next postmaster was white. [14]

1900

Kentucky Governor William Goebel, whose election was so marginal it was decided by the state legislature, was killed in January by men connected with the defeated Republican party. One of the three conspirators was the former Kentucky secretary of state, Caleb Powers. He and the other two, Henry Youtsey and James Howard, were convicted and executed. [1]

1901

William McKinley, in September of the first year of his second presidential term, was greeting people at the Temple of Music at the Pan-American Exposition in Buffalo when twenty-eight-year-old Leon F. Czolgosz, a white handkerchief wrapped around his right hand which held a .32 caliber revolver, approached the president and fired two shots. McKinley died eight days later, and Theodore Roosevelt assumed the presidency.

Czolgosz had attended socialist and anarchist meetings, although evidently he understood the full meaning of neither. His action was inspired, in part, by the assassination at Monza, Italy, of King Humbert I by an anarchist the previous year.

Although there was no evidence whatsoever of a plot by anarchists or anyone else, the press and the new president manipulated Czolgosz' political leanings into antianarchist hysteria, resulting in the arrest of anarchist leaders such as Emma Goldman (whose charges, along with those of other anarchists, were subsequently dropped), antianarchist vigilante groups, and immigration restrictions against anarchists.

Dr. E. C. Spitzka, a psychiatrist who had

testified twenty years earlier that Garfield's assassin, Charles Guiteau, was crazy, suggested that Czolgosz had a female coconspirator because he used a handkerchief to shield the murder weapon, evidence of a feminine touch.

On September 23, 1901, Czolgosz was tried and convicted, and 36 days later was electrocuted at New York's Auburn State Prison. [1, 8]

1905

Ex-Governor Frank Steunenberg of Idaho, who was in office at the end of the nineteenth century, was dynamited to death at his Caldwell home in late December. Although quite pro-labor at the beginning of his term, he invited federal troops into the state to quell labor difficulty involving the Western Federation of Miners union (W.F.M.). From that point on, Steunenberg was pro-management.

Eventually, a man named Harry Orchard, who knew the leaders of the radical mining union, admitted he killed the ex-governor as part of a massive conspiracy to wipe out mining bosses. The kingpins of this alleged conspiracy were Industrial Workers of the World (I.W.W.) activist Big Bill Haywood and W.F.M. officials Charles Moyer and George Pettibone, whose legal extradition to Idaho from Denver was circumvented when Idaho lawmen simply kidnapped them, brought them back to Idaho, and jailed them for eighteen months. In early May 1907, just prior to the trial, huge demonstrations sympathetic to Haywood and his codefendants were held around the country, and with Clarence Darrow defending, a jury acquitted the accused

in July. Orchard, who was allegedly a provocateur paid by the bosses to frame unionists, got life imprisonment. [1, 6]

1908

New Jersey Governor John F. Fort's mail one day contained an envelope with explosives inside. There was no return address, and the bomb did not go off. At the time, Fort's political enemies were those whose business suffered when liquor laws were enforced in Atlantic City. [1]

1910

Another in a long line of disappointed-job-seeker-turned-assassin, John J. Gallagher shot New York Mayor William Gaynor as the latter was embarking for Europe in August. Gallagher was angered that Gaynor would not reverse a ruling calling him incompetent as a dock watchman. Hizzoner died three years later with Gallagher's bullet still in him. [1]

1912

A thirty-year-old retired barkeep, John Schrank, followed Bull Moose presidential candidate Theodore Roosevelt on the campaign trail and shot him from six feet in Milwaukee. The bullet went through a metal glasses case TR was carrying, as well as a fifty-page manuscript (folded over) in his pocket. Bodily damage was a fractured rib, and Roosevelt completed his October evening's politicking before hospitalization.

Schrank viciously opposed anyone seeking a third presidential term, he said, and related dreams in which William McKinley, assassinated eleven years earlier, told him Roosevelt was responsible for his own assassination and that Schrank shouldn't let TR become president. Schrank was declared insane and lived out his life in mental institutions in Wisconsin. [1]

1913
When B. P. Windsor, mayor of Mt. Auburn, Illinois, got into a feud with local newspaper editor Fay D. State over an editorial, the editor ended the argument by killing him. [1]

1917
Three pacifists angered by Massachusetts Senator Henry Cabot Lodge's support of U.S. military involvement overseas, attacked him in Washington. The April assault was evidently not meant to fatally wound him, however. The three were A. Bannwart, Mrs. A. M. A. Peabody, and the Rev. P. H. Drake, the first of whom apologized a couple of days later. [1]

1919
In September Mayor Edward P. Smith of Omaha, Nebraska, was killed by a lynch mob when he attempted to prevent the same gang from attacking a Negro prisoner. [16]

1921
In August, a month after U.S. Senator Lewis Heisler Ball presented a report on vice among sailors at Newport, he received a threatening letter and was shot at. [1, 6]

1921
In November Kentucky Democratic Congressman Robert Young Thomas, Jr., evidently said something that angered his Republican opponent George Baker enough that Baker attacked him. Thomas lived. [1]

1925
An election in Kermit, West Virginia, dealing with local schools led to a big fight with upwards of 200 shots fired. Killed in the melee was Buck Kirk, president of the local school board. Two deputy sheriffs were wounded. [6]

1926
In April Illinois Assistant State's Attorney William H. McSwiggin was machine-gunned to death in Chicago by gangsters riding by in an automobile. McSwiggin, who was called "the hanging prosecutor," had made enemies in the Capone gang and with others in organized crime. His boss was evidently lax with the mob, and McSwiggin's death touched off hot controversy over the Illinois State's Attorney's office. [1, 6]

1926
An aide to Georgia State Solicitor General Boykin, Bert Donaldson was engaged in wiping out gambling and other vices in Atlanta. Previously he had been a convict, a Presbyterian minister, and a social worker. After a number of threats from enemies, Donaldson was killed in August; police suspected one W. B. Sands, working on behalf of local crime honcho Floyd Woodward. [1, 6]

1926
Mayor Jeff Stone of Colp, Illinois, was killed by bootleggers who wanted to maintain their control of the area. No one was ever charged with the November crime. [1, 6]

1926

When West City, Illinois, Mayor J. Adams answered his door one December day, there was a bullet waiting for him. He died soon thereafter. Adams was friendly to one side of a bootleggers' dispute between the Shelton gang and the Birger gang. A month earlier the Adams home was the target of a bomb, but no one was injured. [1, 6]

1929

At the Loray Mill at Gastonia, North Carolina, Police Chief O. F. Aderholt attempted to enter a textile workers union hall after striking workers in June had threatened to remove scab employees from the mill. Before the chief could get in the hall, he was shot dead, and no less than sixteen National Textile Workers Union organizers were indicted. The numerous charges were generally considered to be a frame-up and came amidst hysterical redbaiting by newspapers. [1, 6]

1929

Borger, Texas, an oil town in the Texas panhandle, was the center of much corruption, bribery, and liquor law violations when District Attorney J. A. Holmes embarked on a clean-up campaign. The campaign was under way when Holmes was shot as he left his home one September day. Two men, including a deputy constable, were indicted, and Borger was temporarily placed under martial law. [6]

1930

South Carolina State Senator E. J. Dennis, while running for reelection in July, was shot in Monck's Corner by a man named Thornley, who said he was hired by a political opponent of Dennis's, Glenn D. McKnight. Dennis soon died, and McKnight, who was alternately a prohibition officer and bootlegger, was not convicted. [1, 6]

1933

While President-Elect Franklin Roosevelt was departing Bayside Park in Miami, Florida, following a February speech, thirty-three-year-old Guisseppe Zangara fired shots at him, missing. Hit, among others, was Chicago Mayor Anton Cermak, who died eighteen days later.

Zangara, who lived in Italy the first twenty-three years of his life, disliked capitalism intensely, and saw himself representing the poor working class striking back at a symbol of the ruling elite. He evidently had no feelings about FDR personally. "I go contented because I go for my ideas," he wrote in his hastily compiled autobiography during the thirty-four days between the assassination attempt and his electrocution in Raiford, Florida. "I salute all the poor of the world."

(In September 1974 a *Washington Post* column suggested that FBI ballistics tests on the bullets which killed Mayor Cermak proved that they did *not* come from Zangara's gun at all, and that Cermak was embroiled in a feud with organized crime back home.) [1]

1935

Illinois State's Attorney Thomas J. Courtney

was shot and injured in March by persons unknown. Associates of Al Capone were suspected. [1]

1935

Elmon C. Middleton, Harlan County (Ky.) Attorney, was afraid of being killed because he backed the National Guard action rescuing United Mine Workers' organizers in a tense labor dispute. Middleton's fears came true that September when a bomb wired to his car ignited, with him at the wheel. Other Middleton enemies included slot machine operators, some of whom were arrested in the case. [1, 6]

1935

U.S. Senator Huey "Kingfish" Long, visiting the state capitol in Baton Rouge, was shot by Carl Weiss, a twenty-nine-year-old doctor from a well-to-do background. Weiss evidently feared Long was amassing too much personal power and was on his way to demagogue status. Facts about the September assassination conflict, but it is known that Long died a day after being shot, that Weiss carried a .32 caliber automatic, and that Weiss died of no less than sixty-one bullet wounds in his body, put there by Long's bodyguards. One theory is that bullets from a bodyguard's gun accidentally hit Long.

Weiss' funeral attracted a large showing from prominent Louisianans. [1, 4, 8]

1936

A U.S. military colonel, E.F. Riggs, was killed in February by two Puerto Rican students who were avenging a massacre at the University of Puerto Rico four months earlier. Students Beauchamp and Rosado were charged with the murder and killed at police headquarters. [1, 6]

1936

Illinois State Representative John M. Bolton, from Chicago's West Side, was killed in July by alleged racketeers. [1]

1938

Kentucky's U.S. senatorial campaign was particularly intense, with accusations of dirty politics in the race between Governor Chandler and incumbent Senator Barkley. In August former sheriff Lee Combs of Breathitt County had been killed, and his brother Louis, a county chairman for Chandler, had been injured by a gun shot. [6]

1939

In November Long Beach, New York, police officer Alvin Dooley shot and killed the town's mayor, Louis F. Edwards, claiming that the mayor had successfully prevented him from reelection to the local Police Benevolent Association presidency. [1]

1940

In September a man named Utuado unsuccessfully tried to kill the Speaker of the Puerto Rican House, A.M. Mendez Garcia. Utuado was killed following the incident. [1, 6]

1940

The Secret Service office in Birmingham, Alabama, was raided in November during an investigation of Nazi sympathizers. Left dead in the ruin was Secret Service official Robert Perry, whose papers were stolen at the time. [6]

1945

In January, shortly before he was to testify on bribery charges against fellow state legislators, Michigan State Senator Warren G. Hooper was killed. Four conspirators were charged: Harry and Sam Fleisher, Mike Selik, and Pete Mahoney. [1]

1947

In March Hubert Humphrey, ambitious mayor of Minneapolis, was shot at three times, but never hit. At the time Humphrey was a reformer trying to clean up the city. [1]

1947

Ohio's Senator John William Bricker, who fifteen years earlier had been State Attorney General, was shot at by a constituent who still held a grudge against him for what he was convinced was Bricker's failure to help him out of a financial jam in 1932. William L. Kaiser was charged with the July shooting. [1]

1949

Evarts, Kentucky, Mayor Elihu H. Bailey found twenty-four sticks of dynamite under his bedroom window one April day, leading him to believe that his efforts to drive bootleggers out of business in the area had enraged someone. No one was apprehended. [1]

1950

While President Truman was taking an after-noon nap, two U.S. citizens from Puerto Rico, Oscar Collazo and Grielio Griselio Torresola, attempted to shoot their way into the temporary presidential quarters at Blair House. Neither one made it; Torresola was killed in the gunfire exchange with presidential guards, as was Leslie Coffelt, a guard.

Both attackers were ardent proponents of Puerto Rican nationalism, and hoped to draw attention to that cause by their action that November. After a trial in which Collazo refused to let his attorneys claim he was insane, the remaining attacker was sentenced to die by the electric chair on August 1, 1952.

A week before the execution, Truman commuted Collazo's sentence, and the convicted man now lives at Leavenworth Federal penitentiary. [1, 8, 12]

1954

Three Puerto Rican nationalists made the ultimate commitment to their cause by entering the U.S. House of Representatives visitor's gallery and shooting at members of Congress. Five were hit—Kenneth Allison Roberts (Ala.), Benton Franklin Jensen (Ia.), George Hyde Fallon (Md.), Alvin Morell Bentley (Mich.), and Clifford Davis (Tenn.). Charged with the March shooting were Lolita Lebron, Rafael Cancel Miranda, A. F. Corcera, and I. Flores Rodriguez (later arrested at the bus station). All were found guilty. [1]

1954

Alabama State Attorney General candidate Alfred Patterson was killed in June by Albert Fuller, former Sheriff of Russell County. One of Patterson's campaign promises was to decriminalize Phenix City, the Russell County seat. [6]

1958

As South Carolina State Senator Paul A. Wallace sat listening to election returns renominating him to the Democratic ticket, local County Court clerk Henry Rogers shot and killed him. Two weeks later, in late June, Rogers hanged himself in a state mental hospital. [1]

1959

In April Virginia Governor Lindsay Almond, Jr., was shot at by a "party unknown." Not long before the incident, Almond had taken what was considered at the time a moderate stance on school integration [1, 6]

1963

In November President John F. Kennedy was killed in Dallas, Texas. See previous chapters for details. Likewise Texas Governor John Connally, who was wounded at the same time.

1964

In April Verda Welcome, the only black member of the Maryland senate, was shot at. Assemblyman Young was charged with hiring others to murder her. [1, 6]

1965

A county welfare supervisor in Nebraska, M. J. Schumacher, was shot by a welfare recipient in November after talking about a cut in payments. [6]

1967

Sheriff Buford Pusser and his wife were both fired upon at Selmer, Tennessee, in August. His .wife died, Pusser lived, and the movie "Walking Tall" was based on this incident. [6]

1967

In August a state prosecutor in Georgia, F. Hoard, was killed by a bomb planted in his car. A. C. Park was later found guilty of hiring people to kill Hoard. [6]

1968-1974

At various times public threats were made against Richard Nixon, some of which his Justice Department acted upon, and others of which they didn't. In the former category was a statement by Black Panther activist David Hilliard; the latter group included Groucho Marx's 1971 comment that "the only hope this country has is Nixon's assassination." [6]

1968

Rio Arriba County, New Mexico, Deputy Sheriff E. Salazar was beaten to death in January. The state quickly charged Chicano activists associated with those about to stand trial on political charges. [6]

1968

Linden, New Jersey, Mayor John T. Gregorio had a particularly hectic April weekend. When riding in his car, a bullet just barely missed him; a couple days later his home was firebombed. [6]

1968

On the night after winning the June California Democratic presidential primary, U.S. Senator Robert Kennedy was shot at in Los

Angeles by at least one person, Sirhan B. Sirhan, and died soon thereafter. Sirhan, who used a .22 caliber pistol, was convicted of the assassination.

A number of discrepancies and mysteries continued to plague the case for years, including the number of bullets found, the handling of evidence by Los Angeles police, and the possibility of coconspirators. [1, 6]

1968

In September Jimmy Swan, who had run for governor in Mississippi the previous year as a hard-line segregationist, was fired upon while riding in a car. No assailant was apprehended. [6]

1968

White militant Anthony Imperiale, a Newark, New Jersey, city council candidate, was shot at in October. The assailant missed his target. [6]

1970

In January, a county prosecutor in Morgantown, West Virginia, Joseph A. Laurita, Jr., was injured when a bomb ignited in his car. His attacks on organized crime appeared to be the spark. [6]

1970

In April Los Angeles Superior Court Judge Alfred J. Gitelson was the intended target of a conspiracy by five men who possessed a large cache of weapons. Judge Gitelson had previously ordered the desegregation of Los Angeles schools. [6]

1970

Missouri State Representative Leon M. Jordan was shot to death in July while seeking his fourth Democratic nomination. No one was apprehended. [6]

1970

In August, Marin County, California, Superior Court Judge H. J. Haley was held with three others by seventeen-year-old Jonathan Jackson, whose actions temporarily freed the defendant and witnesses in a case Haley was presiding over. Judge Haley was killed during the ensuing escape attempt, and Jackson along with the defendant and a witness were killed when police opened fire.

Among those charged with conspiracy in the murder was educator Angela Davis, who went underground, was captured, tried, and acquitted. [6]

1971

A January kidnap attempt of South Carolina State Senator John C. Lindsay was foiled because he was not home. His wife was, however, along with eight others; Mrs. Lindsay was wounded in the mass abduction. Allegedly, two men sought to kidnap Lindsay and his family plus other local prominent officials in Marlboro County, South Carolina, and perhaps trade them for Angela Davis, then in prison. The two abductors also went to the home of State Representative Edward Cottingham, but he was not home. Charged in the incident were Charles Scales, who was wounded during capture, and Grover Bennett. [6]

1971

Civil rights worker Frank Stewart was charged in April by local authorities with conspiring to murder Baton Rouge Mayor Woody Dumas. Stewart contended that the prosecution was official retaliation for his civil rights work. [6]

1971

Republican election judge John Mills was shot and killed at the Goose Rock voting precinct in Kentucky. Four people were charged, including Democratic election judge James Smith, who was wounded in the incident. There had been an election day disagreement over voting procedures. [6]

1972

Campaigning in May for the Democratic party presidential nomination, Alabama Governor George C. Wallace was fired upon at a Laurel, Maryland, shopping center. The assailant was a twenty-one-year-old unemployed Milwaukee man, Arthur Bremer, whose recent past had included following ("stalking," in assassination parlance) various presidential candidates around North America while staying at expensive hotels.

Bremer's political views were largely unknown, except that he had attended Wallace rallies, a few radical student meetings, and allegedly been seen in the company of White House operative Anthony Ulasewicz. During the Watergate hearings, Hawaii Senator Daniel Inouye asked Nixon campaign aid Donald Segretti if he had ever known Bremer; Segretti said no.

Immediately following the shooting, Nixon aid Charles Colson suggested that E. Howard Hunt, another White House operative, break into Bremer's Milwaukee apartment and plant left-wing literature.

Bremer was subsequently tried and convicted; no coconspirators were ever indicted. The immediate beneficiary to the assassination attempt was Richard Nixon, whose re-election gained considerable strength as the second choice of millions of Wallace voters. Wallace was paralyzed from the waist down, but remained active in state and national politics. [6, 7, 8]

1973

In May Rockland County, New York, District Attorney Robert Meehan was fired upon during an investigation of official corruption and organized crime. The shot missed its mark. [6]

1973

The former mayor of Camden, New Jersey, Major B. Coxson, was murdered during June in what has become known as "gangland style" (tied hand and foot, shot in the head). Others with the former mayor were also shot, one of whom died later. Suspected in the slaying were organized crime figures tied to narcotics traffic. [6]

1973

Maryland State Legislator James A. Scott, under indictment for transporting heroin, was shot to death in a parking garage. He had been accused of participating in an operation that moved millions of dollars of heroin from New York to Maryland. Near his dead body that June were found leaflets from "Black October," a clandestine group of black militants conducting an extralegal campaign to drive narcotics pushers out of their community. [6]

1973

In May Warden P. Curran and his deputy, R. Fromhold, were stabbed to death at the Holmesburg Prison by inmates F. Burton and J. Bowen when conditions inside the Pennsylvania facilities became unbearable for the two. Cited were massive overcrowding and lack of facilities for religious practice, among other causes. [6]

1973

After leaving a nighttime meeting, Oakland (Calif.) School Superintendent Marcus A. Foster and his deputy, Robert Blackburn, were fired upon; Foster died and Blackburn recovered. A group called the "Symbionese Liberation Army" took credit for the November slaying which was accomplished with cyanide bullets. Arrested two months later were Joseph M. Remiro and Russell J. Little, who were convicted in a 1975 trial. The SLA charged that Foster was implementing police-state type regulations in the city schools. [6]

1974

In June Washington State Superior Court Judge James J. Lawless was killed in his office when a small package containing a bomb exploded in front of him. Convicted of the crime six months later was Ricky Young. [6]

1974

Judge Joseph J. Crescente, on night court duty, was shot at through an open window in Wanaque, New Jersey, while presiding over a case. Two youths were responsible, including one nineteen-year-old who had been ejected from the court earlier that November evening for causing a disturbance. [6]

1975

In September U. S. President Gerald Ford was the target of two assassination attempts in California. The first attempt was carried out in Sacramento by Lynette "Squeaky" Fromme, an associate of convicted murderer Charles Manson. The loaded gun did not go off, and presidential guards seized it and Fromme. Eighteen days later, part-time government informer (FBI and AT&F) Sara Jane Moore shot at Ford in San Francisco, and missed. Both assailants were later convicted. [6, 7]

1976

In January former Union City, New Jersey, Municipal Court Judge Jack Prizzia was seriously wounded when shot in the lobby of the building where he practiced law. At the time, Prizzia was appearing before a grand jury investigating the activities of the city's vice squad while he was a magistrate. He died a month later of a heart seizure. [6]

1976

Baltimore City Councilmen Dominic M. Leone and Carroll J. Fitzgerald were fired upon in April by Charles Hopkins, who entered City Hall with a gun. Leone died, and

Fitzgerald was wounded along with mayoral assistant Kathleen Nolan. Hopkins was critically injured by police gunfire. [6]

1976
In Springfield, Massachusetts, three people were arrested by local police for conspiring to murder Senator Edward Kennedy. The senator was visiting the area in September in his successful reelection bid. Charges were dropped shortly thereafter. [6]

1976
In September Orlando Letelier, a cabinet member and ambassador to the U.S. from Chile's Allende government, was assassinated when a bomb exploded in his car while driving in Washington, D.C. Agents from the military junta which seized power from the elected Chilean government in September 1973 were strongly suspected. At his death Letelier was active in developing studies and plans for Latin American politics and economy, and was an effective spokesman against Chile's ruling regime. [6]

Sources for Chapter 5

1. Kirkham, James J., Levy, Sheldon, and Crotty, William J., *Assassination and Political Violence*. Washington, D.C.: Government Printing Office, 1969. (Chapter 1, based on a paper by Rita James Simon with the assistance of Sondra Phillips, University of Illinois, Urbana, Ill.)

2. Shirley, Andrew, *Plots and Conspiracies*. Westport, Conn.: Greenwood Press, 1975.

3. Heaps, Willard A., *Assassination: A Special Kind of Murder*. New York: Meredith Press, 1969.

4. Havens, Murray Clark, Leiden, Carl, and Schmitt, Karl M., *The Politics of Assassination*. Englewood Cliffs, N.J.: Prentice-Hall, 1970.

5. McConnell, Brian, *The History of Assassination*. Nashville, Tenn.: Aurora Publishers, 1970.

6. *The New York Times* (various dates; check annual Index).

7. Wallechinsky, David, and Wallace, Irving, *The People's Almanac*. New York: Doubleday & Co., 1975.

8. *World Almanac and Book of Facts*. New York: Newspaper Enterprise Association, various years.

9. "American Heritage," August 1964, vol. CXV, no. 5.

10. Brown, Richard Maxwell, *Strain of Violence; Historical Studies of American Violence and Vigilantism*. New York: Oxford University Press, 1975.

11. Adamic, Louis, *Dynamite: The Story of Class Violence in America*. New York: Harper, 1931; Chelsea/Vintage, 1958.

12. Morris, Richard B., ed., *Encyclopedia of American History* (revised edition). New York: Harper & Row, 1961.

13. Broehl, Wayne G., Jr., *The Mollie Maguires*. Cambridge, Mass.: Harvard University Press, 1964.

14. Bergman, Peter M., *The Chronological History of the Negro in America*. New York: Harper & Row, 1969.

15. Morrison, Samuel Eliot, *The Oxford History of the American People*. New York: Oxford University Press, 1965.

16. Ginzburg, Ralph, *100 Years of Lynching*. New York: Lancer Books, 1962.

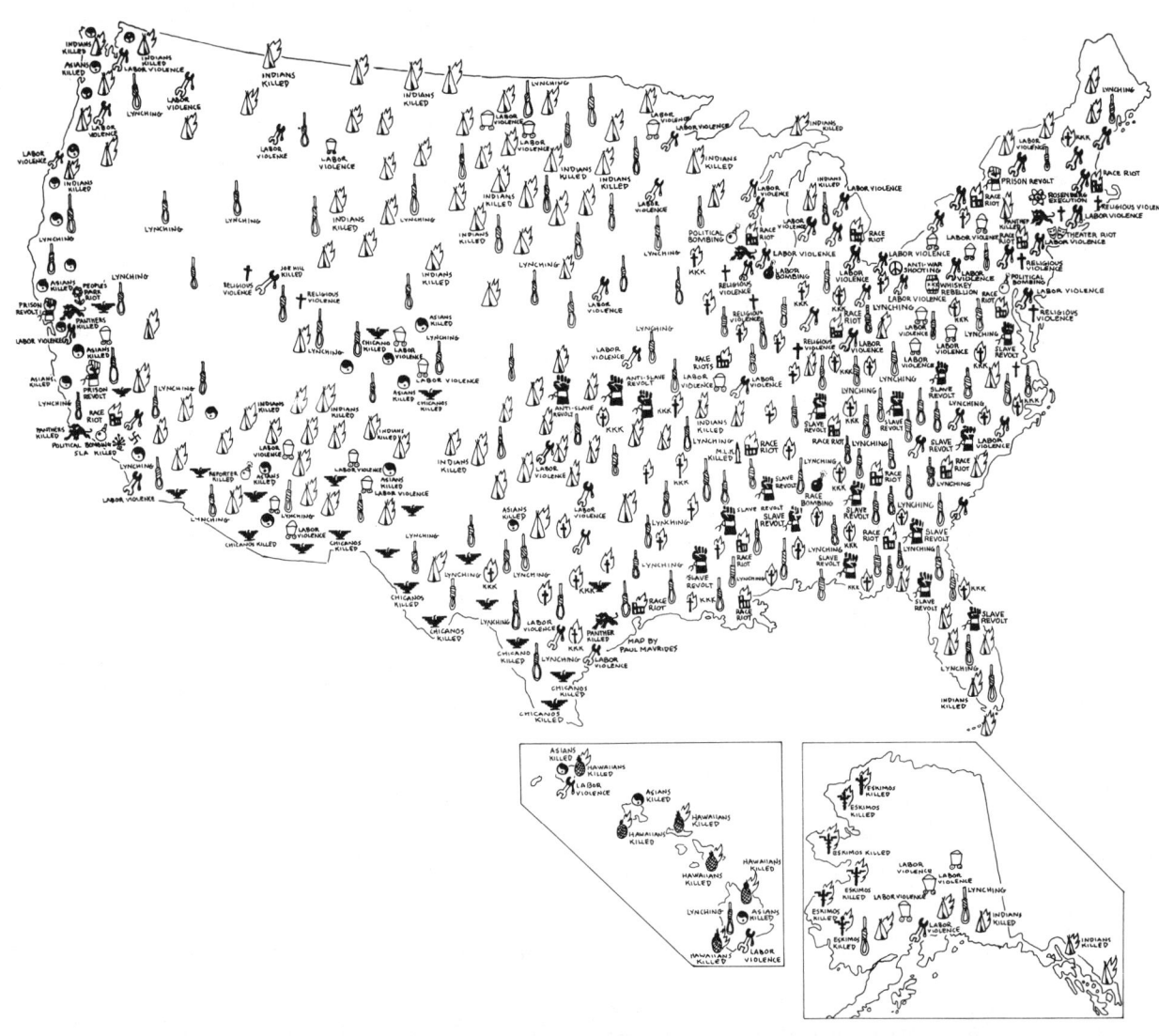

6 EVERYONE ELSE

What is an assassination?

In common usage it is the politically motivated killing of a public official. This is true as far as it goes, but we deceive ourselves when we limit the definition to officeholders exclusively. Politically motivated murders of private citizens often go unnoticed; while this makes them harder to record historically, it does not diminish their significance. One book on the subject simply says "assassination is the deliberate extralegal killing of an individual for political purposes."[1] Hence, any time someone is killed by extralegal means for reason of race, to facilitate land domination, to enforce the political status quo, or radically alter the balance of political power, it is an assassination.

Throughout American history such assassinations have been regularly carried out, often against well-defined groups during certain periods. Violence against Indians, blacks, striking laborers, antigovernment activists, and others has resulted in considerable death for political purposes. In many cases, incidents were so obscure or commonplace that little is known of them today. An Indian killed for interfering with westward expansion was barely a statistic and hardly ever a name. A black person lynched was the victim of political motivation as well, however crude.[2] Information about such killings decreases with the status of the deceased. It is this anonymity which separates assassinations of nonofficeholders from the others; it is this same anonymity which gives them importance.

The list that follows contains at least one record entry for each year since George Washington took office (with the exception of 1803, a year for which there is apparently no recorded incident of an extralegal politically motivated fatality). For most years there were many more assassinations that could have been substituted. The list is not so much intended to highlight specific murders as to demonstrate the extent to which assassination of private citizens has occurred throughout the country's history. Some are rather grisly and not as "sophisticated" as those of officeholders, but their purposes are parallel: For many, to maintain economic superiority or political survival, the only answer has been assassination.

1789

Government surveyors, guarded by U.S. soldiers, plotting townships in Indian territory near the Ohio River, were attacked by local Indians in an early morning August raid. A

---

1. *The Politics of Assassination,* by Havens, Leiden and Schmitt (Englewood Cliffs, N.J: Prentice-Hall, 1970).

2. A November 1933 report of the "Southern Commission on the Study of Lynching" said one cause of lynching was a "consuming fear of Communism."

few soldiers were killed, and the surveyors quickly left the area. [37]³

1790

Several slaves from Africa, who were feared to have supernatural demonic powers, were hanged and shot for this "crime" near Cahokia, Illinois. Among those killed were Moreau and Emmanuel. [38]

1791

After seeing federal troops raise a truce flag during the Whiskey Rebellion, James McFarlane, who had just led an attack on the home of an excise tax collector in Pennsylvania, stepped into the open. The federal troops immediately killed him. [1]

1792

Three slaves in Virginia were executed outright amid rumors of impending slave uprisings. Many whippings also occurred for the same reason. [2]

1793

Slaves as far north as Albany, New York, were accused of setting fire to valuable property. Two women and three men were hanged as a result. [2]

1794

The U.S. military, under "Mad Anthony" Wayne, invaded Shawnee Indian territory at Fallen Timbers, killing many in victory. Re-

3. The number in brackets following each entry refers to a source at the end of the chapter containing supportive information.

treating to the fort, soldiers burned Indian villages en route. [7]

1795

Slaves in Point Coupee, Louisiana, had poorly laid plans for an uprising, and the police came in to wipe them out. Twenty-five slaves resisted capture and were killed. Twenty-five more were executed for being part of the plot. Severed slave heads were displayed along the Mississippi River as an example to others with thoughts of rebellion. [1, 2]

1796

At the Poydras plantation in Point Coube Parish, Louisiana, a slave insurrection nipped in the bud resulted in the assassination of twenty-four blacks. (Whites convicted as accomplices were sentenced to prison.) [28]

1797

A slave "conspiracy," as it was called, was discovered in Charleston, South Carolina, and two blacks were assassinated by hanging. The plot allegedly involved burning down Charleston that November. [26]

1798

Jemmy Jones, a Federalist, was killed in a duel by New York Republican politician Brockholst Livingston in the Hoboken, New Jersey, fields in early May. Earlier, Jones had beaten Livingston on the streets of New York after the latter denounced the Alien and Sedition Bills, which were passed later that year. [47]

1799

Two white escorts of a group of slaves were

killed in Southampton County, Virginia, and four to ten slaves were killed as a result. [2]

1800

In August Gabriel Prosser gathered over a thousand other slaves near Richmond, Virginia, with plans to seize state power using homemade swords, bayonets, and a few guns. They soon realized the logistic impossibility of their goal and disbanded before striking a blow. Local whites learned about the plan, and more than thirty slaves, including Prosser, were hanged in October. [2, 13]

1801

Two slaves in Nottaway County, Virginia, were hanged in January on charges of organizing a slave revolt. [2]

1802

After slave Tom Cooper planned an uprising in May, word leaked out to local whites in Elizabeth County, North Carolina, and fifteen slaves were killed on the spot. [2]

1803

(No recorded incident of an extralegal, politically motivated murder was found for this year.)

1804

Plotters of slave revolts in the countryside around New Orleans were executed. Names of the dead were not available. [26]

1805

At least four slaves were killed—one by burning, the others by hanging—when an uprising was feared by whites in North Carolina. [13]

1806

A white North Carolinian was executed for kidnapping a free Negro and making a slave of him. [13]

1807

Two boatloads of newly arrived slaves from Africa, protesting their enslavement, went on a hunger strike. The strike was never resolved, and they all died. [2]

1808

Slave "conspiracies" were uncovered in Goochland County, Virginia, and a number of slaves were assassinated for their part in these "conspiracies." [26]

1809

At Kaskaskia, Illinois, a political feud erupted between two men, Shadrach Bond and Rice Jones. The feud led to a pistol duel on an island in the Mississippi River. No one was wounded, but as a result, Bond's second at the duel became embroiled in a bitter feud with Jones, and not long thereafter killed him, ending the rivalry and Jones's upwardly mobile political career. [38]

1810

In Greene County, Georgia, a slave "plot" (similar to a slave conspiracy) was revealed, and plotters were killed for it. [26]

1811

A Santo Domingo free born Mulatto, Charles Deslondes, led a partially successful rebellion in January against Louisiana plantation owners, using mainly knives and axes. After killing a few slaveowners, the father of one of the victims counterattacked with other whites. Sixty-six blacks were killed right away, and sixteen more after trials in New Orleans. The original battle took place in St. Charles and St. John the Baptist Parishes. [2]

1812

A slave "conspiracy" was discovered in Rockingham County, North Carolina, and participants were assassinated. [26]

1813

Shawnee Indian leader Tecumseh died fighting for the British forces in U.S. territory. [7]

1814

In the summertime Fredericksburg and Richmond, Virginia, were the scenes of assassinations of slaves charged with plotting revolts. [26]

1815

A white settlement was the object of Osage Indian raids in the summer and fall, when Osage parties seized horses belonging to settlers along the Red River in southern Oklahoma. One settler, Abraham Anthony, was killed in one attack. [36]

1816

Col. Duncan Clinch led a force of U.S. troops and Indians against a fugitive slave fortress at Ft. Blount, Florida. Two hundred seventy fugitive slaves were executed in the ensuing ten-day battle. [2]

1817

White settlers in Florida assassinated many Seminole Indians in November, and some Seminoles replied in kind, leading to the Seminole War of 1817-1818. Whites blamed the Spanish for provoking Indians to attack whites. [23]

1818

In April Andrew Jackson led U.S. troops against a force of Seminole Indians and blacks in Florida, leaving many nonwhites dead. Jackson called the conflict "this savage and Negro war." [25]

1819

For allegedly leading a slave revolt and planning to burn Augusta, Georgia, a slave named Coot or Coco was executed. [2]

1820

Federal troops were used to put down a slave revolt on Talbot Island, Florida. A number of slaves gave their lives in the struggle that March. [26]

1821

A group of abolitionists in Kennett Square, Pennsylvania, killed two Southern slaveowners who had come north to repossess an AWOL employee. [2]

1822

Mobs of vigilantes killed forty-one slaves in July after rumors of an impending slave revolt spread through Charleston, South Carolina. Denmark Vessey, alleged leader of the revolt, was hanged with the others. [1]

1823

Osage Indians under the leadership of Mad Buffalo, or Skitok, made a successful surprise attack on a white hunting party in November. Five were killed by the Osage in the raid, who captured camp equipment, arms, clothing, and horses. [36]

1824

Chippewa Indians on the road to St. Louis reportedly killed and scalped a number of whites. By this time white settlers had established strongholds in Chippewa territory. [30]

1825

In August at Abbeville County, South Carolina, a slave called Negro Jack was convicted by a magistrate on charges of rape and murder. In order to "make of him a dreadful example to his race," the six-man jury (a magistrate and five "freeholders") had the convicted chained to a stake and four days later executed by fire. [31]

1826

A "Free Mason" named William Morgan in Batavia, New York, was killed because it was said he had revealed "secrets" of "The Order of Free Masons," which evidently was frowned upon. The Morgan death was a prime spark leading to the "Anti-Masonic Party." [23]

1827

After a Frenchman had killed two Osage Indians at a Pawnee Indian town, he was him-self killed by the Osage, along with six others in the town. Altogether, five Osage died in the summer skirmish. [36]

1828

Pawnee Indians attacked and killed two soldiers from Ft. Towson in Oklahoma; the fort was charged with protecting settlers from Indians and guarding Indian rights. Later, back at camp, Pawnees were attacked by a posse of settlers, soldiers, and "friendly Indians." Only a few Pawnees escaped death; the battle took place on the Blue River in what is now Bryan County, Oklahoma. [36]

1829

A gang of whites invaded an area of Cincinnati called "little Africa" killing many blacks and driving half of the community's population out of town. [3]

1830

Bostonian David Walker, an active abolitionist, was assassinated in June at his used clothing store soon after the third issue of his "appeal to the coloured citizens of the world" was published. [26]

1831

Nat Turner, having received urging from God as well as fellow slaves, was hanged with more than a hundred other slaves following their August rampage killing of fifty-seven whites in the Southampton, Virginia, area. [15, 35]

1832

Lt. Jefferson Davis led a U.S. Cavalry attack

on Sauk and Fox Indians at the Rock River in Wisconsin. The Indians, who were led by Chief Blackhawk, were looking for a place to plant corn to feed themselves and other Indians. Sauk and Fox Indians of all ages were assassinated in the spring massacre. [24]

1833

The Osage Indians, following unsuccessful territorial treaty negotiations with various tribes including the Kiowa at U.S. Fort Gibson in the Southwest Territory, attacked a defenseless Kiowa encampment leaving many dead. The campsite, at the mouth of Rainy-Mountain Creek, a southern tributary of the Washita, was near Ft. Sill, Oklahoma. All Kiowa warriors were out hunting the Osage, and the dead were all elderly men, women, and children. [33]

1834

Mobs of whites ran through the black section of Philadelphia looting and burning black homes and businesses. Among the dead from the community was Stephen Jones. [2]

1835

Angry citizens attacked the homes of persons they thought were responsible for the collapse of the Bank of Maryland in August. Baltimore's mayor led a "citizen's militia" counterattack, leaving ten to twenty dead and one hundred wounded. [1, 4]

1836

A free Mulatto, imprisoned for having stabbed a deputy sheriff in an attempt to free a black man from custody, was taken from a St. Louis, Missouri, jail in April to the outskirts of town and burned to death as he hanged. [35]

1837

When abolitionist newspaperman and Presbyterian minister Elijah P. Lovejoy attempted to prevent a mob from burning his presses in November at Alton, Illinois, he was murdered. A grand jury refused to indict the accused. [2, 4, 35]

1838

Hundreds of Cherokee, Choctaw, Chicasaw, Creek, and Seminole Indians died on a forced march to "Indian Territory" (Oklahoma). The fall march became known as the "Trail of Tears." [5, 34]

1839

Eight miles above the mouth of the Coloosahatchie (or Synabel) River in Florida, a Col. William S. Harney attempted to set up a trading post on land within an area designated for Indians by a treaty completed a few months earlier. In July, eighteen of the party setting up the post were attacked and killed by Spanish Seminole Indians. Forty-five Indians were imprisoned a week later and put aboard a steamship bound for Ft. Moultrie. [34]

1840

In August it was reported that a group of Indians had landed on an island in the Florida Keys and killed most of the black inhabitants.

The massacre took place on Indian Key. [30]

1841

In Kansas an intertribal battle resulted in death for a number of Pawnee Indians at the hands of the Kanzas Indians. [30]

1842

A white gang attacked participants at a peaceful parade in Philadelphia celebrating the abolition of slavery in the West Indies. Two died as a result. Black businesses were also attacked. [2]

1843

In the Cherokee Nation the reelection of Chief John Ross provoked threats against some of his supporters in one voting precinct, leading to the death of Isaac Bushyhead and the wounding of two others. Four people accused in the plot were captured, and two more—one a white man—were sought. [30]

1844

In Philadelphia thirteen persons died in battle between Irish Catholics and "Nativist" Protestants. Two Catholic churches were burned in the July fight, and many Irish homes were destroyed. The combatants used cannons; the conflict ended only after U.S. Cavalry interfered. [4, 6]

1845

In the year following the killing of Mormon prophet Joseph Smith at Carthage, Illinois, a local group called "The Fire and Sword Company" destroyed hundreds of dwellings, driving Mormons out of another Illinois community, Warsaw, where one Franklin B. Warrell was ambushed and killed. [30]

1846

Slaves living in southern Maryland, en route to Pennsylvania in an escape attempt, were captured by a white gang near Washington and summarily assassinated by bullet and rope. [24]

1847

A government agent rounded up one hundred seventy Indians belonging to the "Six Nations" of Indians in New York State from their homes and herded them west of the Mississippi to what was called "undiscovered territory." Within a couple of months approximately eighty of the Indians had died of sickness and malnutrition. [30]

1848

Twenty-six members of the Des Chutes Indian tribe died in battle with a "scouting expedition" led by a Col. Gilliam. (The Des Chutes had been retaliating against white settlements encroaching on Indian lands in the area along the Dallas River in Oregon.) The following month fifty more Indians were killed in similar battles. Nine "Americans," as white settlers were called in the press, were also killed in the battle. [30, 40]

1849

A crowd of people gathering outside the Astor Place Opera House in New York, where *Macbeth* was playing, was fired upon by National Guardsmen called in by Mayor Woodhull to quell a growing disturbance. The controversy arose out of a minor dispute involving a British actor a few days earlier, but soon grew into a riot of major proportions. Twenty-one New Yorkers were killed by the guard, including curious passers-by. [30]

1850

The sheriff, mayor, and five others in Sacramento, California, were killed by a group of "squatters" after the sheriff tried to evict a local farmer in August. [1]

1851

Slaveowner Edward Gorsuch was killed in September by an integrated crowd when he tried to recapture some former black employees who had secretly moved to Christianna, Pennslyvania. Those charged in the killing were acquitted. [1]

1852

In July a suspected Mexican bandit, Mariano Hernandez, was captured by a notorious vigilante committee in Santa Cruz, California, and promptly hanged. The next day the committee charged another Mexican with crimes and hanged him. [46]

1853

About seventy-five Yahi and Maidu Indians in north-central California along the Feather River were assassinated by bullet and rope by local vigilantes who made sporadic scalping raids into Indian territory. [41]

1854

In New York City following rumors in August that Catholic churches were really arsenals, a group of self-proclaimed "Native Americans" burned and looted Irish homes, slaughtering eight people inside one of the churches. [4, 6]

1855

Following provocative remarks by "Know Nothings," a mob fired a brass cannon into the Irish section of Louisville, Kentucky, which started a two-day August riot, leaving twenty Irish immigrants dead. [4, 6]

1856

Pro and antislavery guerilla warfare in "Bleeding Kansas" left 200 dead in the state between May and September. The first open warfare was in Lawrence, an antislavery center, when proslavers ransacked the town. In quick retaliation John Brown and his party executed proslave forces at Pottawatomie Creek. [7, 19]

1857

At Mountain Meadows, Utah, in September, some Mormons offered to escort a party of non-Mormons across the dangerous state —whereupon the adults in the traveling party were lined up and shot. [27]

1858

Proslavery forces at Marias de Cygne, Kansas, added to the death count in the episode known as "Bleeding Kansas" by executing five abolitionists in May. [1]

1859

Hoping to spark a general uprising among slaves, John Brown and an integrated following of twenty-one others captured the federal arsenal at Harpers Ferry, killing the mayor and taking hostages. In mid-October troops commanded by Robert E. Lee and J.E.B. Stuart captured the abolitionists, including Brown. Twelve abolitionists were killed in battle, and others, including Brown, were tried for treason and later executed at Charlestown, Virginia. [1, 7, 19]

1860

When local vigilantes heard a rumor that Indians along the Eel River in California were supplying the Bald Hills Indians with arms and ammunition, they attacked the peaceful tribe. Two hundred Indians were left dead in the nighttime raid. The rumor later proved to be false. [22]

1861

When a Navajo protested to U.S. soldiers about cheating during a Ft. Wingate, New Mexico, horse race, he was killed. Many Navajo who protested the September murder were themselves killed by the soldiers. [5]

1862

Mescalero Apaches were offered foodstuffs in September by U.S. soldiers in southern New Mexico and then were murdered when they came to pick up the goods. [5]

1863

Objecting to unfair draft laws (the rich could evade the draft by paying a $300 fee for a substitute), some 50,000 protesters, mainly poor and working class Irish, rioted in New York City. They attacked draft offices, police, and wealthy homes as well as blacks who were mistakenly blamed for the war, which brought the draft about in the first place. Federal troops from Gettysburg, Pennsylvania, were brought in to quell the riot; over a thousand people died during the uprising. [1, 4]

1864

Over one hundred thirty members of the Santee Sioux tribe were killed in November by the U.S. Cavalry at Sand Creek, near Ft. Lyon, Kansas. Earlier the local sheriff had assured the Indians, mainly women and children, that they would be left alone. Dead Indian bodies were mutilated and scalped. [5]

1865

Fifty Sioux Indians living in a village near the Tongue River in South Dakota were attacked and murdered by U.S. troops in September. [5]

1866

Anti-reconstruction violence of a racist nature occurred in the South following the Civil War. In one such incident in the spring, 46 blacks were killed in Memphis. In late July, New Orleans police, firemen, and Confederate veterans attacked a political meeting of blacks; 50 blacks died and another 150 were injured.

Cheyenne Indians living on the Washita River in Oklahoma were killed by U.S.

troops commanded by General Phillip Sheridan. One hundred three Indians, mainly women, children, and old men, were killed that Thanksgiving weekend. [5]

1867

A Goodlettsville, Tennessee, Reconstruction Republican named William Scruggs was shot at his store one July evening. Earlier that day he had hosted a "radical" meeting. [22]

1868

At a Fourth of July gathering at Butte, Montana, miners in the employ of Anaconda celebrated by hanging a Chinese coworker. [32]

1869

Two hundred Cheyennes, trying to leave their settlement in the Dakota Territory in order to avoid white settlers, were killed by troops commanded by Eugene Carr in July. [5]

1870

Rioting whites attacked the Chinese community in Denver just prior to election day, destroying most of the buildings. At least one Chinese man was killed, and most others were jailed "for their own protection." [8]

1871

White mobs attacked the Chinese community in San Francisco, killing at least twenty Chinatown residents. Lynchings took place in the streets. [8]

1872

Over Thanksgiving weekend, Major James Jackson's soldiers shot a baby and an old woman in the Modoc Indian tribe at Lost River, California. [5]

1873

Twenty-three Comanches were assassinated in September at McClellan's Creek, Texas. U.S. Cavalry troops attacked without apparent provocation. [5]

1874

Apache leader Delshay, accused of aiding a group of Indian raiders, was killed by mercenary soldiers in the New Mexico territory. The heads of two Indians, both alleged to be Delshay, were brought in and mounted on posts at Camp Rio Verde and Camp San Carlos as "examples" to other Apaches. [5]

1875

A race riot in the Yazoo City, Mississippi, area left many blacks dead; others fled the area. [44]

1876

Newspapers and opportunistic politicians, spreading anti-Chinese sentiment, spurred vicious attacks on Chinese communities throughout northern California in the spring of 1876. Numerous Oriental immigrants died violently as a result. [8]

1877

The Great Railroad Strike of 1877 boiled over in July as President Hayes ordered federal troops to keep train terminals open at strike locations in Buffalo, New York, Reading and Pittsburgh, Pennsylvania, Baltimore and Cumberland, Maryland, and elsewhere. Over thirty strikers were killed by troops. Civilians who supported strikers fought the federal troops alongside strikers in Pittsburgh and elsewhere. [1, 9]

1878

En route to testify about election fraud before a federal grand jury in New Orleans, Lott Clark and Bill Whute were killed in December near Caledonia, Louisiana. [22]

1879

After five days in January without heat, water, or food, one hundred Cheyenne tried to leave Ft. Robinson in the Dakota Territory. Each of the one hundred was killed by federal troops in what was called an "escape attempt." [5]

1880

Frontier justice was evident in Socorro, New Mexico, when vigilantes apprehended and hanged a Mexican card dealer because two of his employees had incensed them. There is no evidence that the two employees were likewise hanged. The vigilantes had been receiving payoffs of twelve dollars daily to allow the gambling tables to remain open. [39]

1881

A black woman in Spartanburg, South Carolina, Ann Cowan, was hanged by a white mob after accusations that she set fire to a white man's barn. [22]

1882

Following rumors in May that Galeyville, New Mexico, had been burned down by Apache Indians, U.S. Cavalry troops under a Captain Tupper were let loose on the Indi-

ans, killing forty of them. Later, it was determined that Galeyville had not, in fact, burned down. [22]

1883

A government campaign, headed by General George Crook, to eradicate the Apache Indian warriors, resulted in the death of many Apaches. An agreement with Mexico, which allowed Crook to enter that country "in hot pursuit" of Apaches from New Mexico and Arizona, contributed to Crook's success, which resulted in the surrender of 285 Apaches, including Geronimo. [42]

1884

After a murderer's sentencing, which Cincinnati residents felt was less severe than it should have been, a crowd burned the courthouse to the ground, and the state militia came in to quell the disturbance. Forty-two died as a result of the March riot. [4]

1885

In December at Caldwell, Kansas, a "whiskey peddler" was hanged by a vigilante committee comprised of temperance partisans, who were trying to drive all vestiges of alcohol out of the community by any means possible. [39]

1886

Major demonstrations by laborers throughout the Midwest, South, and Southwest occurred in the spring, highlighted by the "Haymarket Massacre" in Chicago. Soldiers opened fire on strikers at the McCormick Harvester Works, killing at least four and injuring others. The following day, as police attempted to break up a labor rally, a bomb exploded killing seven policemen. Although there was no evidence to support charges, four anarchist labor organizers were convicted and executed for the bombing. Other cities where significant labor agitation occurred included Milwaukee, where a few strikers were killed by police, East St. Louis, and Ft. Worth. These insurrections led to the establishment of May Day as an international labor and socialist holiday. [9, 10]

1887

Charley Greene and William Edens, two men who dared speak out against the vigilante "baldknobbers" at Kirbyville, Missouri, in March, were killed for their words. [11]

1888

Louisiana Governor McEnery, up against challenger General Nicholls in a re-election bid, lost the endorsement of a key supporter when Patrick Mealey defected to the Nicholls camp. In retaliation, a gang of McEnery's men attacked and killed Mealey in a New Orleans bar. [22]

1889

A black janitor for the Defiance, Ohio, schools, J. H. Mull, was killed by a white mob in February following his accusations that the white superintendent of schools had been in "compromising positions" with young women teachers. Mull's body was mutilated, and his black assistant was reportedly also killed. [22]

1890

Sioux Chief Sitting Bull, erroneously identi-fied as the leader of the Ghost Dances, was killed by officials sent to arrest him. The action was an attempt to end the Ghost Dance movement, a prophesy of a return to Native power, which was sweeping Indian tribes everywhere. The murder took place at the Standing Rock Reservation in the Dakota Territory. Later that December at Wounded Knee, the U.S. Cavalry murdered 300 Sioux who had just surrendered to them, earning eighteen cavalrymen Congressional Medals of Honor for "gallantry and bravery." [5, 7]

1891

In March eleven Italians accused of complicity in the murder of the New Orleans police chief were themselves murdered by a mob before being brought to trial. [35]

1892

At Homestead, Pennsylvania, management brought in Pinkerton guards to break up a steel mill strike. The Pinkertons then collected recruits from the surrounding area and attempted to invade the town by barge—unsuccessfully. Intervention by the state militia finally quelled the rebellion, but not before a few deaths on both sides occurred. The next month, July, Pinkertons working for mine owners in Coeur d'Alene, Idaho, killed union members during an attempt to halt laborers from organizing. Before the union uprising was over, the scene was a virtual guerilla war, with the Army finally declaring martial law. [1]

1893

Two quarreling groups of Choctaw Indians started fighting over tribal election results in

March near Antlers, Texas. Twenty-one Indians were dead by the end of the fighting, which included hundreds of federal troops brought into the area for the purpose of ending the conflict. [22]

1894

A national Pullman car workers strike provoked President Grover Cleveland to call out strike-breaking troops in July, resulting in laborers' deaths all over the country. U.S. deputy marshals and Illinois National Guardsmen fired into picketing strikers as well, killing a few dozen. Also, there were rebellions by iron and coal miners throughout the Great Lakes region, resulting in deaths when police and militia intervened. [1, 10]

1895

In November a white mob in Madisonville, Texas, lynched a black man for supposedly riding his horse over a white girl. After the murder, facts showed that the man had wrongly been accused. [12]

1896

In June, when the Georgia Supreme Court asked that Bill Miles and James Slayton, both black, be tried a fourth time on charges of raping a white woman, a white mob at an Atlanta courthouse assumed jury duty and lynched the duo. [22]

1897

In September twenty striking coal miners at Hazelton and Latimer, Pennsylvania, were assassinated by sheriff's deputies when the deputies fired into a crowd of picketers. Eventually the coal companies agreed to an eight-hour work day, semimonthly pay, and abolished the company store. [23]

1898

In what was called a massacre, a white mob killed one hundred blacks in Wilmington, North Carolina, in November and followed up by forming its own rump governing body for the town. [4]

1899

Approaching a gathering at a bar in Weir City, Kansas, black miner George Wells was told that the bartender had just been killed. The crowd turned on Wells, proclaimed him the guilty party, and lynched him. [12]

1900

In June at Mississippi City, Mississippi, a white mob, angry that no suspects had been picked up in the murder of a white girl, happened upon Henry Askew and Ed Russ, two local black citizens. The sheriff observed the two being murdered but later could not identify anyone in the lynching gang. [12]

1901

At Pierce City, Missouri, Eugene Carter and a friend named Godley were lynched in August, having been accused of murdering a white woman. In a frenzy, the attackers shot at the dead bodies, misfiring occasionally into their own crowd. One young white boy was killed. The mob moved onto the "colored quarter" and burned houses down with occupants still inside, fired at others, and drove every blackskinned citizen from town. [12]

1902

Police in the Pennsylvania coal fields shot at striking miners, killing one Antonio Giuseppe. The July strike was eventually settled by arbitration unfavorable to the miners. [9]

1903

In June a Belleville, Illinois, school teacher, David Wyatt, was beaten, burned, and hanged to death for allegedly taking a shot at the local school superintendent in June. Although Wyatt was already imprisoned, police refused to stand in the mob's way, fearing injury to someone in the crowd. [12]

1904

A June battle between striking miners and the Colorado state militia ended in death for six of the union pickets at Dunnville. [4]

1905

In Tallahachie County, Mississippi, a black man named William James was lynched. It was reported that his crime was "informing." [29]

1906

A pogrom against black Atlantans started on Decatur Street on September 22 and lasted six days. With the support of local militia and police, white mobs ravaged black neighborhoods, leaving twenty-five dead (one white died as well) and hundreds injured. Over a thousand blacks fled the city. The atmosphere for the attack was set by a heavily racist gubernatorial campaign and a local newspaper which, having regularly accused black males of raping white women, suggested that such men be castrated. [44, 45]

1907

In a May race riot at Reidsville, Georgia, five blacks were assassinated by whites. [29]

1908

Race riots in Springfield, Illinois, led to black and white deaths. The disturbance started when a black defendant in a rape case was moved to a nearby town for safety, with whites retaliating by attacking the black section of Springfield. [3]

1909

Miners on strike at McKee's Rocks, Pennsylvania, were attacked in the summer by an "elite" battalion of the Pennsylvania state militia that specialized in strikebreaking. The soldiers, forerunners of more recent S. W. A. T. units, were called the "Cossacks." Twelve Industrial Workers of the World (I. W. W.) miners were killed, and fifty more were wounded. [9]

1910

The antiunion Los Angeles Times was hit by a bomb blast, killing ten employees. Ironworker union officials John and James McNamara admitted arranging the October bombing, which severely retarded labor organizing in Los Angeles by the A. F. of L. and the Ironworkers. [9]

1911

After laws were enacted preventing I. W. W. (Wobbly) organizers from public speaking, a December clash between San Diego police and union men left one Wobbly dead. The death led to immediate victory for the union, which was immediately back organizing on the streets. [9]

1912

A January textile strike battle at Lawrence, Massachusetts, left union members Anna Lo-Pizzo and John Ramy dead. The latter was bayonetted by police, creating a strikers motto: "Bayonets cannot weave cloth!" The I.W.W. strike was victorious. [10]

1913

A migrant farm workers struggle in the summer left four people dead after the I.W.W. attempted to organize the laborers. Two of the dead were hop pickers near Wheatland, California, and the other two were local law enforcement officials. [1]

1914

Marie Scott, a black woman, tried defending herself against an attacking gang of young white men, and stabbed one of them. In retaliation, she was chased into the black section of Muskogee, Oklahoma, and lynched.

Elsewhere that spring, National Guard troops called in to break up a lengthy strike at the Rockefeller-owned Colorado Fuel and Iron Co. at Ludlow fired machine guns at tents and tunnels improvised by the strikers. Some tents caught fire, burning (or smothering) some strikers and their families. [1, 12]

1915

Jailed on charges that he murdered a Salt Lake City store owner, I.W.W. organizer Joe Hill was set for execution at the Utah State Prison. Pleas for clemency from President Wilson and Wobbly sympathizers across the country went unheeded, and in November a firing squad killed Hill. Earlier in the year strikes at factories in Perth Amboy, Elizabeth,

Roosevelt, and Bayonne (Standard Oil) led to company guards killing numerous strikers. [9]

1916

In April a preliminary evidentiary hearing in an Idabel, Oklahoma, courtroom convinced white observers that black defendant Oscar Martin was guilty of assaulting a white girl. Martin was immediately hanged from a courtroom balcony. [12]

1917

In Butte, Montana, a Wobbly organizer, Frank Little, was lynched for trying to organize workers at an Anaconda copper mine. Little, a half-Indian ("half-Indian, half-white man, all I.W.W." went the saying), was also unpopular in certain quarters for his militant opposition to the World War. [7]

1918

A black man in Estill Springs, Tennessee, Jim McIlherron, was tortured with a red hot crowbar, and then burned to death for allegedly killing a white man who was found dead earlier in February. [12]

1919

Labor violence in steel mills at West Natrona, Farrell, Hammond, and elsewhere in Pennsylvania led to many deaths at the hands of the "Cossacks" and private guards hired by U.S. Steel and other companies. One United Mine Worker organizer, Fannie Sellins, pleaded with company thugs to stop beating a picketer and was killed as a result. Steel companies said demands for better working conditions, higher wages, and an eight hour day were inspired by "Bolsheviks and the Red element." Further west in Herrin, Illinois, striking coal miners killed nineteen scabs brought in to take their jobs. A coroner's jury blamed the deaths on mine owners who had imported the strikebreakers. [1, 9]

1920

Beginning in October and lasting apparently a year, Ku Klux Klan violence in New York State left many blacks wounded, leaving at least four dead. [6]

1921

In March masked white men seeking to insure that blacks took no more jobs on the Yazoo and Mississippi Valley Railroad, shot and killed Howard Hurd, a black trainman, at Lake Cormorant, Mississippi. It was the culmination of a terrorist campaign against black railroad workers. Hurd's overalls contained a note saying, "take this as a warning to all nigger railroad men." [12]

1922

In December Streetman, Texas, was the scene of a 1,500 strong white mob intent on lynching George Gay, a twenty-five-year-old black man. Gay was accused of assaulting a white woman, although charges were not pressed and the woman could not identify him. The mob dragged Gay from police protection and shot him on the highway, and then burned the one black hotel in town. Gay was the fourth black killed by a white mob in this central Texas town in four months. [12]

1923

In June Henry Simmons was lynched by local whites in Palm Beach, Florida, for his outspoken views on how blacks were treated at the hands of whites. [12]

1924

Five persons, including Frank Capone, brother of gangster Al Capone, were killed by police on election day in the spring. Threatened by reformist candidates, the Capones and other gangsters in Chicago brutalized voters at polling places until local police caught up with them. Brother Al escaped the shoot-out and was never charged; the gangster-supported candidate won the election. [43]

1925

Following his acquittal in a December murder trial, Lindsay Coleman, a black man, was dragged from a Clarksdale, Mississippi, courtroom and hanged in the street. [12]

1926

Bertha and Demon Lowman and their cousin Clarence were killed in October by an irate white mob when it appeared that the three black defendants on trial for murdering the local sheriff in Aiken, South Carolina, would be acquitted. [12]

1927

Bartolomeo Vanzetti and Nicola Sacco were executed in August after being convicted of murder as a result of protesting the death seven years earlier of a Brooklyn printer. The printer, Andrea Salsedo, had been arrested on "suspicion of radicalism" and later was found dead. Italian and labor groups were sympathetic to Sacco and Vanzetti's situation, and world-wide protests called for commutation of their execution sentence. Although the two were most evidently framed, their judge was quite antilabor and antiimmigrant, referring to the defendants as "those anarchist bastards." [9]

1928

Members of the Industrial Workers of the World on strike against a coal mining company at Walsenburg, Colorado, were parading to meet with the state Industrial Commission in January, when local authorities ordered them to disperse. In the ensuing shooting, one striker and one youth were killed. The previous fall, the city's town council ordered all Wobblies to leave town, and the Walsenburg mayor led a mob attack on the local I.W.W. headquarters. [39]

1929

Ella May Wiggins, one of many national textile workers gathering at Gastonia, North Carolina, in support of striking union members on trial, was killed by private guards working for mill owners. The June trial stemmed from an earlier clash between local police and strikers in their tent encampment—during which the police chief was killed. [9]

1930

A black prison trustee at Thomasville, Georgia, Willie Kirkland, was accused in October of attacking a local white girl and was hanged by a mob. According to the sheriff, however, Kirkland had been locked in the stockade at the time he allegedly attacked the girl. [12]

1931

In January a young black man was chained atop a school building in Maryville, Missouri, doused with gasoline, and along with the school itself, burned. The youth was accused of killing a school teacher a few weeks earlier. [12]

1932

Four protesters, among thousands of demonstrators outside the Ford plant at Dearborn, Michigan, were assassinated by police. Hundreds more were wounded in the March labor action. [14]

1933

Three thousand whites, wanting to lynch black prisoner George Armwood, fought fifty state police in October at Princess Anne, Maryland. Eventually, Armwood was dragged from his cell and hanged on the front lawn of the judge who earlier tried to placate the mob. Local American Legionnaires had earlier refused a request from the governor to protect the prisoner. [12]

1934

Two strikers and one sympathizer were killed when San Francisco police were called in to prevent longshoremen from stopping cargo shipments. Two days earlier, another striker had been killed, and by the middle of July, a general strike virtually shut the city down.

At the same time, there was a general strike in Minneapolis, begun by the Teamsters. A police attack on a strike convoy through town caused two deaths and scores of injuries. The attack failed to break the strike, which eventually gained total victory.

Two months earlier, Ohio National Guard troops killed two strikers at the Electric Auto-

Lite Company (Toledo), and as a result of public opinion, strikers' demands were met. [9]

1935

The Rev. A. B. Brookins of Marked Tree, Arkansas, a Southern Tenant Farmers Union organizer, was the target of a white lynch mob. Finding Brookins not home, they settled for his daughter whom they killed. The gang was organized in March by wealthy land owners who opposed tenant farmers organizing. [1]

1936

In April, while awaiting trial on charges of attempted assault of a white girl, Lint Shaw was taken from the Royston, Georgia, jail and lynched. [12]

1937

A Memorial Day battle between striking steelworkers and Chicago police left ten laborers dead. A police claim of self-defense was found to be false by a congressional investigation which determined that the steelworkers had no weapons. [1]

1938

Although the Wiggins, Mississippi, sheriff had serious doubts about a seventy-four-year-old woman's credibility, her charge in November that a twenty-four-year-old black, W. McGowan, had assaulted her led quickly to young McGowan's death by lynching. [12]

1939

Two nonunion strikebreakers at the coal fields near Harlan, Kentucky, were killed during the "Bloody Harlan" riots. Treed Bates was shot by "persons unknown," and his fellow scab, Elbert Clark, was killed by a deputy sheriff in the May incident. [22]

1940

Brownsville, Texas, NAACP leader Ebert Williams was killed during "racial strife." Many other black citizens were forced to flee. [22]

1941

Dragged from an unguarded ambulance after being charged with assaulting a twelve-year-old white girl, A. C. Williams, a black man, was lynched in Quincy, Florida. [12]

1942

Shortly after President Franklin D. Roosevelt's February directive that Americans of Japanese extraction be detained in relocation camps, a gang of whites in Stockton, California, assassinated an American, Shigemasa Yoshioka, whose parents were Japanese. [22]

1943

Race riots in Detroit, Michigan, caused by white workers angry at blacks getting defense plant employment, left twenty-five blacks and nine whites dead. Right-wing extremists and white supremacists did much to inflame whites prior to the conflict. [3]

1944

Black minister Isaac Simmons, who owned 220 acres of Mississippi farmland, was lynched by a mob in August because he hired a lawyer to protect his land title. Local whites thought that there was oil beneath the Simmons spread and hoped to take the land from him. [12]

1945

Army private Clarence W. Bertucci, using a machine gun, killed eight German P.O.W.s and wounded twenty more at Salina, Utah, in July. [4]

1946

When twenty-seven-year-old Roger Malcolm, a black man in Monroe, Georgia, was suspected of having stabbed his former employer, who was white, he and friend George Dorsey were shot and killed by a white mob. Wives of the two and sisters were murdered at the same time when one of them recognized one of the attackers. [12]

1947

In April New York docks head stevedore Anthony Hintz was killed by racketeers attempting to take over longshore operations on the waterfront. [22]

1948

When Vidalia, Georgia, black Robert Mallard disregarded the advice of local whites that he not vote in the fall election, he was assassinated. [2]

1949

In August, after black Hollis Riles told a group of whites not to fish in his pond near Bainbridge, Georgia, he was shot dead. [22]

1950

In March eighteen-year-old black Willie Carlisle, in the custody of Lafayette, Alabama, police, was beaten to death. Two white policemen were indicted and subsequently acquitted despite the fact that one of the defendants publicly admitted beating the deceased. [22]

1951

An articulate black leader in Sanford, Florida, Harry T. Moore, was killed with his wife in a bomb blast in December. [4]

1952

Teamsters Union official John Acropolis was killed in his Yonkers, New York, home following controversial actions by the state union. [22]

1953

Ethel and Julius Rosenberg, convicted for passing "atomic secrets" to the Soviet Union, were electrocuted in June at Sing Sing, New York. Evidence obtained in the 1970s by their sons under the Freedom of Information Act has demonstrated overwhelming official deceit and doctored evidence in the case. [15]

1954

William W. Remington, a former Commerce Department economist, was murdered in the Lewisburg (Pa.) Federal Penitentiary by fellow inmates. Thirty-six-year-old Remington had been convicted of perjury for denying to a federal grand jury that he had passed out classified data for transmission to Russia, and for denying that he knew about a Dartmouth College unit of the Young Communist League in the 1930s. Said the Lewisburg acting warden about the November killing: "You'll get pretty much of the same reaction concerning loyalty in a prison climate as in any other community." [22]

1955

Soon after fifteen-year-old black Emmett Till waved at a white woman, members of the woman's family kidnapped him, shot him, and dumped him in a river at Greenwood, Mississippi. Two men charged with the murder were later acquitted by an all-white jury. [12]

1956

In the wake of an attack upon antiracketeering columnist Victor Riesel, in which acid was thrown at his eyes, several murders were committed to cover up all traces of the atrocity. The hit man, Abraham Telvi, was killed in July because he himself had been badly scarred by the acid, and subsequently, his own assassins, J. J. Roberts and R. M. Langone, plus a friend, were killed. [22]

1957

After declining on three occasions to cooperate with an FBI investigation, Stanford University scientist William Sherwood was subpoenaed by the U.S. House Committee on Un-American Activities. His suicide note in June said he could not face the ordeal of the impending televised hearings. [16]

1958

At Chester, New York, Alfred Dugan, an organizer for local #1 of the Interstate Industrial Union, was shot in the back by the president of the cable company whose employees he was trying to organize. The assassin, Malcolm White, had reportedly obtained Dugan's police record, and drove off with him to "discuss" it. Said White after the November shooting: "It was better for me to do this than for my workers to suffer. They are loyal humble people." [22]

1959

A black man, Mack Charles Parker, two days away from an April rape trial, was lynched by a white gang. The Poplarville, Mississippi, grand jury declined to look at evidence gathered by the FBI, denying that a lynching had taken place. [2]

1960

After several men dressed as Nazis picketed a Sammy Davis, Jr., concert, Los Angeles City News Service night editor Roby Heard started investigating a young Nazi-type gang in L. A. In mid-investigation Heard was assassinated. Two men previously interviewed by Heard for the story were picked up for the November murder. [22]

1961

United Industrial Workers Union president John Kilpatrick was shot and killed in his car; charged in the October death was Anthony Inisco, "alleged racketeer," who had recently been ousted by the Kilpatrick forces from the union presidency for misuse of funds. [22]

1962

In September, when student James Meredith tried to enter the University of Mississippi over the objection of Governor Ross Barnett, rioting broke out leaving a twenty-three-year-old black student, Ray Gunther, and a fellow student dead. A journalist representing Agence France-Presse, Paul Guilard, was also killed. [2, 22]

1963

A bomb went off in September inside the Sixth Street Baptist Church at Birmingham, Alabama, killing four black girls: fourteen-year-olds Cynthia Wesley, Carol Robertson, and Addie Mae Collins, and eleven-year-old Denise McNeis. Three months earlier Mississippi NAACP Field Secretary Medgar Evers was shot in the back at Jackson, Mississippi. [15]

1964

Three civil rights workers, James Chaney, Andrew Goodman, and Michael Schwerner, were murdered in Philadelphia, Mississippi. Their bodies were found in a nearby earthen dam, apparently put there after being tortured and shot. Charged with the June slayings were twenty-one men, six of whom were Ku Klux Klan members. Of eighteen who stood trial, seven were convicted, including the Imperial Wizard of the White Knights of the Ku Klux Klan, and a Neshoba County deputy sheriff. [15, 22]

1965

In February, black activist Malcolm X was killed as he began an address at the Audubon Ballroom in New York. A year earlier Malcolm had left the Black Muslims and formed his own organization which taught black supremacy until weeks before the assassination, when Malcolm adapted a racial coexistence line. Originally it was believed that Black Muslims were responsible for the murder, although later speculation put government-financed provocateurs in the plot. [48] In the summer, a week-long riot took place in the Watts section of Los Angeles; thirty-four were killed. A government commission headed by CIA director John McCone blamed the disturbance on "social misfits." [1] In November, Norman Morrison, a pacifist, died of self-immolation in front of the Pentagon in protest of the escalating war against Vietnam. [22]

1966

In January black civil rights worker Vernon F. Dahmer was firebombed to death in Mississippi. An all-white jury found Ku Klux Klansman Cecil V. Sessum guilty. Court testimony said that KKK Imperial Wizard Sam Bowers had ordered the killing because Dahmer was "getting too many niggers to vote." [6] Large-scale riots in the Hough area of Cleveland and in Chicago's black ghetto left many dead and injured during the summer. [3]

1967

The "Long Hot Summer" saw black uprisings of various sizes in numerous cities, including Detroit, Los Angeles, New York, Atlanta, Newark, Houston, Jackson, Mississippi, towns in northern New Jersey, and elsewhere. A number of blacks died as well. [3] In August American Nazi Party leader George Lincoln Rockwell was killed in Arlington, Virginia. The man charged and convicted of the slaying has since put forth convincing evidence that he is not guilty of the murder. [17]

1968

Martin Luther King, Jr., a militant pacifist civil rights activist, was killed in April at Memphis, Tennessee, while participating in a sanitation workers strike. Convicted of the assassination was James Earl Ray; no coconspirators have yet been apprehended. Following King's death, black rebellion broke out in more than one hundred cities leaving scores dead. [3, 15] Labor violence at the Masonite Corp. in Laurel, Mississippi, led to the death of five strikers, as management circulated rumors which divided white and black workers. [1] A gun battle in September at a Berea, Kentucky, National States Rights party rally left one black and one white man dead. [6] Four weeks earlier three members of the Black Panther party were killed by Los Angeles police in a shootout. [6]

1969

Students, streetpeople, and other residents of Berkeley, California, defending a vacant block they developed called "People's Park," suffered injuries at the hands of state forces trying to reclaim the land on behalf of the Board of Regents. One James Rector was killed in the battle. In December county for-

ces in a 4:30 AM raid killed a sleeping Fred Hampton, head of the Chicago Black Panther party, at his apartment, along with Mark Clark. The chief of security for the Panthers turned out to be a police agent, and the raid appears to have been part of the FBI's Counter-Intelligence Program (CO-INTEL-PRO). [22, 48]

1970

In January Joseph Yablonski, reform candidate for the United Mine Workers Union presidency, was killed at his home; charged and convicted were Tony Boyle, Yablonski's opponent, and his hirelings who carried out the plot. [15] In March three members of the Weather Underground, Teddy Gold, Diana Oughton, and Terry Robbins, were blown up in a Greenwich Village townhouse as they experimented with bomb manufacturing. Surviving members of the group called this part of the "military error" in their analysis. [7] In May thirteen Kent State University students were shot by National Guardsmen who were on campus to quell a protest of Nixon's invasion of Cambodia. Four of them died: Allison Krause, Jeff Miller, Sandy Scheuer, and William Schroeder. [22] In July chairman Carl Hampton of a Houston group called Peoples party II, similar to the Black Panther party, was killed by a city police sniper squad. Hampton, a popular leader, had been speaking to a rally in the city's ghetto. [15, 18]

1971

A September rebellion by inmates at a New

York state prison at Attica resulted in the death of thirty-two prisoners and nine hostages, all killed by state troopers sent in by Governor Nelson Rockefeller. [15]

1972

In November at Southern University in Baton Rouge, students, including Leonard Douglas and Denver A. Smith, occupied the administration building demanding better conditions on campus. Sheriff's deputies fired into the crowd of students, and Brown and Smith died as a result. Police claimed that blacks were plotting to blow up the state capitol and kill Governor Edwards. No one was prosecuted for the killings. [22]

1973

When members of the American Indian Movement seized the South Dakota town of Wounded Knee in April, protesting the treatment of Indians by the U.S. government, federal troops and U.S. marshals surrounded the town. One Indian, Buddy LaMonte, was assassinated when, staggering from an AIM bunker hit by CS gas projectiles, a bullet struck him. Marshals were heard to say over the radio at the time, "There's one flushed out of that bunker . . . get him . . . he's a good target." [25]

1974

In May six fugitive members of the guerilla Symbionese Liberation Army died when the house they were living in was firebombed by Los Angeles police. Killed in the televised houseburning were Donald DeFreeze, Camilla Hall, Willie Wolf, Angela Atwood, Nancy Ling Perry, and Nancy Soltysik. [15, 22]

1975

Sam Giancana, long-time organized crime manipulator, was killed at his home just outside Chicago prior to scheduled testimony before a congressional committee investigating links between CIA and political assassination, including the attempts on Fidel Castro and John Kennedy. Giancana was proven to be such a link. No suspects were apprehended. [15] In September Ohio State University professor Charles Glatt, who had been assigned by a federal court to draw up desegregation plans for Dayton .public schools, was assassinated at his federal-building office in Dayton. Pleading guilty to the murder was Neal Bradley Long, who said he became angry "because of the busing of school children kids and integration." Long was sentenced to end-to-end life terms for murdering a federal official and interfering with the civil rights of Dayton students. [22]

1976

In June *Arizona Republic* reporter Don Bolles was fatally maimed when a bomb detonated in his car. Bolles was, at the time, investigating links between organized crime, racetrack operations, and politicians. [15] Ronnie Moffitt, active in developing studies and plans for Latin American politics and economics, was killed in September when a car in which she was riding exploded. Accompanying her was Orlando Letelier, a former official from Chile's Allende government, who was also killed. Letelier was an articulate and outspoken critic of the junta, which three years earlier overthrew Allende's democratically elected government. Suspected in the Washington, D.C., bombing were foreign agents of Chile's military dictatorship. [15]

1977

In March members of the Hanafi Muslims, a small sect that had broken away from the Black Muslim religion, killed broadcast journalist Maurice Williams, as the group seized control of the District of Columbia Building in Washington, D.C. The action occurred during an unsuccessful attempt to gain vengeance for transgressions by religious rivals. [22]

Sources for Chapter 6

1. Hofstadter, Richard, and Wallace, Michael, *American Violence: A Documentary History*. New York: Vintage Books, 1971.

2. Bergman, Peter M., *The Chronological History of the Negro in America*. New York: Harper & Row, 1969.

3. *Report of the National Advisory Commission on Civil Disorders*. Washington, D.C.: Government Printing Office, 1968.

4. *The Official National Lampoon Bicentennial Calendar for 1976*. New York: The National Lampoon, 1975 (a day by day listing of violent episodes in American history).

5. Brown, Dee, *Bury My Heart at Wounded Knee: An Indian History of the American West*. New York: Holt, Rinehart and Winston, 1971.

6. *Political Extremism and Violence in the United States*. New York: manuscript form, 1968 (a Report by the Anti-Defamation League of B'Nai Brith to the National Commission on the Causes and Prevention of Violence, Task Force on Political Assassination).

7. The Weather Underground, *Prairie Fire; Political Statement of the Weather Underground*. San Francisco and New York: The Communications Co., 1974 (first edition privately published).

8. Sung, Betty Lee, *Mountain of Gold: The Story of the Chinese in America*. New York: Macmillan, 1967.

9. Adamic, Louis, *Dynamite: The Story of Class Violence in America*. New York: Harper, 1931; Chelsea/Vintage 1958.

10. Yellen, Samuel, *American Labor Struggles*. New York: Monad Press, 1974.

11. Castleman, Harvey, *The Bald Knobbers*. Point Lookout, Mo.: School of the Ozarks Press, 1944.

12. Ginzburg, Ralph, *100 Years of Lynching*. New York: Lancer Books, 1962.

13. Jordan, Winthrop D., *White Man's Burden: Historical Origins of Racism in the United States*. New York: Oxford University Press, 1974.

14. Manchester, William, *The Glory and the Dream*. New York: Little Brown, 1974.

15. Historical Record (events acknowledged as fact through observation, verified by supporting literature and documentation).

16. Donner, Frank J., *The Un-Americans*. New York: Ballantine, 1961.

17. Rode, Meredith, address to the "Decade of Assassination" conference. Washington, D.C.: 1973.

18. Sweeney, Scoop personal file.

19. Morris, Richard B., ed., *Encyclopedia of American History* (revised edition). New York: Harper & Row, 1961.

20. "The Salem (Mass.) Gazette."

21. "The New York Herald."

22. "The New York Times" (various dates, check annual Index).

23. Carruth, Gorton, and Associates, ed., *The Encyclopedia of American Facts and Dates* (4th edition). New York: Crowell, 1966.

24. Morrison, Samuel Eliot, *The Oxford History of the American People*. New York: Oxford University Press, 1965.

25. Burnette, Robert, *The Road to Wounded Knee*. New York: Bantam Books, 1974.

26. Grant, Joanne, *Black Protest*. Greenwich, Conn.: Fawcett Publications, 1974.

27. Sloan, Irving J., *Our Violent Past: An American Chronicle*. New York: Random House, 1970.

28. Carroll, Joseph C., *Slave Insurrections in the United States 1800-1865*. New York: Negro Universities Press, 1968.

29. National Association for the Advancement of Colored People, *Thirty Years of Lynching*. New York: Negro Universities Press, 1969.

30. "Niles National Register."

31. Tetters, Negley K., *"...Hang By the Neck..." The Legal Use of Scaffold and Noose, Gibbet, Stake, and Firing Squad From Colonial Times to the Present*. Springfield, Ill.: Charles C. Thomas, 1967.

32. Hollon, W. Eugene, *Frontier Violence, Another Look*. New York: Oxford University Press, 1974.

33. Foreman, Grant, *Pioneer Days in the Early Southwest*. Cleveland: Arthur H. Clark, 1926.

34. Foreman, Grant, *Indian Removal—The Emigration of the Five Civilized Tribes of Indians*. Norman, Okla.: University of Oklahoma Press, 1932.

35. Cutler, James Elbert, *Lynch-Law; An Investigation Into the History of Lynching in the United States*. New York: Negro Universities Press, 1969.

36. Foreman, Grant, *Indians and Pioneers; The Story of the American Southwest Before 1830*. Norman, Okla.: University of Oklahoma Press, 1930, 1967.

37. Hildreth, S. P., *Pioneer History*. New York: Arno Press and the New York Times, 1971 (reprint from 1848).

38. Reynolds, John, *The Pioneer History of Illinois*. Chicago: Fergus Printing Co., 1887.

39. Graham, Hugh Davis, and Gurr, Ted Robert, *Violence in America: Historical and Comparative Perspectives*. New York: Bantam Books, 1969 (A report submitted to the National Commission on the Causes and Prevention of Violence).

40. Dunn, Jacob Piatt, *Massacres of the Mountains: A History of the Indian Wars of the Far West*. New York: Harper & Brothers, 1886.

41. Kroeber, Theodora, *Ishi in Two Worlds*. Berkeley, Calif.: University of California Press, 1961, 1976.

42. Tebbel, John Williams, *The Compact History of the Indian Wars*. New York: Hawthorn Books, 1966.

43. Furriel, Vincent J., *Organized Crime: History and Control* (California State Peace Officers Training Series). Sacramento: California Community College Chancellor's Office, 1976.

44. Brown, Richard Maxwell, *Strain of Violence; Historical Studies of American Violence and Vigilantism*. New York: Oxford University Press, 1975.

45. "The Journal of Negro History," Washington, D.C., #53 and #54.

46. Kinnard, Lawrence, *History of the Greater San Francisco Bay Region*. New York: Lewis Historical Publishing Co., 1966.

47. McMaster, John B., *A History of the People of the United States From the Revolution to the Civil War*. New York: D. Appleton and Co., 1888.

48. Wallechinsky, David, and Wallace, Irving, *The People's Almanac*. New York: Doubleday, 1975.

from the poem
The Age
by Ed Sanders

This is the Age of Investigation, and every citizen must
investigate! For the pallid tracks of guilt and death,
slight as they are, suffuse upon the retentive
electromagnetic data-retrieval systems of our era.
And let th' Investigators not back away one micro-unit
from their investigations—for the fascist hirelings
of gore await in the darkness to rise up this year
to shoot away the product of the ballot box

And if full millions do not investigate, we will see the
Age of Gore, and the criminals of the right will rise up
drooling with shellfish toxin, to send their berserker
blitz of mod manchurian malefactors mumbling with
motorized beowulfian trance-instructions, to chop
up candidates in the name of some businessman's moan
of national security

And this is the Age of Investigative Poetry, when verse-froth
again will assume its prior role as a vehicle for the
description of history—and this will be a golden era
for the public performance of poetry: when the Diogenes
Liberation Squadron of Strolling Troubadours and Muckrakers
will roam through the citadels of America to sing
opposition to the military hit-men who think the United
States is some sort of corpse farm

And this is the age of leftwing epics with happy endings! Of
leftwing tales/movies/poems/songs/tractata/manifestoes/
epigrams/calligrammes/graffiti/neonics and Georges
Braque frottage-collage-assemblage Data Clusters which
dangle from their cliffs the purest lyricals e'er
to hang down a hummingbird's singingbard throat

This is the Age of Garbage.* And we're not talking here about
        Garbage Self-Garbage—but an era of robotic querulousness—
        how at the onset of a time when the power of a country
        is up for grabs, the Garbage Hurlers, attired in robes
        of military-industrial silk, arise to hurl, as swift
        in their machinations as a chorus in the Ice Capades:

        and none of us will trudge this era without a smirch-face
        waft of thrilly offal dumped upon our brows of social
        zeal—and the pus-suck provocateurs armed with orbiting
        plates of dog vomit will leap at us while we stand
        chanting our clue-ridden dactyls of KNOW THE NEW FACTS
        EARLY! Know-the-new-facts-early, know-the-new-facts-
        early! And do not back away one micro-unit just because
        some CIA weirdomorph whose control agents never ended
        WW II invades your life with a mouthful of curdled
        exudate from the head of the Confederate Intelligence
        Agency &

This is the Age of Nuclear Disarmament—when the freeroam roamers
        of the Hills join hands with the nesters of the Valley
        Wild, to put an end to nuke puke w/ a zero-waver total
        transworld Peace Walk—that never again will the
        patriarchs ship nodules of plutonium on the railroads
        of explosion

        o that it not unduly scare the Office of Naval Intelligence
        when a legally Constituted assembly of freely elected
        representatives sloshes 37 tons of mule mucous down into
        the missile hatches of the Polaris submarines!

        & this: o hardened silos of North Dakota, thy destiny
        of recreation land for those who wish to roam the
        summer. . . .

*Poet's note: pronounced "garbahzhe"

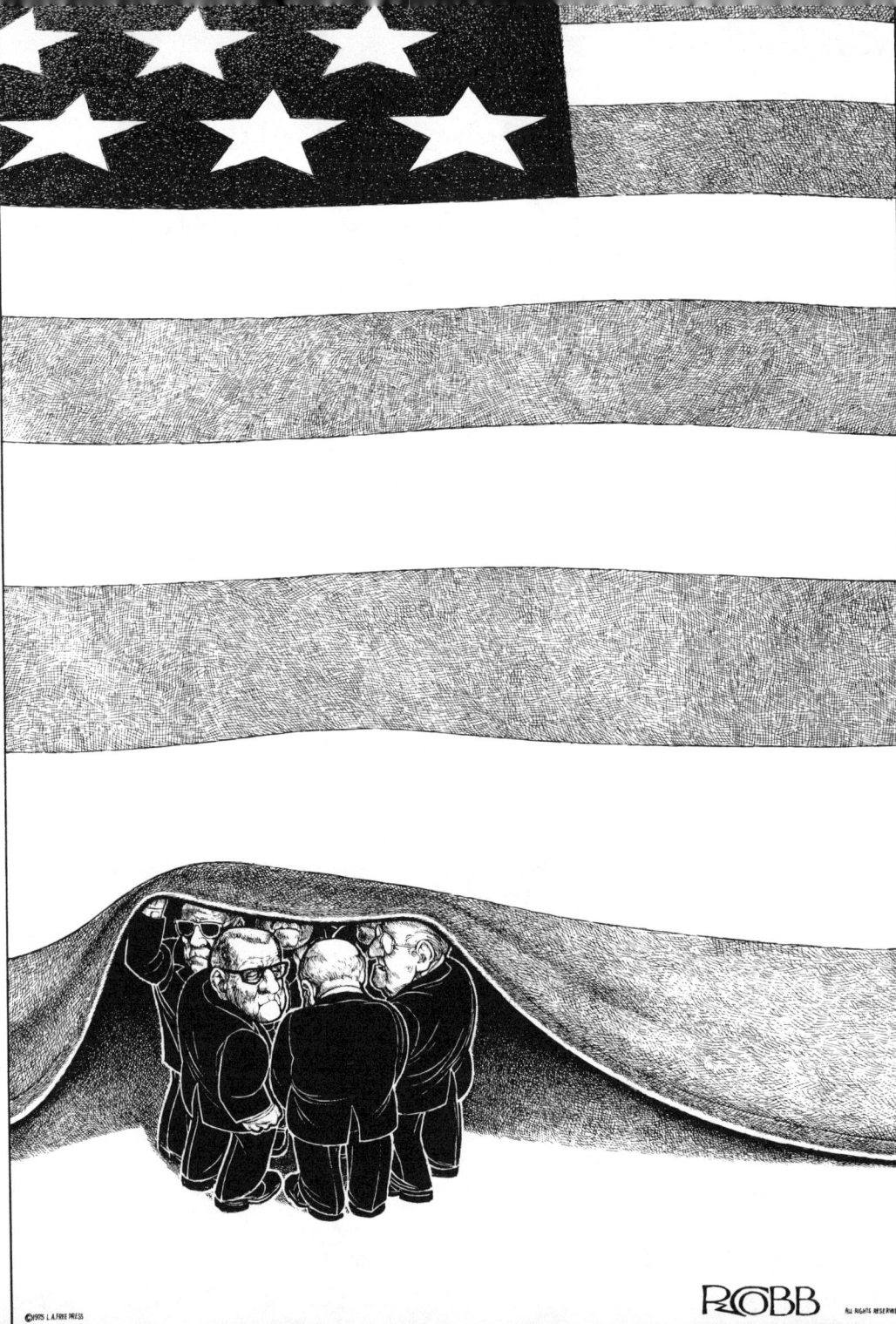

ROBB

INDEX